IMAGES of America

FULTON

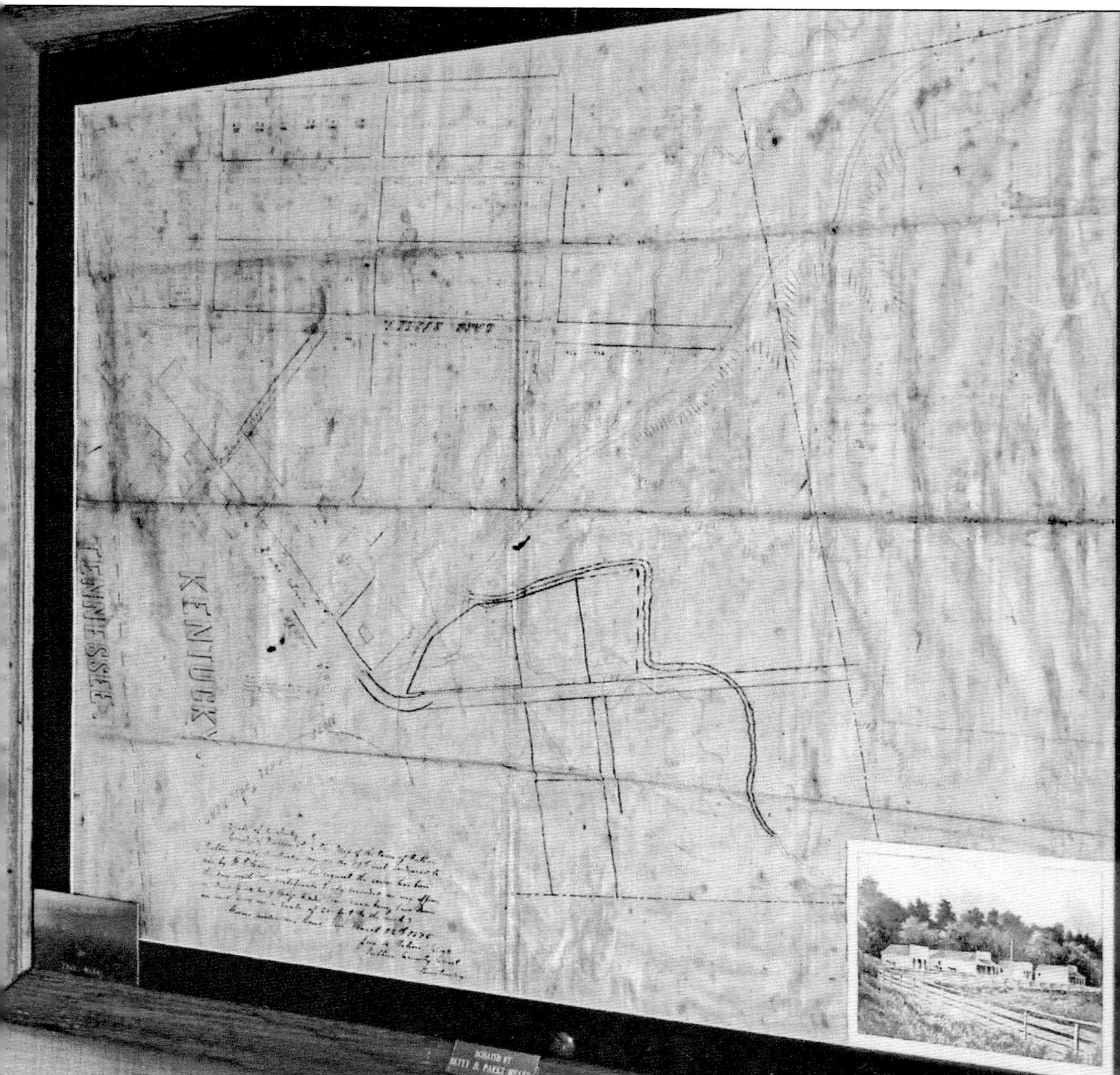

The original plat for Fulton, Kentucky, hangs in a private home, preserved behind glass. Over time, the initial 160-acre land grant, which had brought the Benjamin Franklin (B.F.) Carr family to the area from the Carolinas, was enlarged to include a total of 1,100 acres. A picture of the "village" of Fulton, as it appeared around the 1860s, is in the far right hand corner of the frame.

IMAGES
of America

FULTON

Elizabeth R. Jones

ARCADIA
PUBLISHING

ISBN 978-0-7385-1699-8

Published by Arcadia Publishing
Charleston, South Carolina

Printed in the United States of America

Library of Congress Catalog Card Number: 2004108738

For all general information contact Arcadia Publishing at:
Telephone 843-853-2070
Fax 843-853-0044
E-mail sales@arcadiapublishing.com
For customer service and orders:
Toll-Free 1-888-313-2665

Visit us on the Internet at www.arcadiapublishing.com

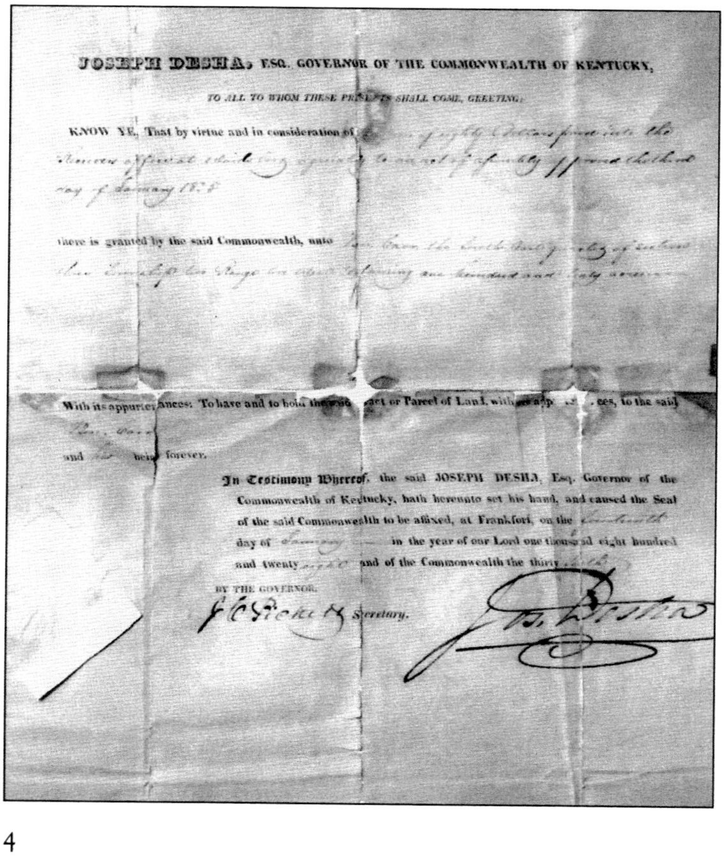

JOSEPH DESHA, ESQ. GOVERNOR OF THE COMMONWEALTH OF KENTUCKY,

TO ALL TO WHOM THESE PRESENTS SHALL COME, GREETING:

KNOW YE, That by virtue and in consideration of

there is granted by the said Commonwealth, unto

With its appurtenances: To have and to hold the said Tract or Parcel of Land, with its [illegible], to the said

and [illegible] heirs forever.

In Testimony Whereof, the said JOSEPH DESHA, Esq. Governor of the Commonwealth of Kentucky, hath hereunto set his hand, and caused the Seal of the said Commonwealth to be affixed, at Frankfort, on the day of in the year of our Lord one thousand eight hundred and twenty and of the Commonwealth the thirty

BY THE GOVERNOR.

Secretary.

The Commonwealth of Kentucky, wishing more settlers for what is now Fulton County, offered land grants to pioneer settlers. B.F. Carr was the first person to make such a purchase in 1828. The original grant, consisting of 160 acres, sold for $80. Carr made additional grant purchases through 1831, resulting in a total of 1,100 acres for $440. Seen here is the original land grant signed by Joseph Desha, Esq., governor of the Commonwealth of Kentucky, to Mr. Carr on January 14, 1828. It hangs in a private home in the community.

CONTENTS

ABOUT THE IMAGES

The images for this book were derived from a variety of sources. Through community donation, newspaper and library archives, family photos, and genealogical publications, this pictorial history came to be. It is the author's hope that the book will generate an interest in the rich history of Fulton and encourage others to embrace the legacy it holds for future generations. Please overlook any shortcomings in documentation, as the endeavor was not so much to record historically accurate facts and figures but to give the reader a glimpse into a time gone by. Countless hours have been spent on the compilation of this book for publication, and the assistance provided by the citizens of the Twin Cities would be impossible to note individually. I am indebted to you all. May the future hold continued blessings for this special community and the people who call it home.

Elizabeth R. Jones
September 2004

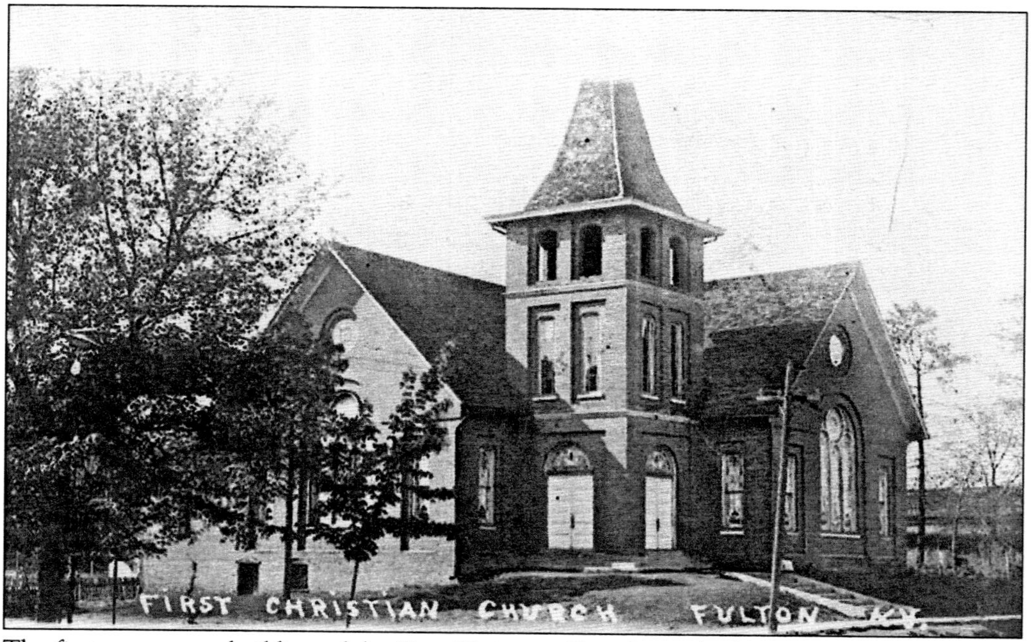

The first permanent building of the First Christian Church was built on its present site at 108 Carr Street, a lot donated by W.W. Carr, in 1875. The building was remodeled and enlarged in 1909, and the Sunday school rooms were added in 1925. This image depicts the church in the 1920s. The church was destroyed by fire in 1928. Little was salvaged, but a beautiful new sanctuary was immediately commissioned, which still stands today.

INTRODUCTION

Native Americans knew Kentucky as the "dark and bloody ground, " where they hunted and fought other tribes. The extreme western end of Kentucky and the northwest corner of Tennessee abounded in some of the finest game in all of America, partly because the land was burned off each year by the Chickasaw tribe to promote growth of grass and suppress the growth of forest. Large areas of prairies came to exist and there was a ready supply of grazing elk, bison, and deer. Relics abound, but there is no sign that permanent residence was ever taken by any tribe or nation.

The community known as Fulton, Kentucky, was first called "Pontotoc" by the Chickasaw, meaning "Land of the Hanging Grapes." Tribes wandered in and out, using the region for sustenance, and the coming of the white man created much animosity. The first known white men to the area arrived between 1780 and 1800. Davy Crockett mentions visiting the land that became Fulton County in his biography. A treaty was entered into in 1818—ratified by the U.S. Senate in January 1819—by Andrew Jackson, who purchased thousands of acres, including the land on which Fulton and South Fulton stand, from the Chickasaw Indians for the price of $3,000. For reasons unknown, the Indians chose to deal with Andrew Jackson instead of Kentucky's governor when arriving at a settlement. This sale became know as the Jackson Purchase. The earliest records of Fulton date to 1828, when Benjamin Franklin Carr acquired a land grant of 160 acres for 50¢ an acre. By 1831, Mr. Carr had acquired a total of 1,100 acres. The Paschall family settled on the Tennessee side. The first settlers were farmers, and as others realized the rich resources and the strategic location between the Mississippi and Tennessee Rivers, more covered wagons arrived and settled in the county. The earliest known post in the area was a *c.* 1850 station called Pontotoc, where mail was dropped. The mail route came by horseback, from Old Feliciana in Graves County to Pontotoc and eventually on to Jacksonville, Tennessee, which is now near Harris Station, Tennessee. The Fulton Post Office was established in 1862.

The first railroad deed was sold in 1857. Construction reached Pontotoc in 1859 over the Paducah-Memphis line. For a long time, the United States government referred to Fulton as "The End of the Line," and all mail was addressed in this manner. Passengers rode to Fulton, got off at the crossing, and took a stagecoach to Jacksonville. With its original name of Pontotoc, Fulton had aroused a great deal of acrimony among the residents of Pontotoc, Mississippi, who wanted a "clear" title to the name. It seemed an opportune time and place, because of its proximity to the mighty Mississippi, to recognize the popular inventor Robert Fulton, who had just built the first steamship. Thus Pontotoc changed its name to "Fulton" in honor of the man, with the county being named Fulton as well. The town of South Fulton was first incorporated in 1895.

In 1861, this little tip of western Kentucky and Tennessee found itself on the dividing line between the North and the South. The greatest casualties of the war in the area were experienced at Camp Beauregard when an epidemic of measles took the lives of many local Confederate soldiers. The closest battle was fought at Columbus, Kentucky, 23 miles away.

By 1896, the railroad lines in the area were owned by the Illinois Central Railroad (IC), and the district and division offices were located in Fulton. Fulton became a hub of the IC, with its north-south lines converging in the city. In 1918, the IC built one of its most modern roundhouses in Fulton as a repair terminal for steam engines. More than 30 passenger trains and 3,000 freight cars picked up or delivered to the yards daily. The most important development that led to Fulton's moniker of "Banana Crossroads of the U.S." was the refrigerated rail car that enabled the shipping of bananas out of New Orleans to Canada around 1890. Fulton was the railroad town tying the Deep South to the North, and it quickly became the redistribution site for all bananas in mid-America. Until the 1960s, Fulton handled over 70 percent of the bananas brought to the United States. From this sprang the renowned International Banana Festival in the 1960s and the annual preparation of a one-ton banana pudding.

It is through this pictorial that we hope to capture the exciting story of the growth and development of the twin cities of Fulton, Kentucky, and South Fulton, Tennessee. Straddling two states, it has sometimes been difficult for the community to find unity and prosperity in the division. Most of the residents like to think of it as a "point-of-interest" line and not a "dividing line." It serves as a reminder that the cities share common problems and concerns and that the need to work together should be foremost in all minds. It is hoped that with funds raised by the sale of this book, projects for the preservation and beautification of the unique history of this township can benefit future generations. Tremendous gratitude goes out to my fellow members of the Heritage Committee of the Twin Cities Chamber of Commerce. Without their assistance in gathering the pictures and history of our community, this book could not exist. A special thank you to the Chamber of Commerce director, Lois Birk, for her unwavering patience and support as I completed this project. It was important to have someone believe in the possibilities. And finally, my sincere appreciation goes out to all the citizens of the Fulton, Kentucky and South Fulton, Tennessee community, who have served as my inspiration for compiling this history—especially the children, from whom we've inherited the responsibility for preserving their roots.

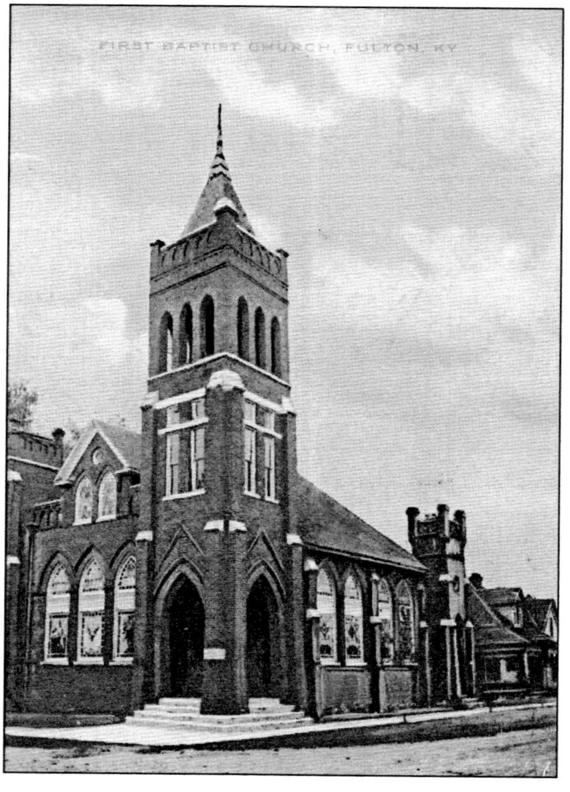

A permanent building for the First Baptist Church was erected on a lot donated by W.W. Carr at the corner of Second and Eddings Streets in the early 1880s. The sanctuary pictured is representative of the church's appearance until the 1920s.

One

Faces of the Past

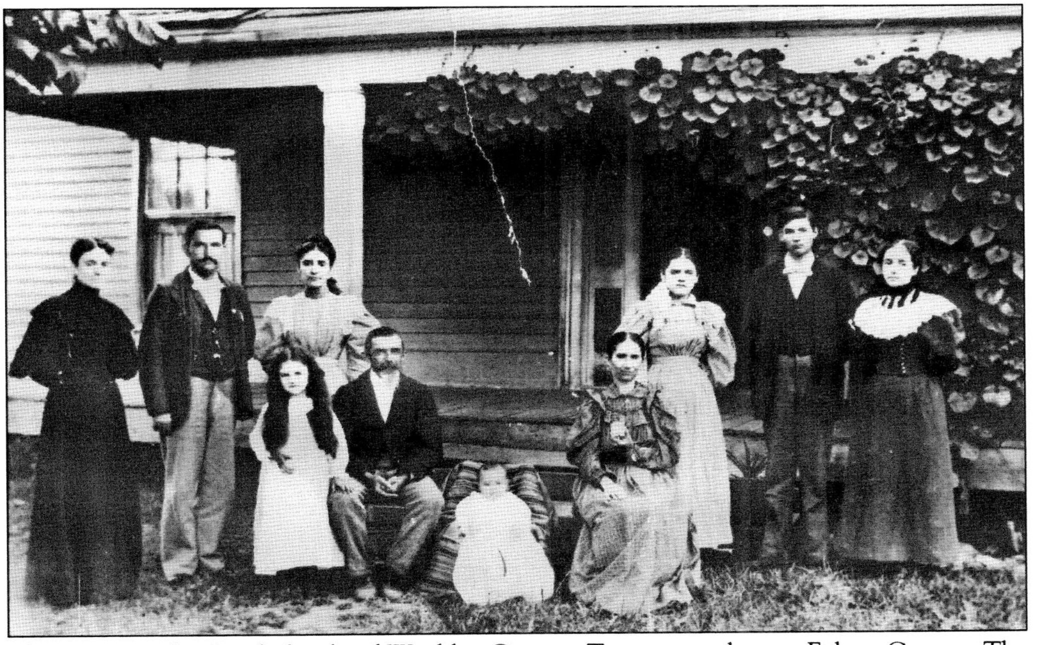

This image is the Smith family of Weakley County, Tennessee, close to Fulton County. The young girl with long hair third from left is Cornelia Wayne Smith. Seated to her left is father Cornelius Neal Smith, infant sister Nell Smith, and mother Rebecca Myrick Smith. In the mother's hand is a small, framed photo of a deceased child, son Hortence Smith. Cornelia later became the wife of John Lloyd Jones Sr., who moved to Fulton County from Weakley County when he graduated dental school. The Jones family continues a third-generation dental practice in Fulton to this day.

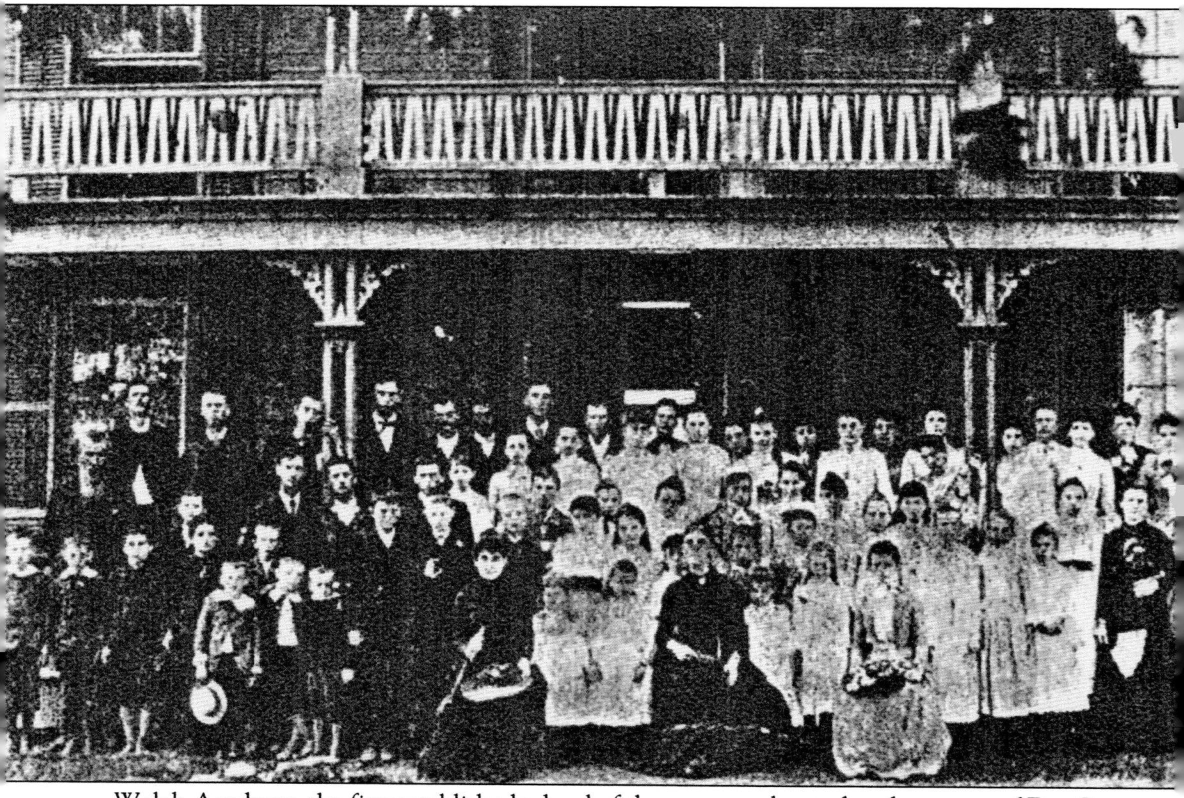

Welch Academy, the first established school of the area, was located at the corner of East State Line Road and Forestdale Avenue. A prestigious, two-story building housing classrooms and a beautiful dormitory, it boasted Christian education for primary and secondary grades. Mrs. Sarah H. Welch ran the school with teachers S.W. Welch, Nannie Witt, and Leila Weaver. There was even a college education offered at the cost of $30 tuition. Seen here is the graduating class of the 22nd session, in 1889. Much emphasis was put on "how to mind your manners," as well as courses such as astronomy, physiology, reading, writing, arithmetic, music, art, and Greek. There was even a course on moral and mental philosophy.

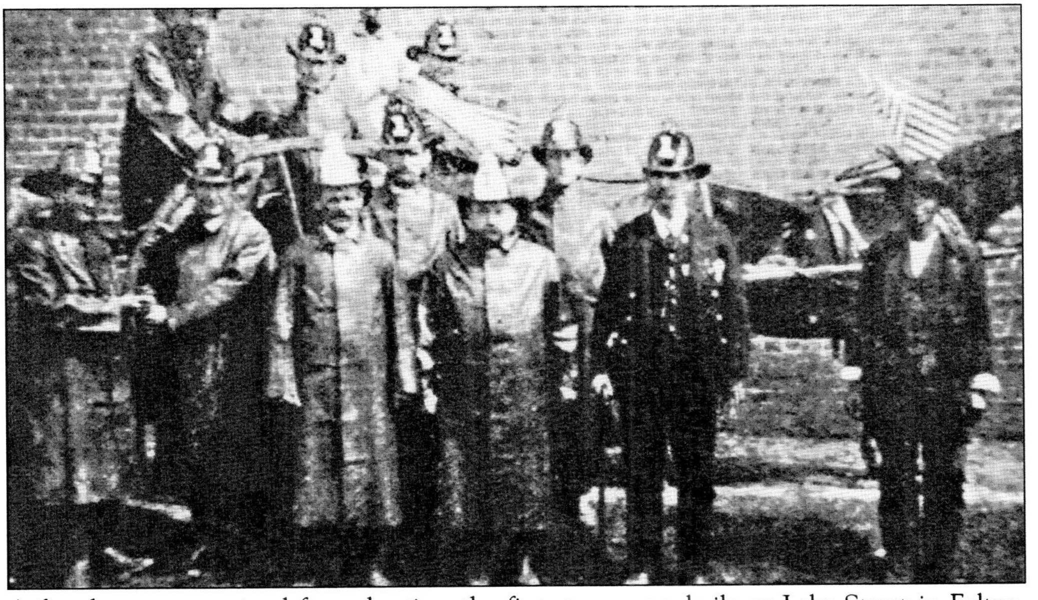

A fire department existed from the time the first stores were built on Lake Street in Fulton. Organized in 1892, the fire department used a "bucket brigade" to fight the flames—a series of wells were dug at intervals on Lake Street, with buckets hanging beside them. Pictured here is one of the earliest fire departments, comprised of Jessie Walker, Harve Johns, Bob May, Jim Cullen, Jake Roberts, Juston Harpole, Will Templeton, Bob Nolen, Gerod Sellers, and John Huddleston.

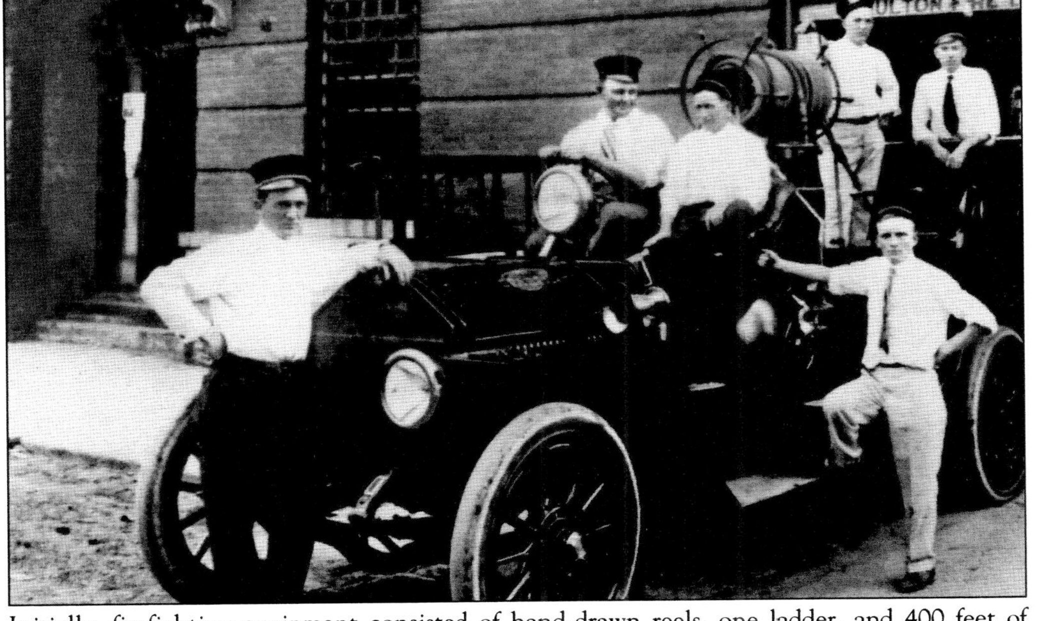

Initially, firefighting equipment consisted of hand-drawn reels, one ladder, and 400 feet of hose. Later, a horse-drawn cart replaced the hand-drawn reel, and in 1913, a motor truck was purchased from the American LaFrance Company. The new equipment included 1,110 feet of hose, carried 10 men, and had a 40-gallon chemical tank. The fire department occupied the northwest corner of the ground floor of Fulton City Hall on Main Street.

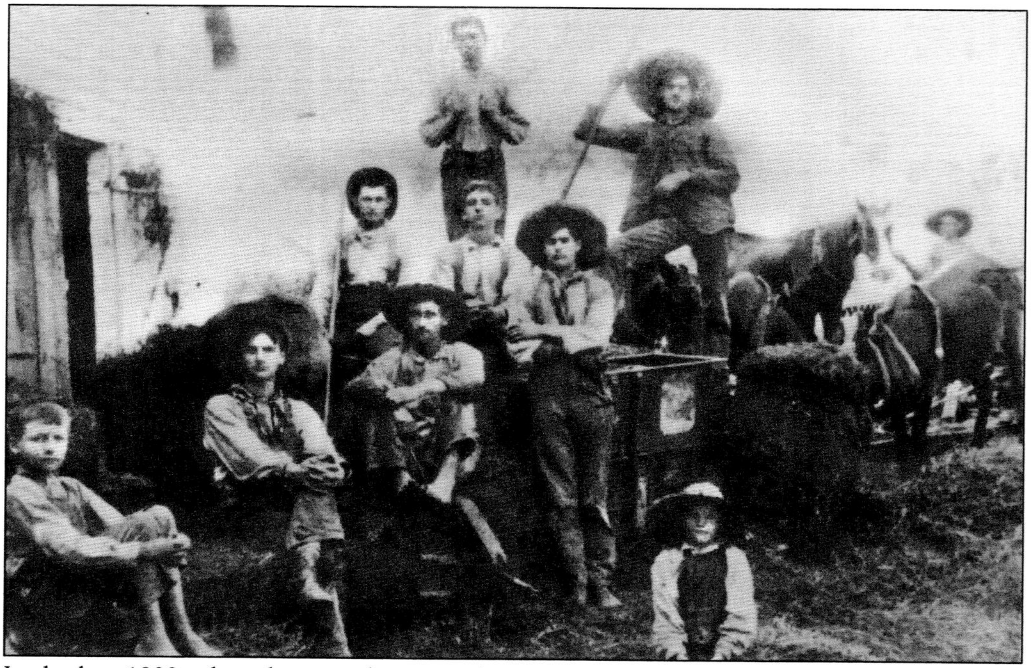

In the late 1800s, the tobacco industry was booming in Fulton. It furnished work for both the farmers and the railroad. Seen here are farmhands from the Chestnut Glade community of Weakley County. Second from left is a young John Lloyd Jones, who helped harvest tobacco to pay his way through dental school at the University of Tennessee at Nashville in the early 1900s. Dr. Jones later came to Fulton with his wife, Cornelia Smith Jones, to practice dentistry and raise his family.

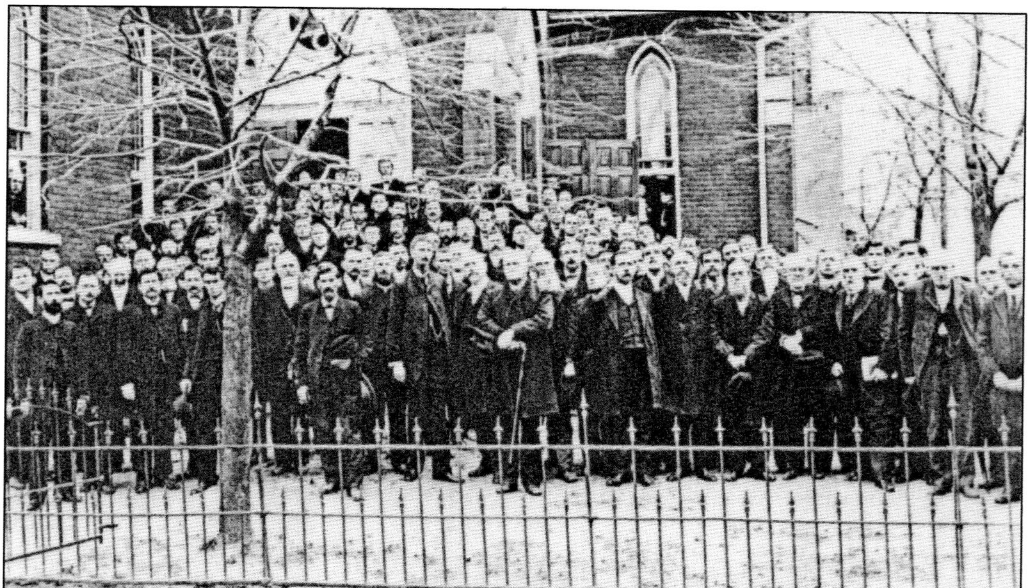

The First United Methodist Church was organized in Fulton in 1870 by Rev. T.L. Beard with 18 charter members. Seen here is a gathering of Methodist men at a conference dated 1888.

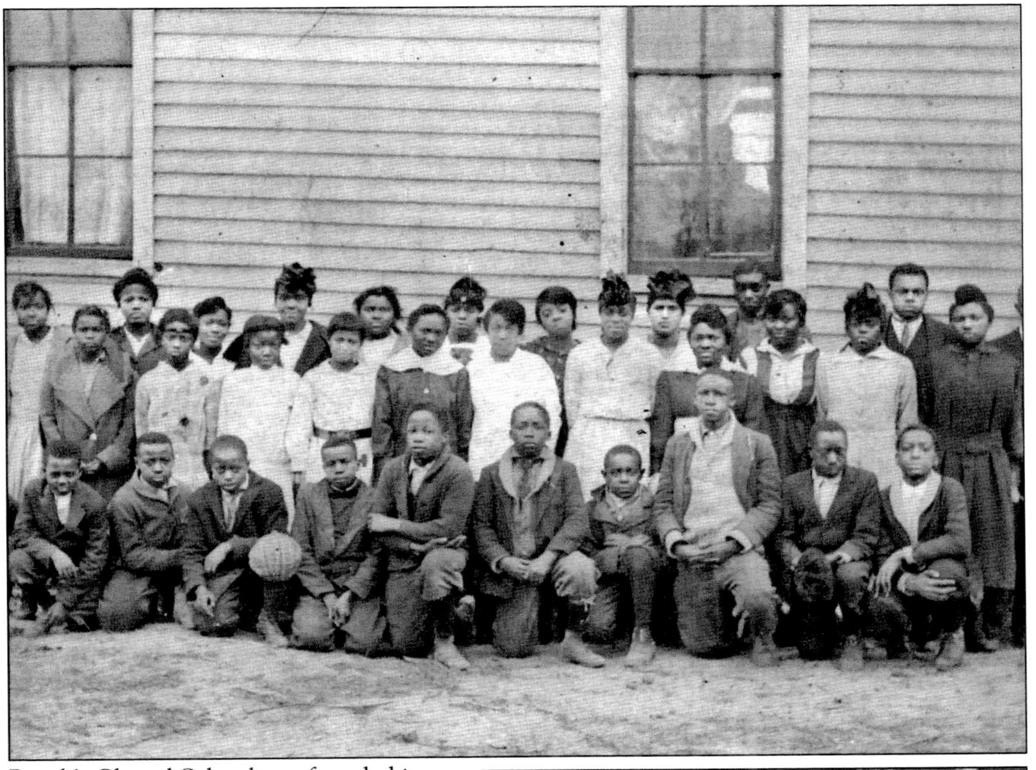

Brook's Chapel School was founded in 1887 to educate African Americans from Fulton County and the surrounding area. It was named after Elder Steven Lee Brooks, the pastor who organized and taught there. In this image are children from Brook's Chapel School in 1888. In the late 1920s, the school was burned down by the Night Riders, a vigilante band of men associated with the Ku Klux Klan opposed to the education of African Americans. Classes were then held in the chapel until the opening of "colored schools" by the Fulton County School Board.

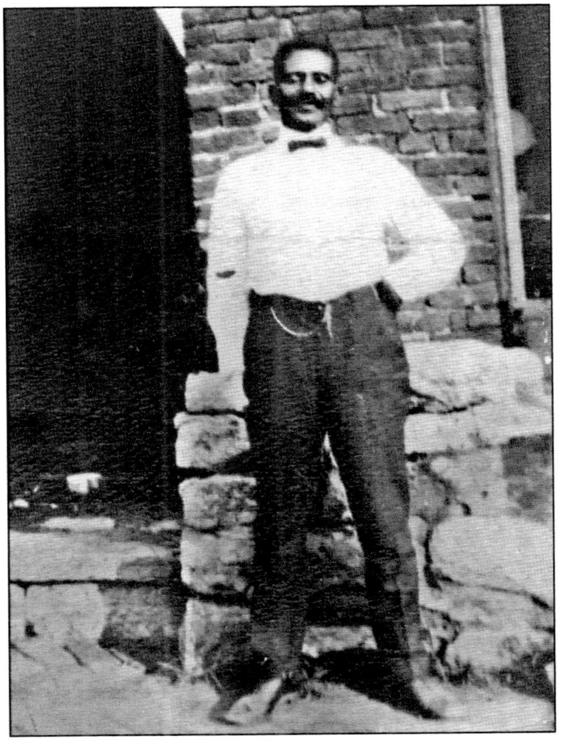

Thomas Columbus Henry Heard John-the-Conqueror Patterson moved to Fulton from the Eagleville, Tennessee area. A well-known herbalist in the African-American community, he ran Patterson's Store in Missionary Bottom in the early 20th century.

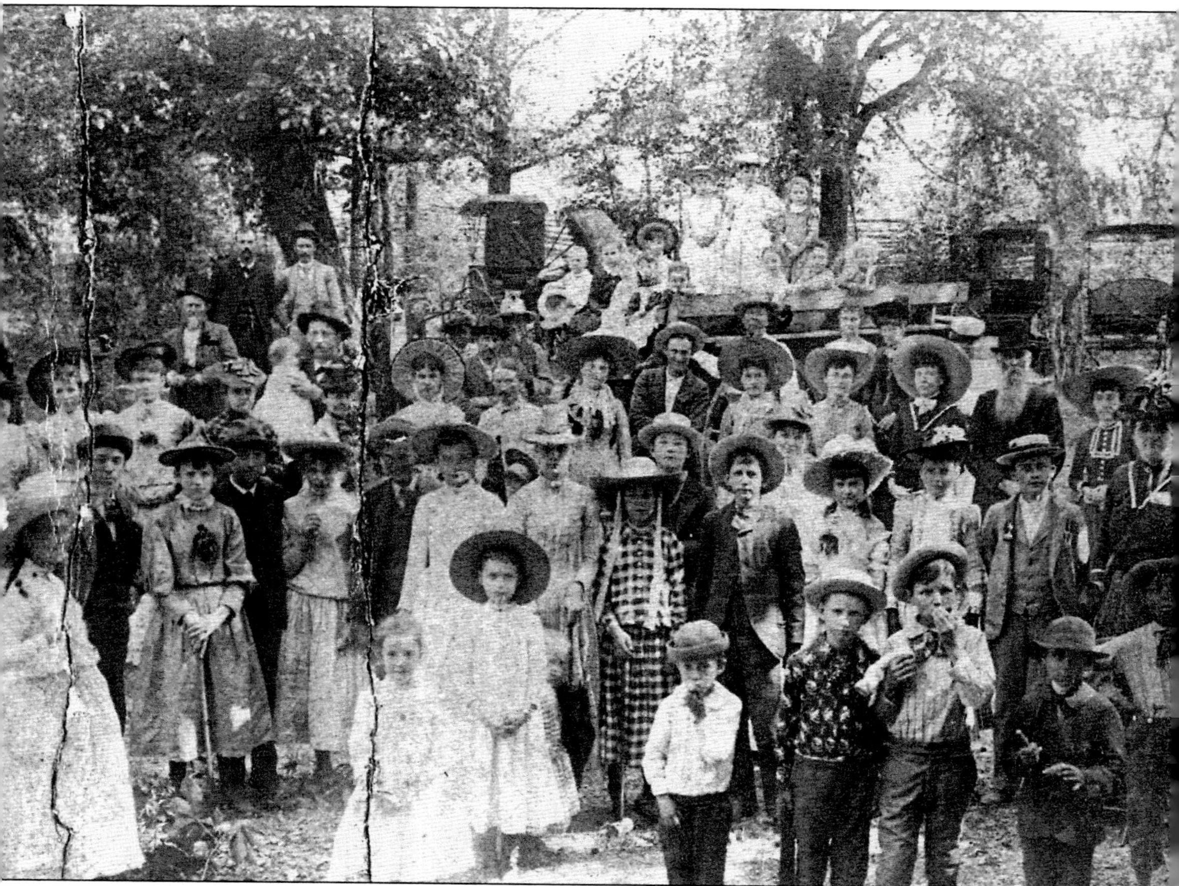

Elder R.A. (Robert Alexander) Cooke organized the First Christian Church in 1874 with 33 charter members. A lot donated by W.T. Carr on Carr Street was used for the first church building, and as the congregation grew it was not uncommon for them to enjoy "dinner on the grounds" at Carr's Park, adjacent to the church building. This photograph from 1886 includes Mrs. W.T. (Kate) Carr and children; the children are, from left to right, (front row) Mary, Annie, Frank, and Herbert. Elder Cooke is seen on the far right hand side in a top hat with a long white beard. Carr's Park existed from about 1875 to 1950. It is unclear as to whether or not W.T. Carr deeded the land to public use or whether the acreage evolved over time. Of interest is the fact that this image was taken from the double radial bow windows of the W.T. Carr house at 209 Second Street—the windows having been specifically designed to give the Carr family a panoramic view of the verdant park.

On June 14, 1902, 22-year-old Jim Archie Roper was accidentally shot and killed in Fulton by his friend Harlan Soloman while trying to convince Harlan to buy his .32-caliber Smith and Wesson revolver in the back of Phipp's Jewelry Store. Soloman and Roper were reportedly the best of friends. The shooting left behind a young wife of less than a year and a daughter, Annie Viola "Jimmie" Roper. The story was featured prominently in a 1902 edition of the *Fulton Daily Leader*.

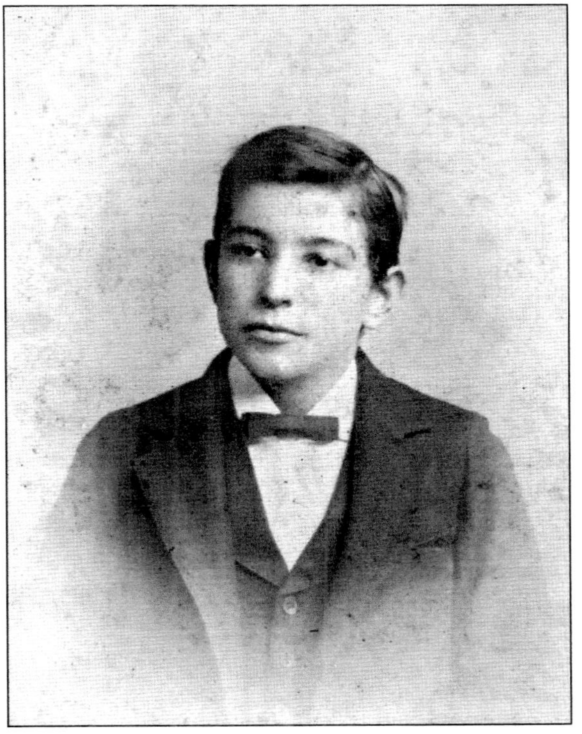

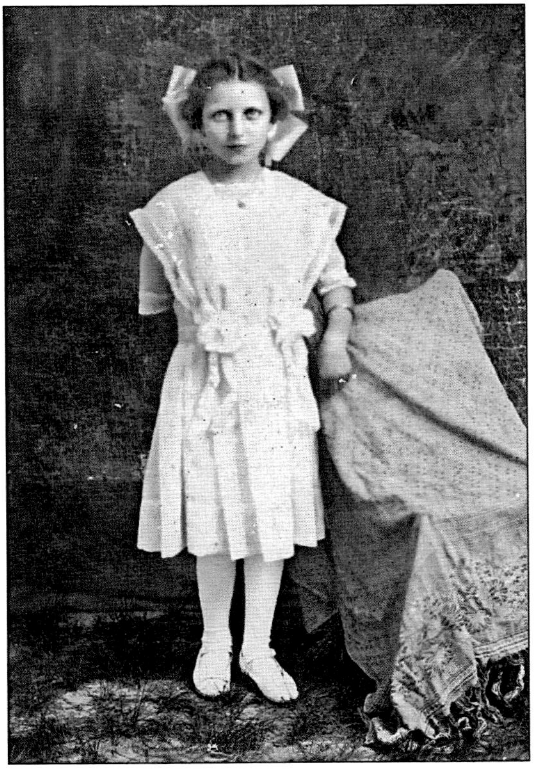

As the only child of Jim Archie Roper, Viola came to be known as Jimmie in honor of her father after his accidental shooting in her infancy. Jimmie was raised by her father's sister, Marion Lucretia "Lou" Roper Bondurant and Marion's husband, Elbert Eugene Bondurant.

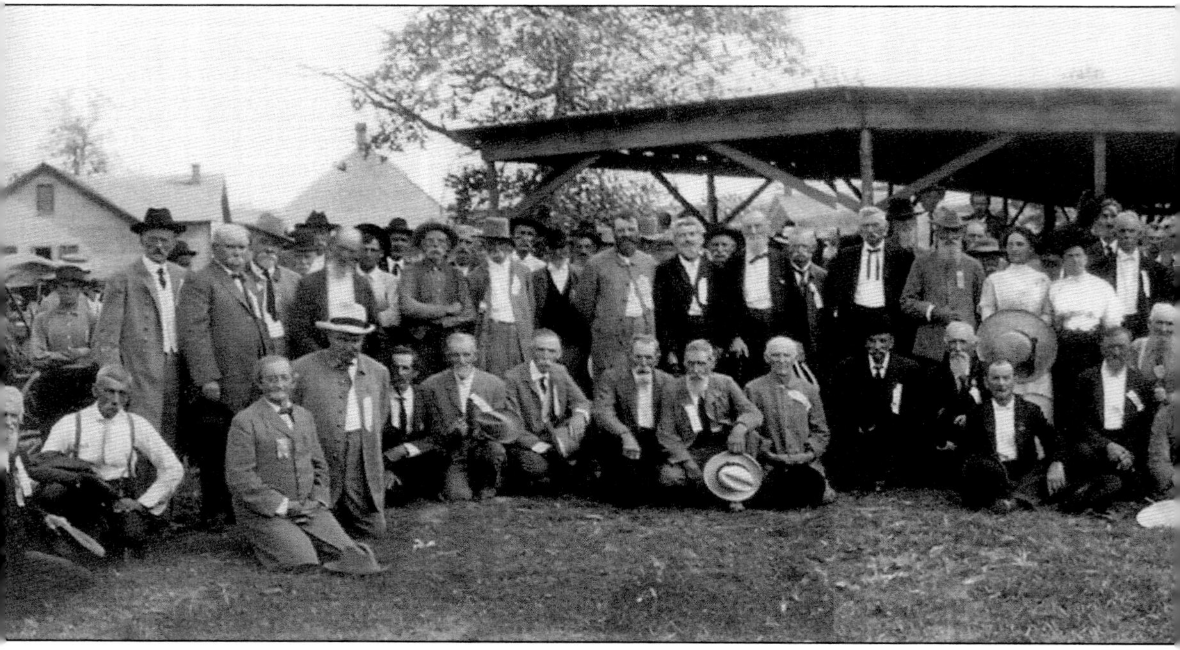

James G. Pirtle Chapter #990 of the Confederate Veterans held a camp reunion on September 22, 1916. Named after the company commander for the 7th Kentucky, James G. Pirtle, this Fulton chapter of veterans was one of the largest Confederate camps in the area. They were described as a "gallant band of heroes who wore the gray and immortalized southern valor." They

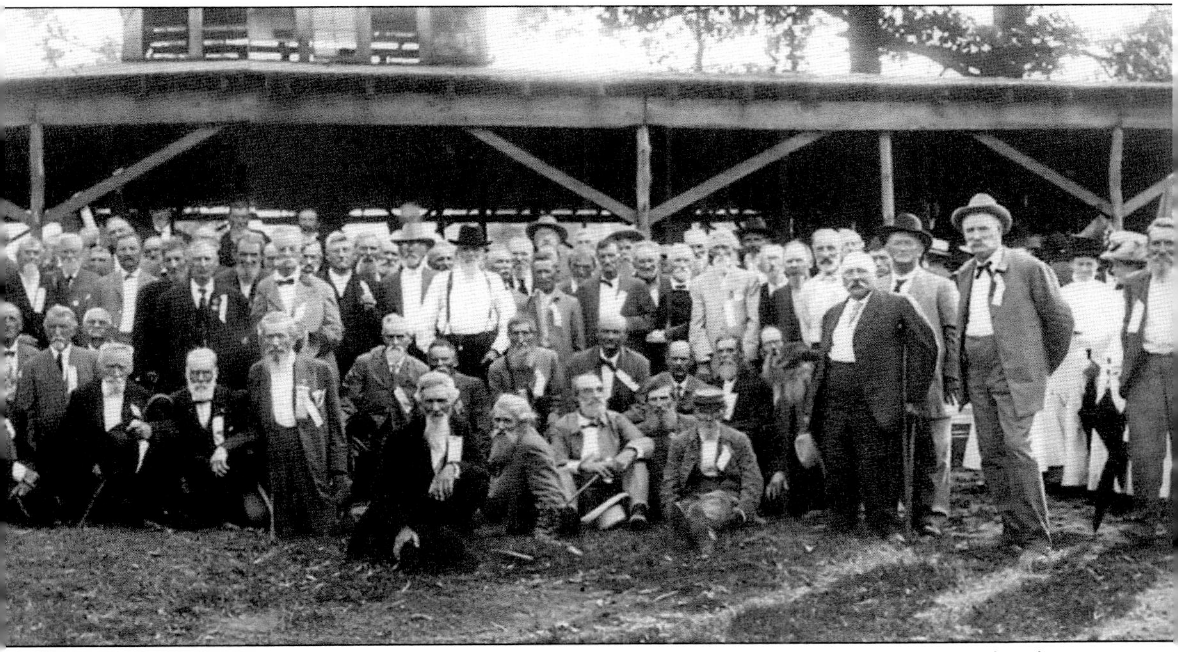

often spoke together of the time when they would "cross to the other side and rest under the shade of the trees with Stonewall Jackson and others gone before," as written in a 1911 souvenir edition of the *Fulton Daily Leader*. It was not until 1911 that the Kentucky Legislature passed a law to pay the Confederate soldiers and their families a pension for their service in the war.

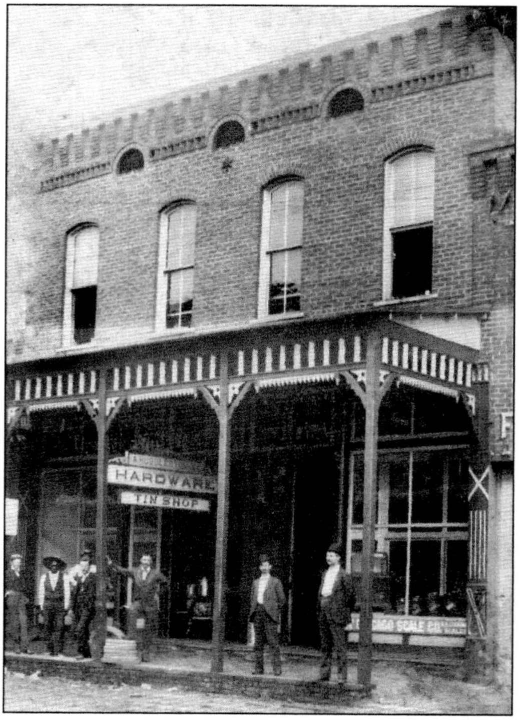

Founded in 1893 and known as one of Fulton's oldest and most popular mercantile establishments, A. Huddleston's Hardware Company and Tin Shop was popular among citizens of the community, chiefly thanks to its original proprietors, Arch Huddleston and George T. Beadles. Around 1950, Huddleston erected an electrical appliance store next door to an old livery barn that was razed to form the "new" hardware and electrical store, which is still in business to this day.

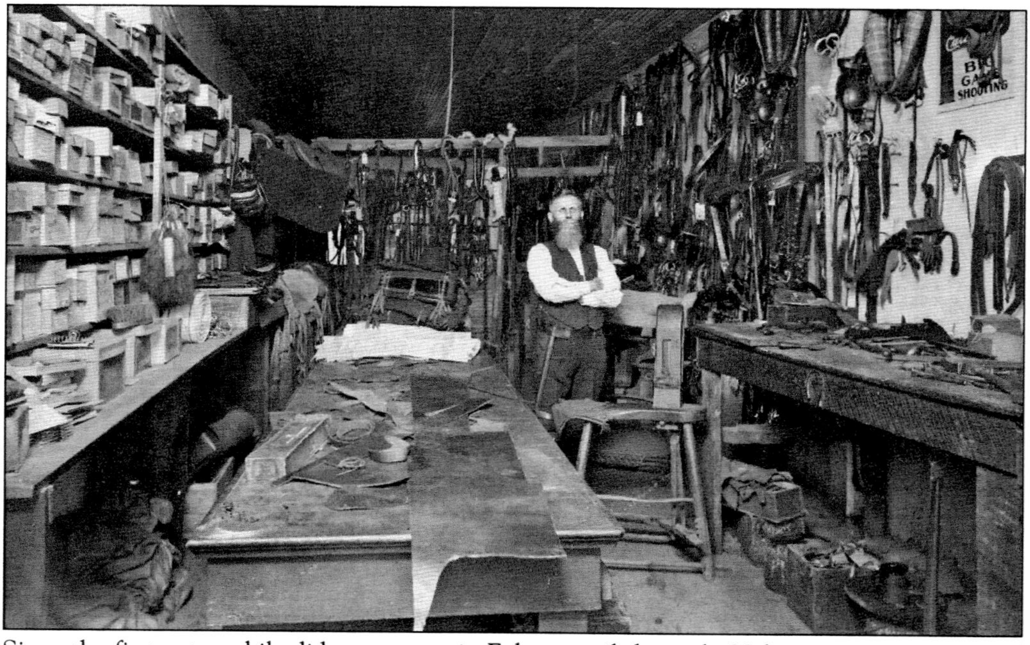

Since the first automobile did not appear in Fulton until the early 20th century, carriages and walking were the two prominent forms of transportation. The construction of a dirt racetrack at the fairgrounds around this time brought horse owners following the fair circuit in need of supplies. Seen in this image is harness maker J.H. Brown, who ran a harness shop on the east end of Lake Street.

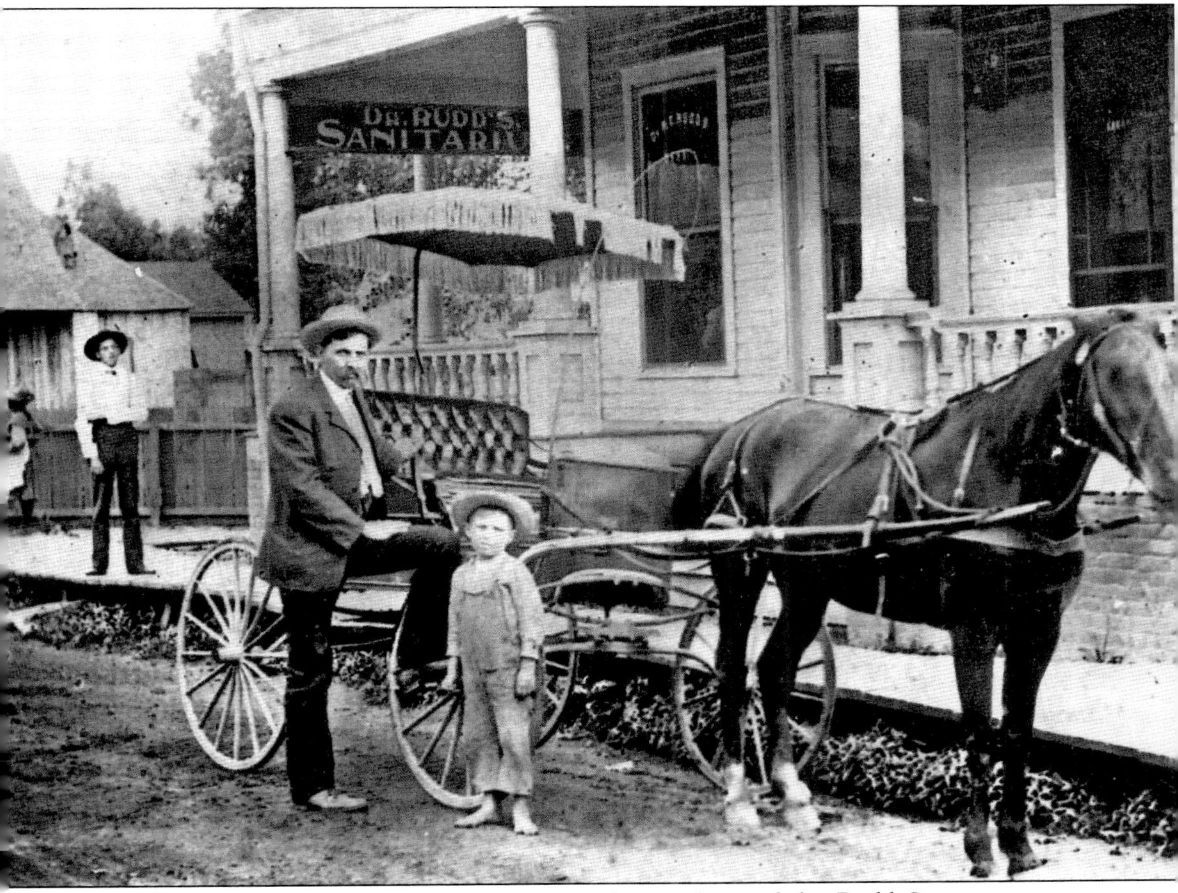

Dr. R.T. Rudd and young son Russell stand together in front of the Rudd Sanitarium on Commercial Street in Fulton. R.T. Rudd's brother, Vester, is visible in the background. Vester operated a drug store in Hickman, Kentucky. The date of this photograph is unknown.

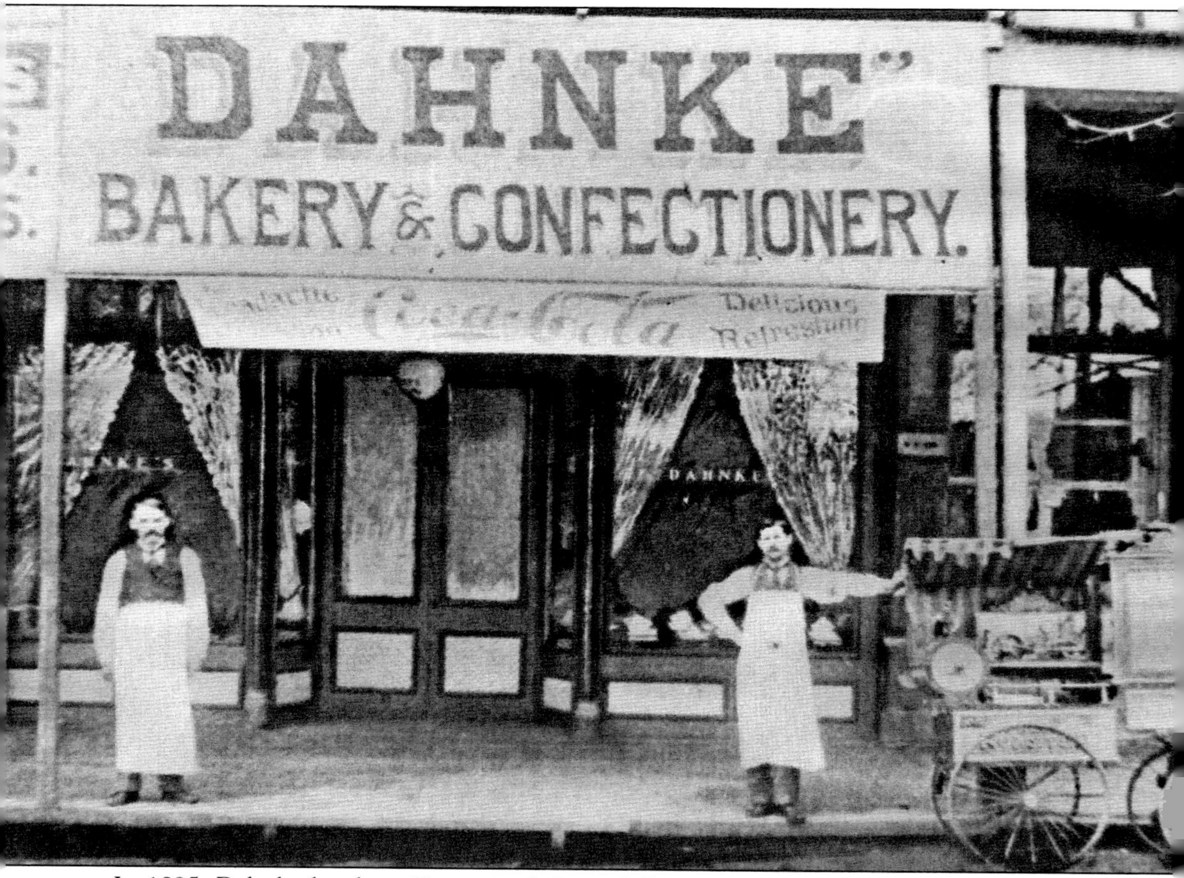

In 1895, Dahnke brothers George and Conrad (known as C.F.) opened a confectionary and bakery on Lake Street in Fulton. Noted for their brand of "cream bread," the brothers also had successful establishments in Union City and Dyersburg.

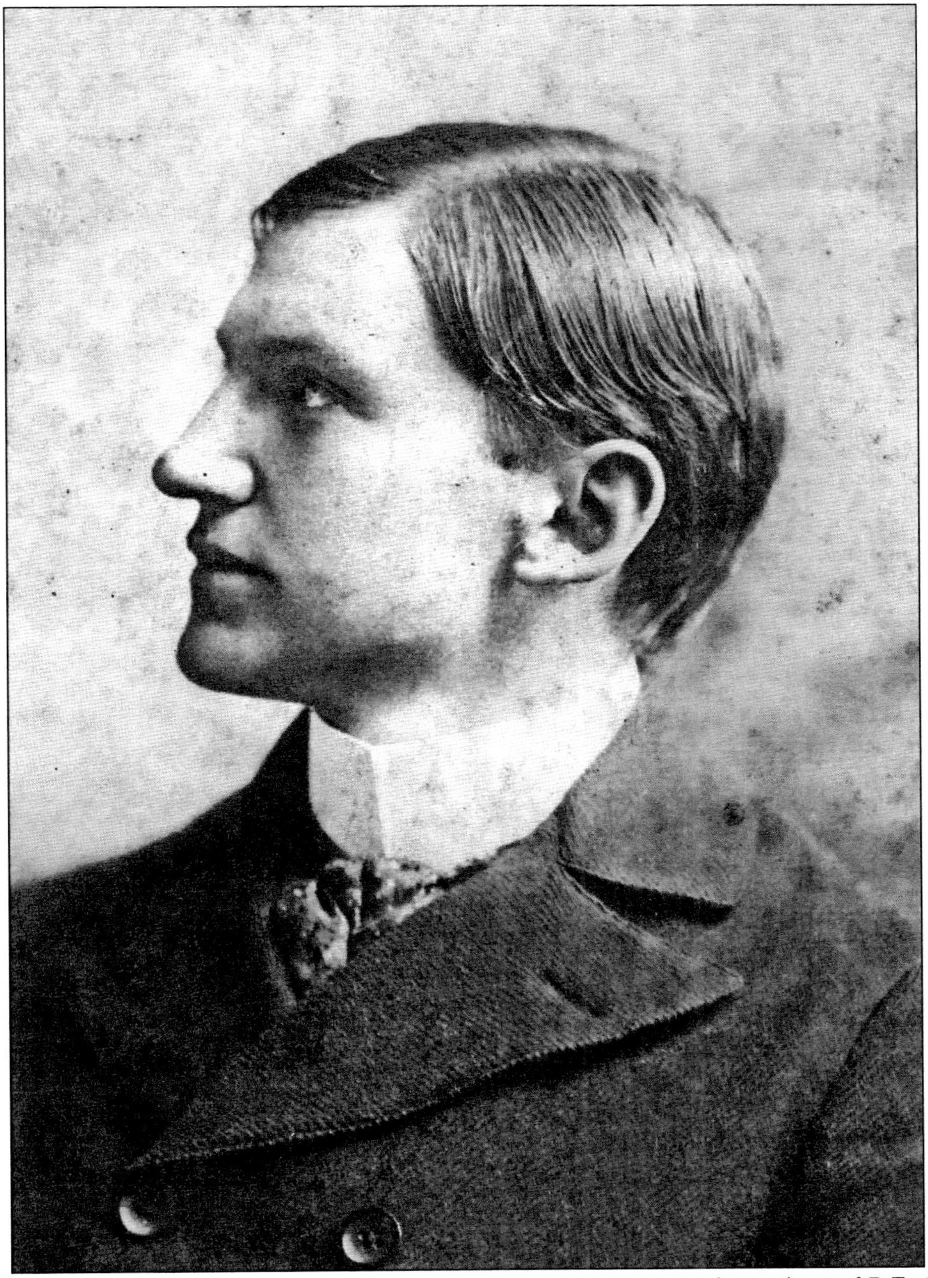

Born in Fulton in 1875, Herbert Carr was the son of W.T. Carr and grandson of B.F. Carr. Herbert graduated from Vanderbilt University in 1898 and became a lawyer. He married Myrtle Skeen of Bell Buckle, Tennessee, returned to Fulton, and together they had two children. In 1900, he was elected judge of the city court, served eight years, and then returned to private practice in 1909 as senior member of the firm Carr & Carr. The junior member of the firm was his younger brother Frank. The firm was the local attorney for the Illinois Central Railroad and prospered. It was Judge Carr who moved the B.F. Carr home on Eddings and Second Streets to its present-day location when he was given the residence from his father as a wedding present.

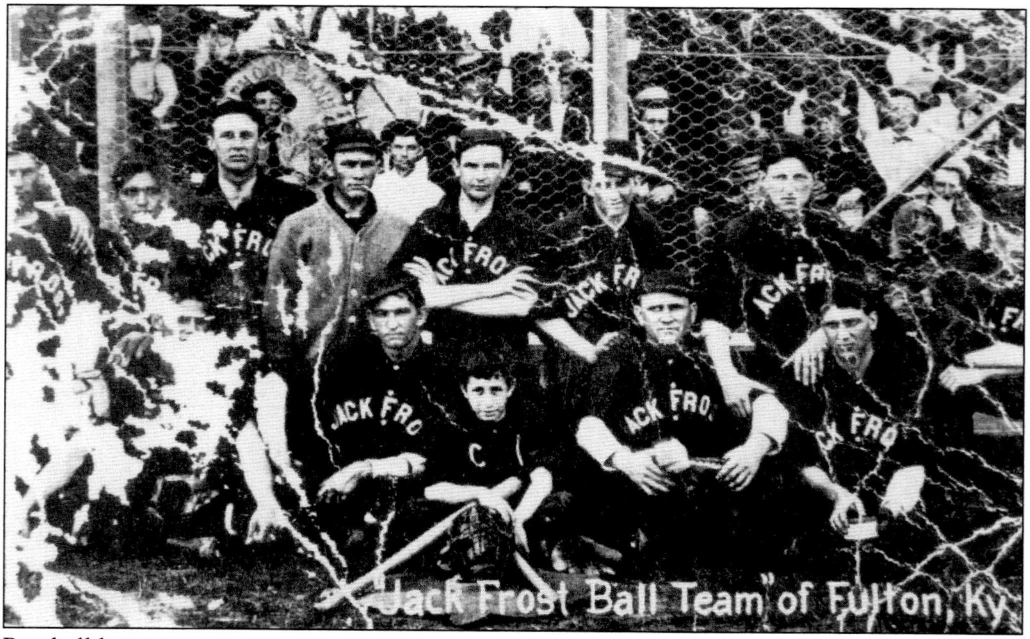

Baseball became an institution in 1908, when the never-to-be-forgotten "Jack Frost" team was organized. Team members included Boot Shepherd, Sam Edwards, L.O. Diguid, Tom Mahory, Ed Roach, Collin Cowardin, and Hub Williams. Millard Cohn was mascot. They played to a grandstand located on Taylor Street in Fulton.

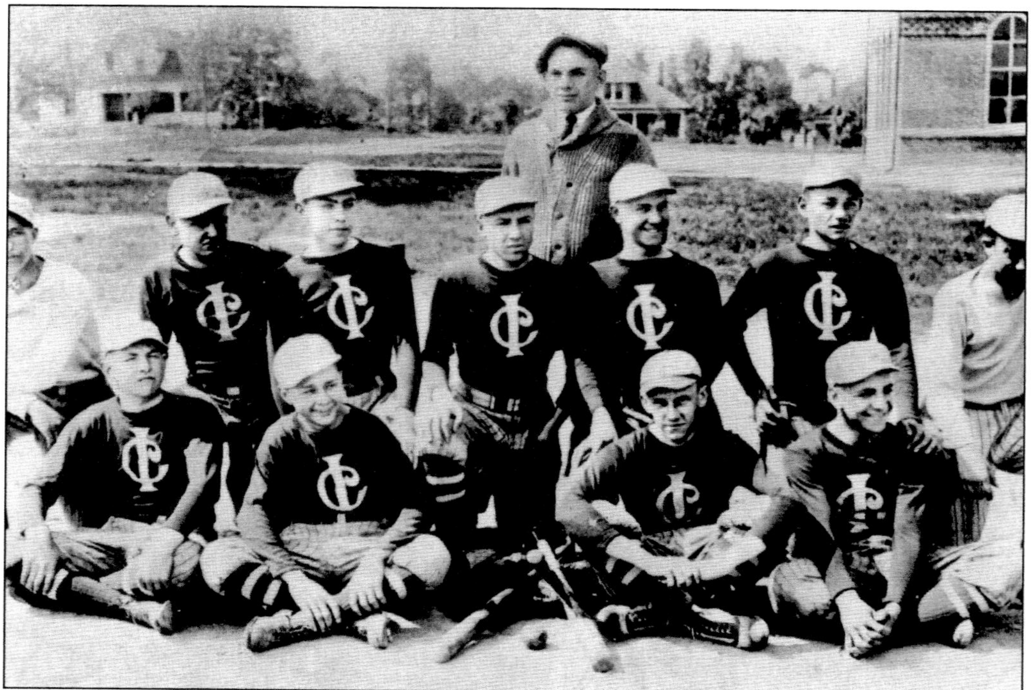

With the C.I. logo emblazoned across their uniform tops, these team members were among the earliest players of organized sports at Carr Institute in the year 1922.

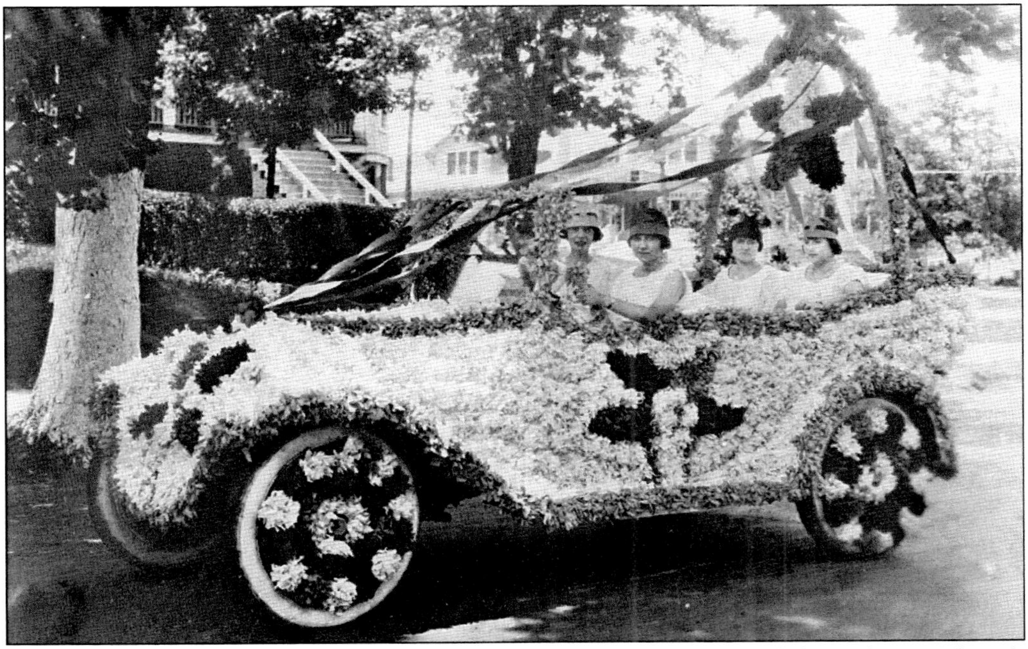

Fulton City Chapter No. 41 of the Order of the Eastern Star was founded April 7, 1905, with 15 charter members. The O.E.S. accepted petitions for membership from Masons and the wives, widows, sisters, daughters, and mothers of Masons. Seen here are unidentified members of the O.E.S. with their parade entry on July 4, 1923.

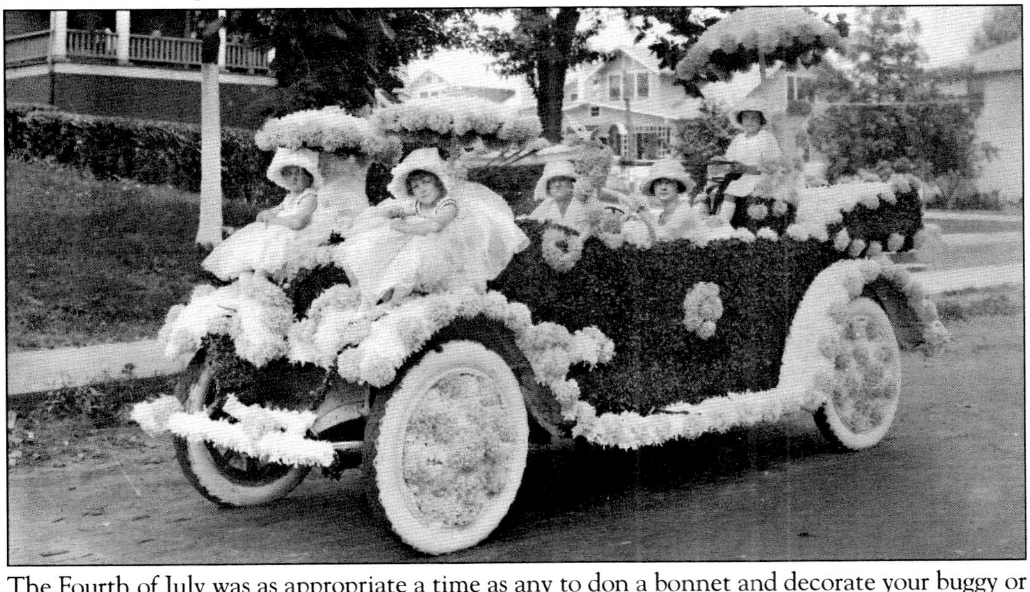

The Fourth of July was as appropriate a time as any to don a bonnet and decorate your buggy or automobile for entry in the parade on Lake Street. Featured here is a 1918 touring car owned by P.H. Weaks. The photograph was taken at the corner of Carr and Third Streets near the home of Dr. Cohn. On the front fender are Martha Moore Mahan, left, and Jane Scates Edwards, right. In the passenger and driver seats respectively are Virginia Fields Gattney and Carmen Parks Weaks. In the rumble seat is Sarah Alexander.

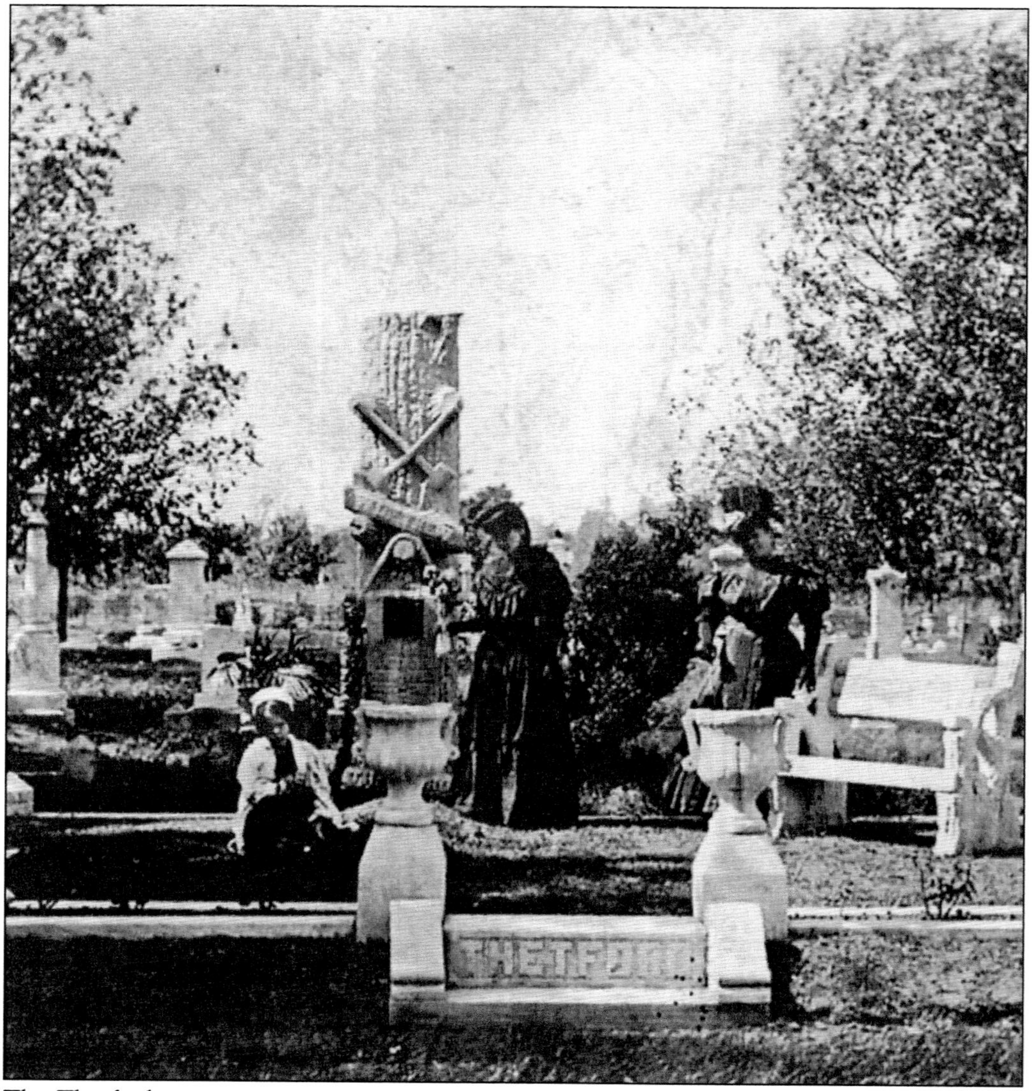

The Thetfords were an enterprising family, including brothers E.N. and James Harmon, who dealt primarily in furniture and coffins. James handled the undertaking business, and E.N. was a director at Carr Institute. Here the Thetford women are in Fairview Cemetery reflecting at the family burial site. The young girl seated on the left is Monette Thetford Willingham as a child.

Pictured here are two of the four children born to Emma Josephine Bondurant Donoho (1859–1955) and Hayden Donoho. Seated is daughter Jessie, and standing is son Dr. Glen Donoho. Their dress depicts typical children's fashion at the turn of the century—very proper, dark-colored fabric with a high lace collar, stockings, and ankle boots for Jessie and her brother in a dark wool suit, bow tie, and ankle boots.

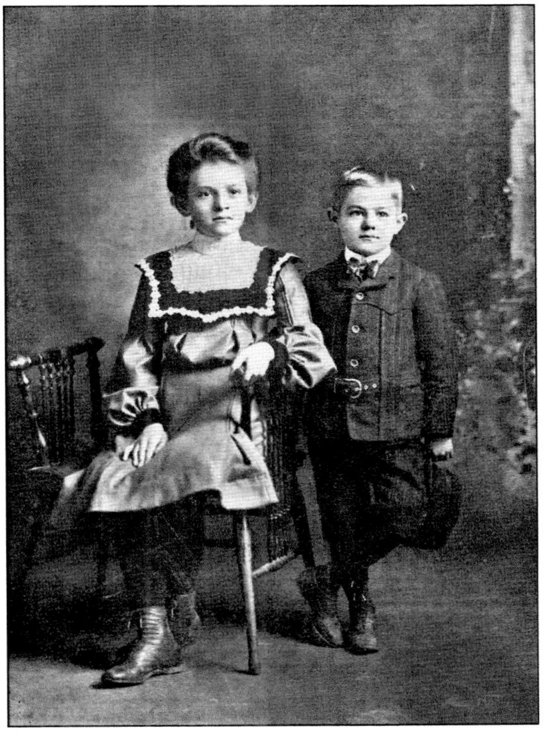

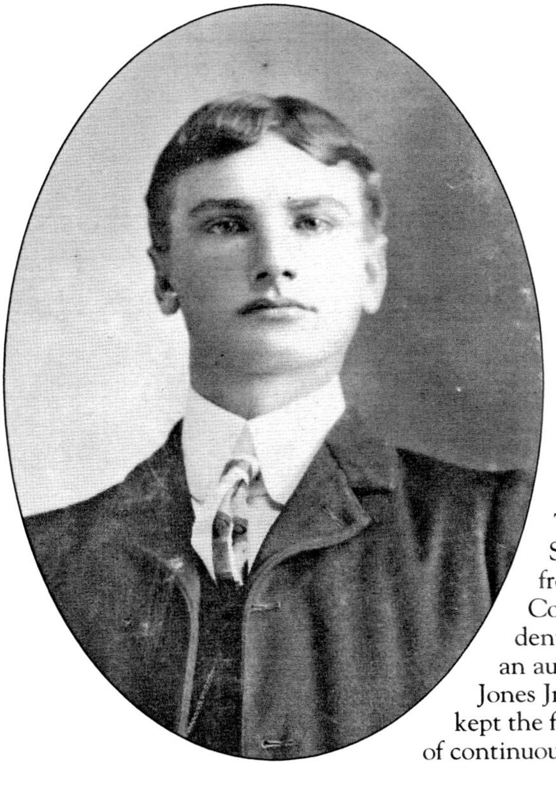

This photograph of Dr. John Lloyd Jones Sr. was taken in 1909 at his graduation from the University of Tennessee Dental College in Nashville. Dr. J.L. Jones practiced dentistry in Fulton from 1929 until his death in an automobile accident in 1950. His son Dr. J.L. Jones Jr. and his grandson Dr. Alan W. Jones have kept the family practice in existence for over 77 years of continuous dental care in the Twin Cities.

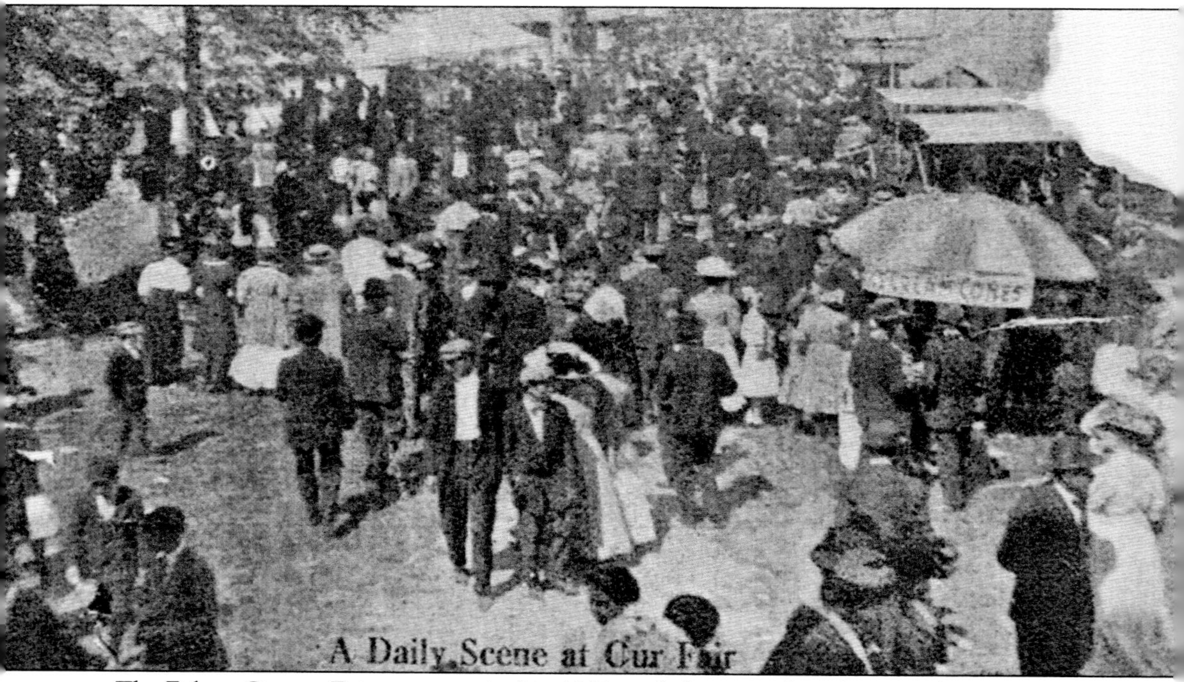

The Fulton County Fair was organized in 1911, with fairgrounds embracing about 35 acres. The grounds were located on property sold to the Fair Association by E.C. Reeds at the present day site of the Lions Club Fulton City Park. Every day was a big one at the fair. It was not uncommon for 10,000 or more adult tickets to be sold at the gate in one night. The adult admission price was 50¢. The fair usually ran about five days and featured—besides the very popular harness racing—entertainment such as balloon ascensions, to the pleasure and apprehension of the crowd, as well as animal acts like a troop of trained chickens in 1912 that were reported to do "marvelous" stunts.

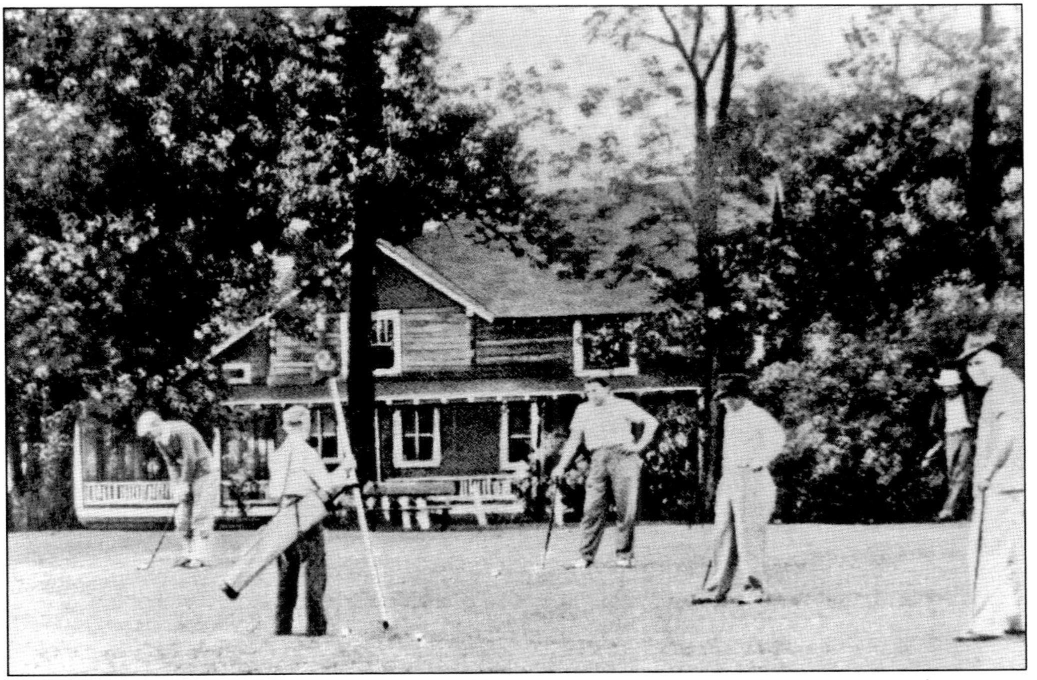

Tennis was a popular sport in Fulton in 1920, but it was destined to give way to another sport, golf, already gaining in popularity. Golfers originally played on a nine-hole course on Water Street behind what was known as the old Dick Thomas House. In 1925, the Fulton Country Club was organized. A log cabin (seen in the background) served as the clubhouse. This was then the only golf course between Memphis and Fulton.

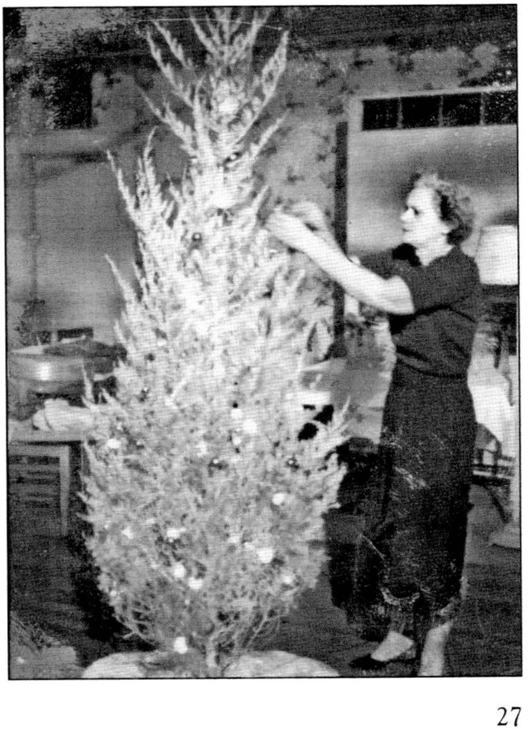

Conveniently located on the corner of Lake and Fourth Streets, Smith's Café was known throughout the community as a fine dining establishment and the best place in town to get a steak. Opened originally in 1901, Howard and Lucille Adams were the owners from 1950 to 1960. This Fulton landmark closed its doors for good in 1962. Shown here is a Christmas postcard featuring Lucille Adams trimming a tree. Postcards were a popular mode of advertising for the day.

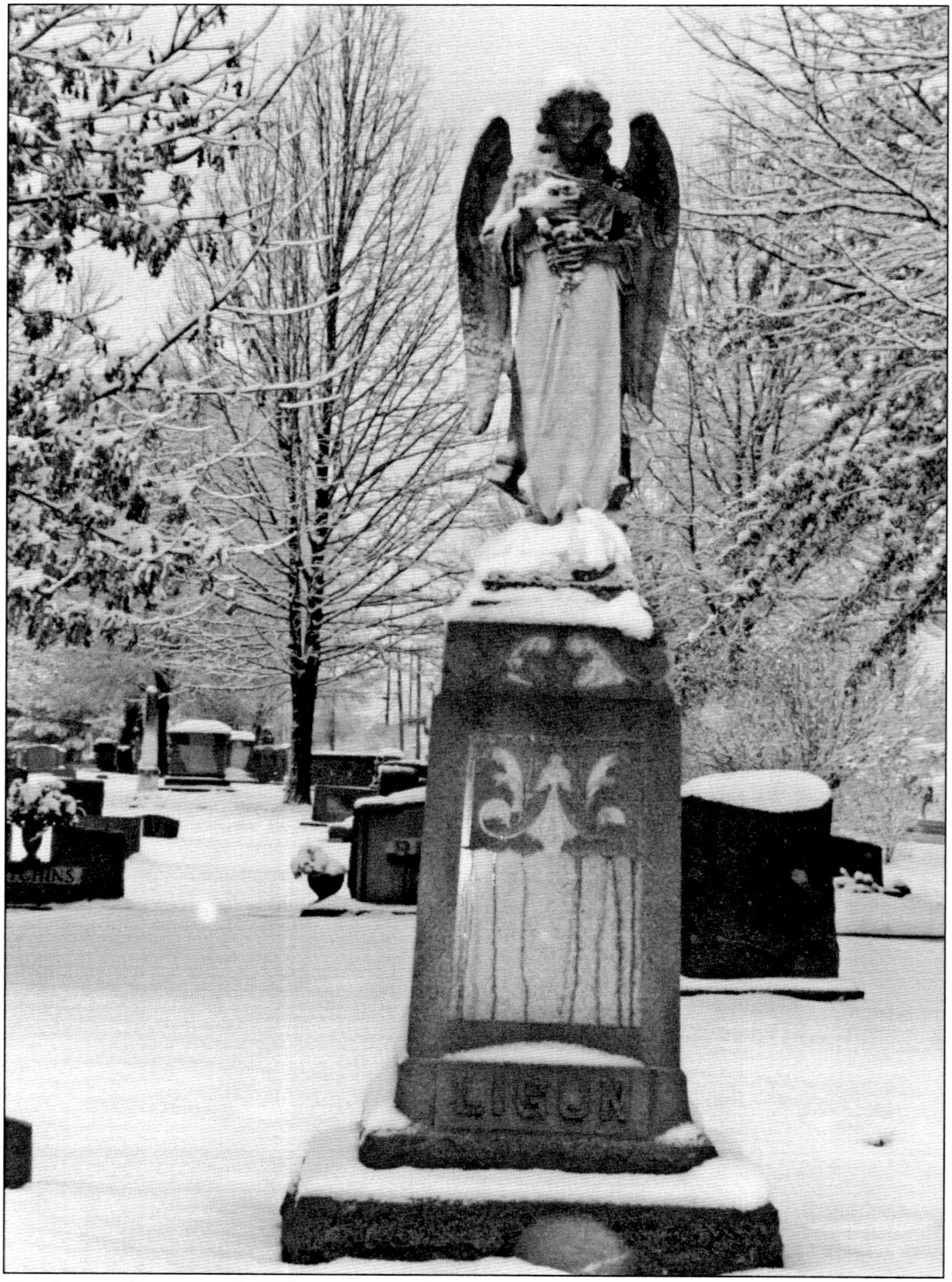

An object of beauty in the February snow, this angel keeps timeless watch over Fulton's Fairview Cemetery, established in the late 1800s. The grounds contain many fascinating markers, monuments, and statuary, all paying tribute to loved ones from the community. The earliest recorded burial is that of cemetery organizer G.E. McFall in 1881.

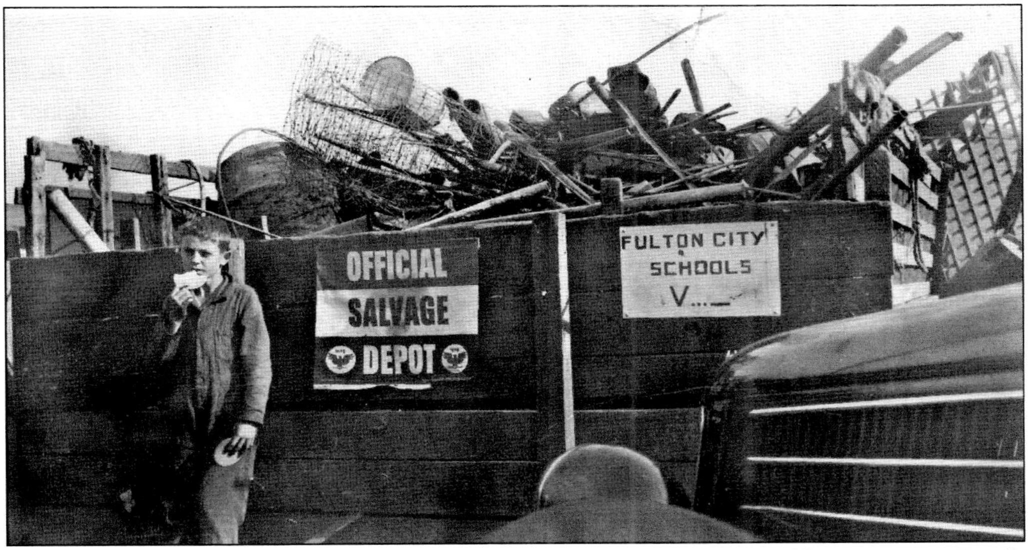

Pearl Harbor was bombed December 7, 1941. Memories of the First World War were still with everyone. Fulton responded to the draft board with the best of her youth, and those left behind did all they could to help the war effort. Seen here is a scrap-metal collection site located on the grounds of Fulton High School, where citizens were asked to contribute items that could be put to use in the American war machine.

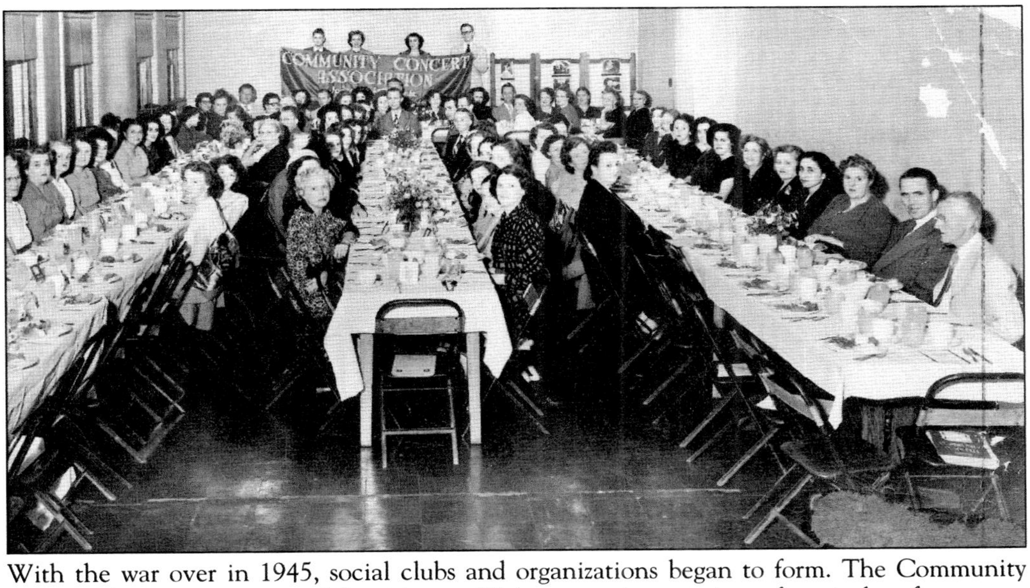

With the war over in 1945, social clubs and organizations began to form. The Community Concert Association arranged for citizens of Fulton to enjoy a variety of musical performances, usually held at the gymnasium at the Carr school building.

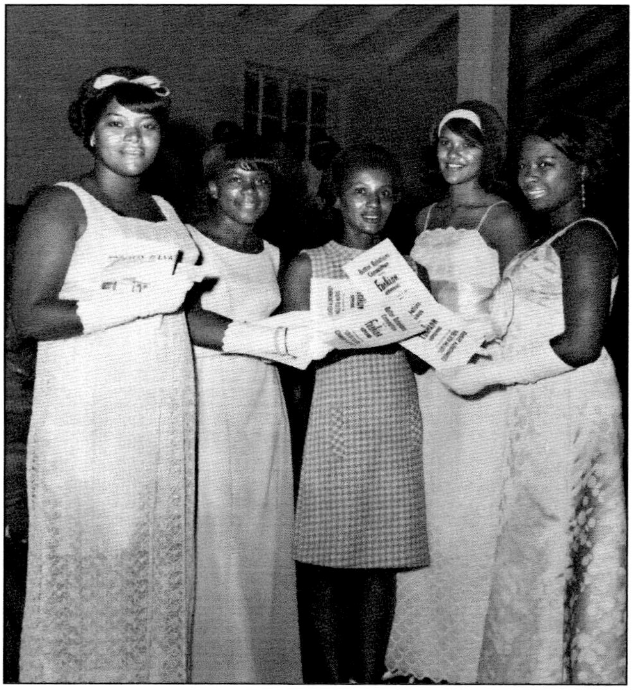

The Better Relations Committee, c. 1960s, sponsored a "fashion happening" for the community at large. Those participating in the show included, from left to right, Beulah Williams, Cathy Walker, Lily Jones, Kay Stunson, and Beatrice Heans Wilcox.

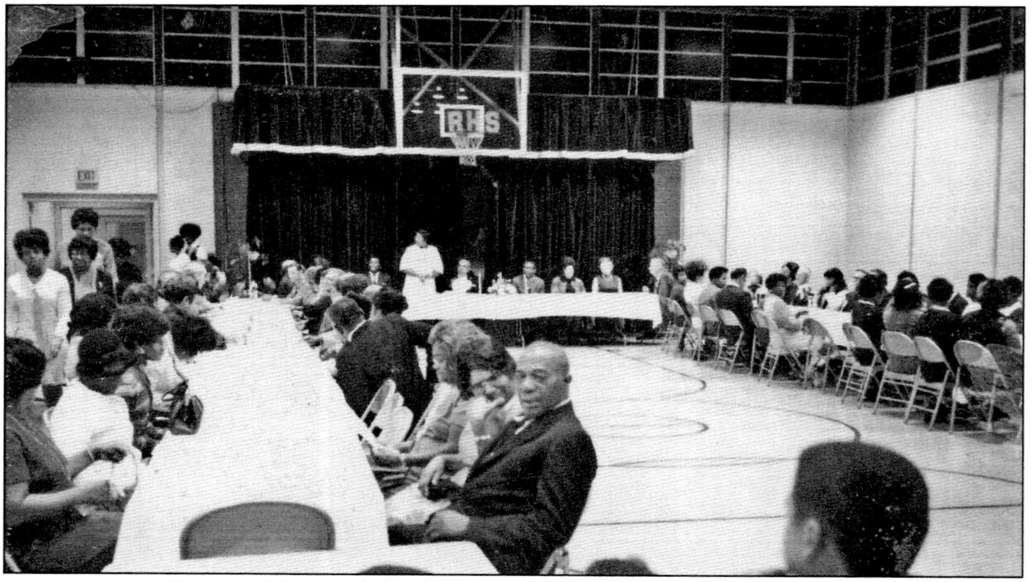

South Fulton's Rosenwald School, built from a grant to assist African-American communities in constructing rural elementary schools, originally housed classrooms and a gymnasium under the same roof. In 1953, a separate gymnasium, seen here, was built to the left of the first school building. In the 1960s, a third building for science was erected. The last class graduated from Rosenwald in 1963. The original building burned, but the gymnasium and science building were saved. The gymnasium is now the Ken Tenn Community Center. It is hoped that the gym may be added to the National Register of Historic Places, as there are so few Rosenwald buildings remaining.

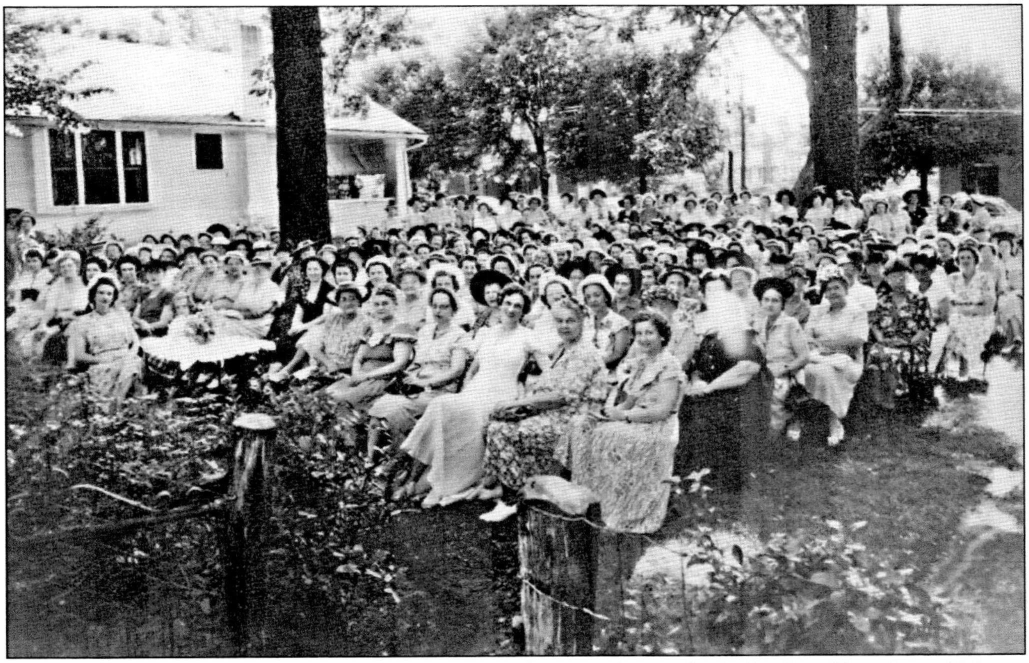

This group of women is thought to represent the First United Methodist Church in Fulton, gathered to spend time socially in someone's backyard garden, a popular way to spend a Saturday or Sunday afternoon.

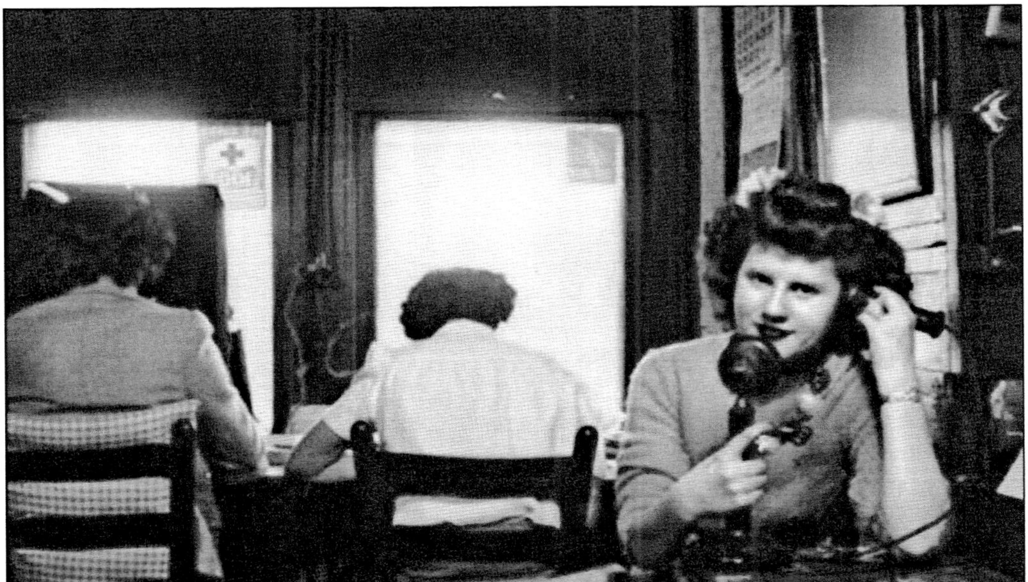

The Bell South Telephone Company has had a part in Fulton's progress since the first telephones were invented. As early as 1898, advertising was in place to "get on line" by the West Kentucky Telephone Company of Mayfield, Kentucky. In the 1950s, work as a Southern Bell switchboard operator was much sought. "Number please" was a familiar phrase until the conversion to dial-phone service took place after 1961.

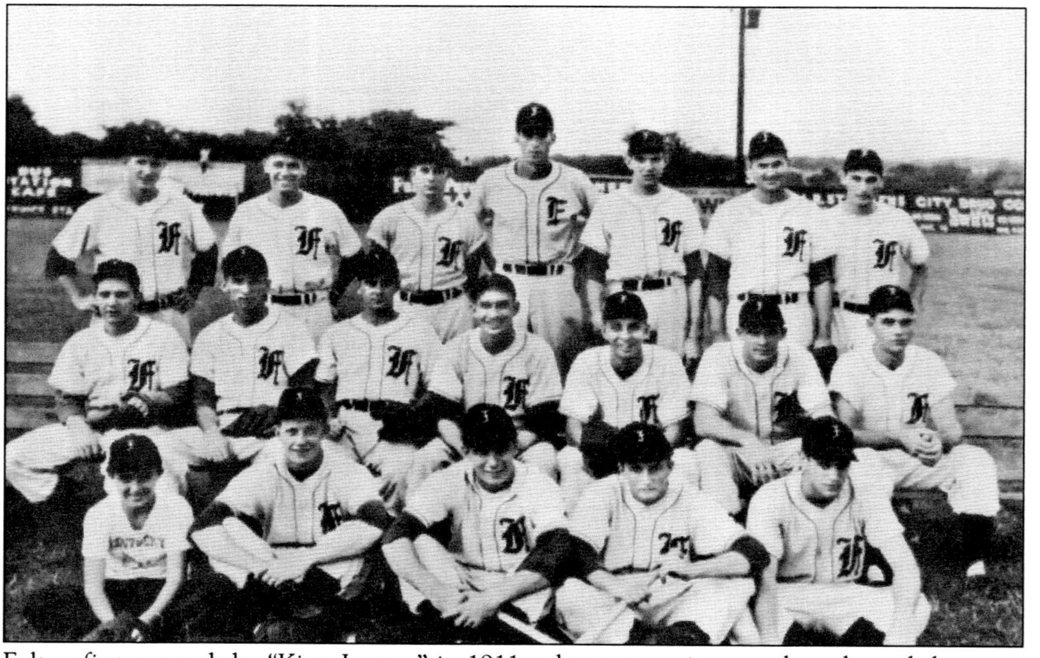

Fulton first entered the "Kitty League" in 1911—the community warmly embraced the game of baseball, as evidenced by the popularity of the Jack Frost team, and laid claim to being the "smallest city in organized baseball" when the Fulton Railroaders formed in 1949. Home games were played at Fairfield Park, known today as Lohaus Field, home to the Fulton High School baseball squad. After three consecutive pennant winning seasons—1951, 1952, and 1953—and after a name change to the Lookouts in 1952, television broadcasts of major league baseball brought about a decline in public interest for minor league action.

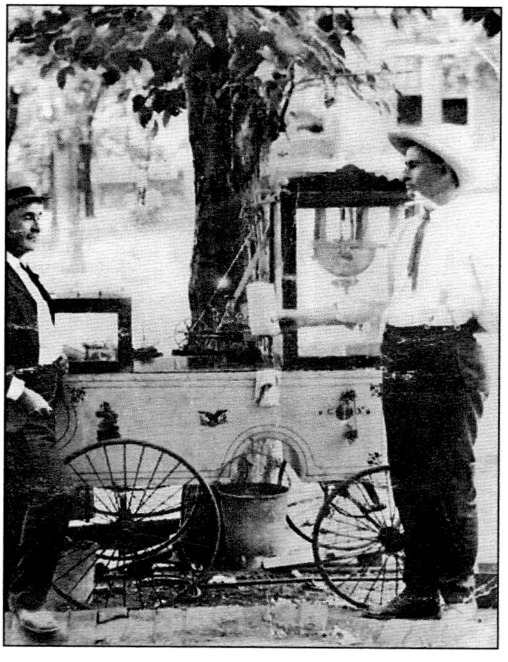

A popular sight on the streets of Fulton was Gilbert Moon, who sold popcorn to customers passing by on Lake Street.

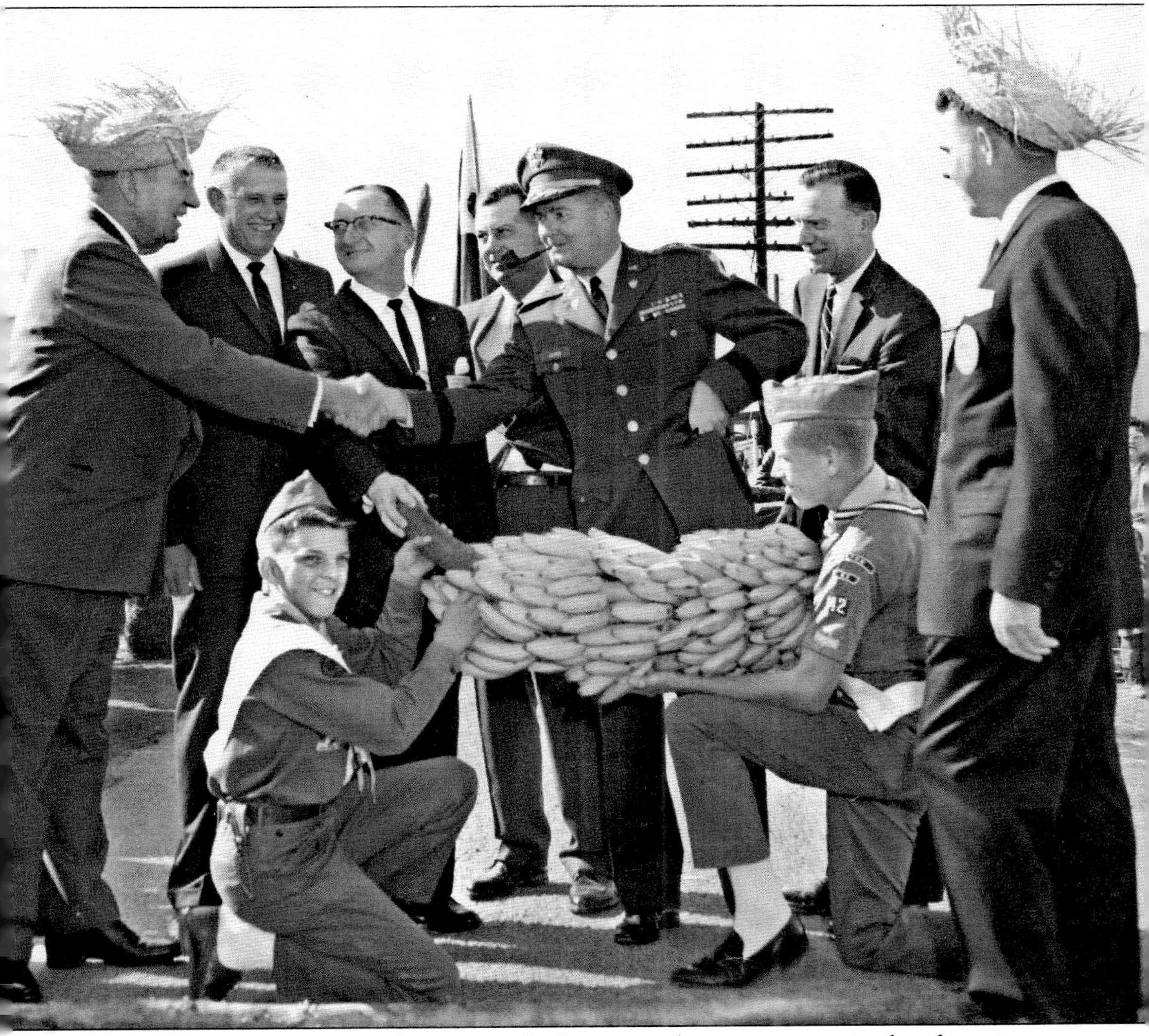

In 1962, a giant festival paying homage to the banana industry was conceived and put into motion by the citizens of the Twin Cities. The annual celebration spanned 30 years and focused on the railroad history of the Illinois Central Gulf, which maintained large facilities in Fulton to ice down rail cars and send tropical fruit from the port cities to Midwesterners. In this photo, Boy Scouts of troop 42 hold bananas from Latin America while, from left to right, two unidentified men, Fulton mayor Gilbert de Myer, unidentified, a Washington diplomat, 1st District congressman Frank Albert Stubblefield, and Banana Festival president Nathan Wade look on.

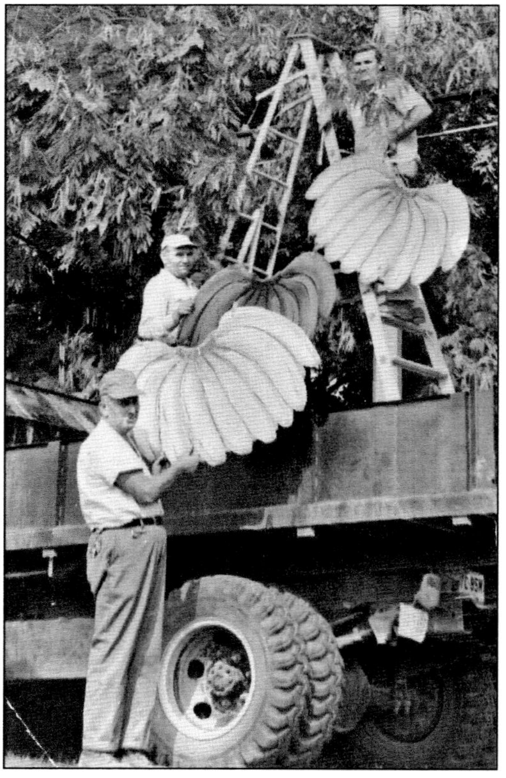

It was truly a community effort for the International Banana Festival, as citizens went all out to decorate the Twin Cities for the event. Seen here are men hanging cardboard bunches of bananas from fronds as festive decoration in preparation for the week-long schedule of activities.

These members of the Civitan Club and their wives are "bananas" for the fun. The club worked long hours to make colorful decorations that added a festive air to downtown. Free fruit was even "growing" out of the parking meters during the three-day 1964 International Banana Festival. From a carnival and midway to arts and crafts, the Banana Box Derby, beauty pageants, a parade and even an Inter-American Music Fiesta, there was something for everyone. Miss America 1965, Vonda Van Dyke, made an appearance in the fall of 1964 to help serve the world's largest banana pudding to the festival crowd after the grand parade.

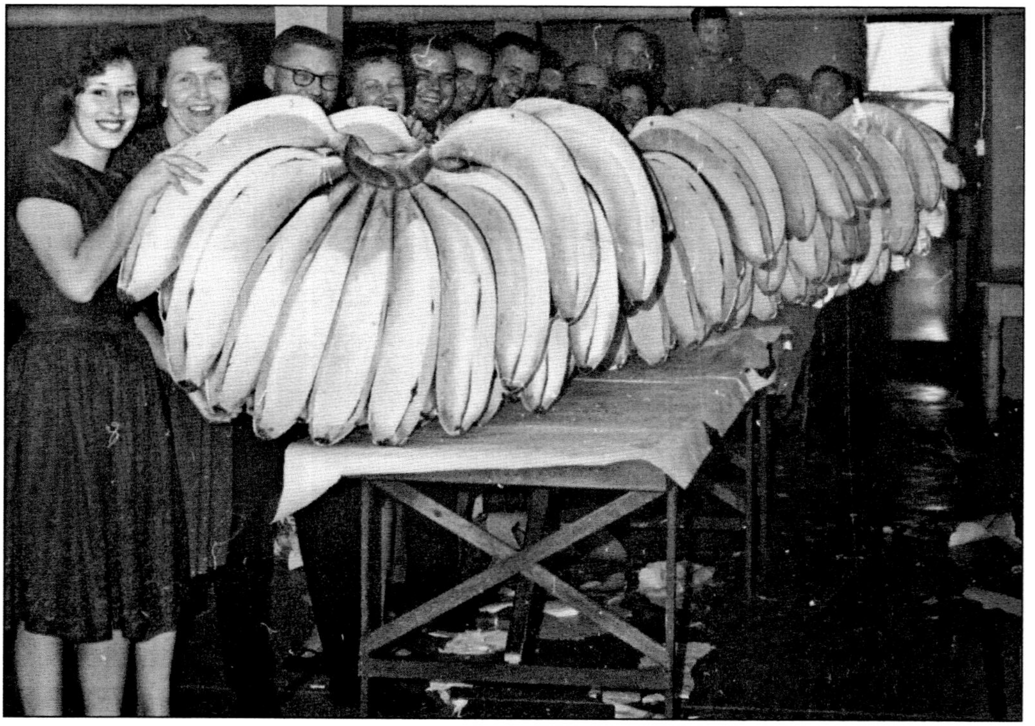

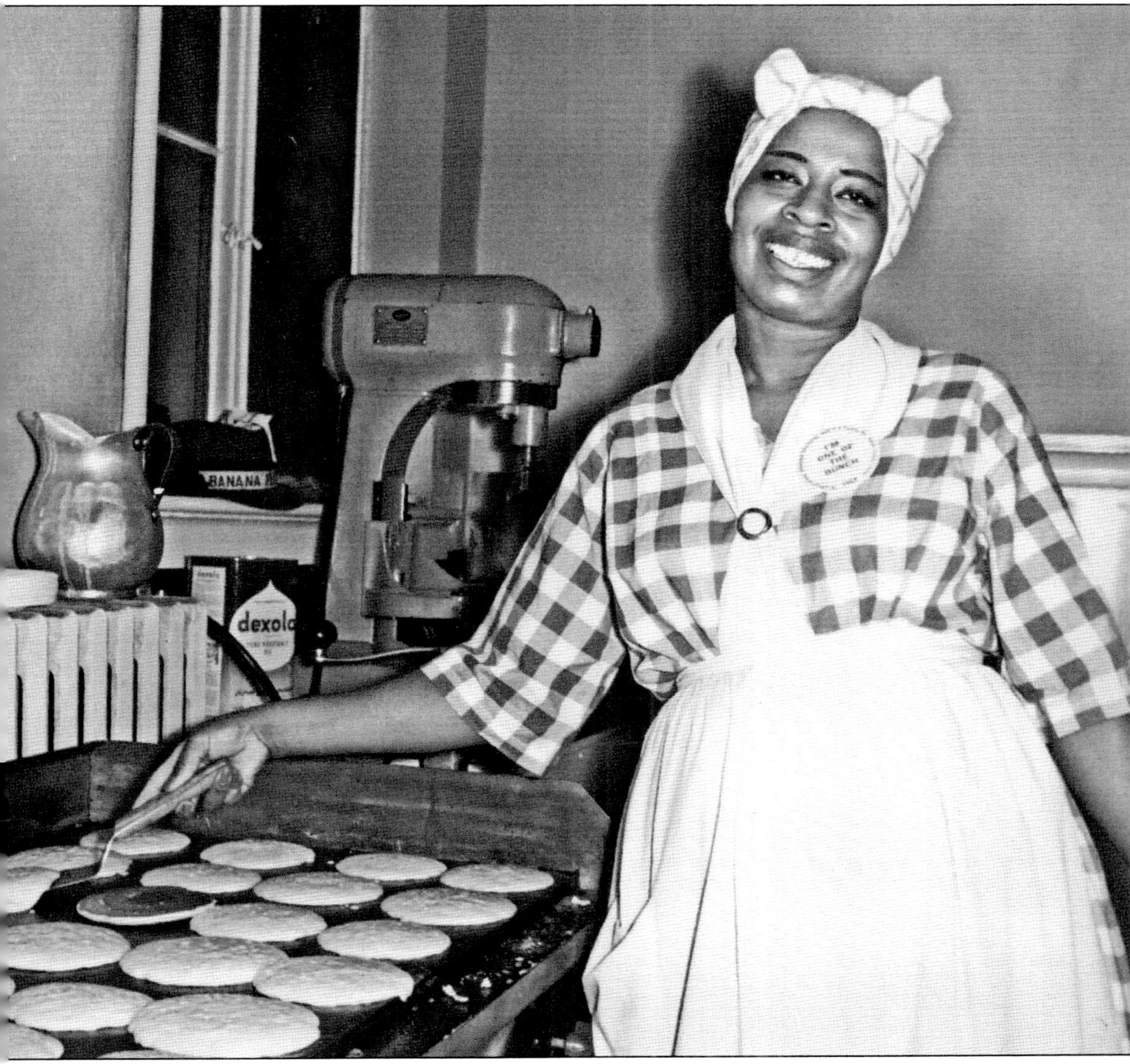

Aunt Jemima made annual appearances at the Twin Cities International Banana Festival. Her performances were much anticipated and well attended by the residents of Fulton and South Fulton. She traveled throughout the United States on behalf of the Quaker Oats Company. She traditionally performed mostly African-American spirituals, which have their own unique place in music history.

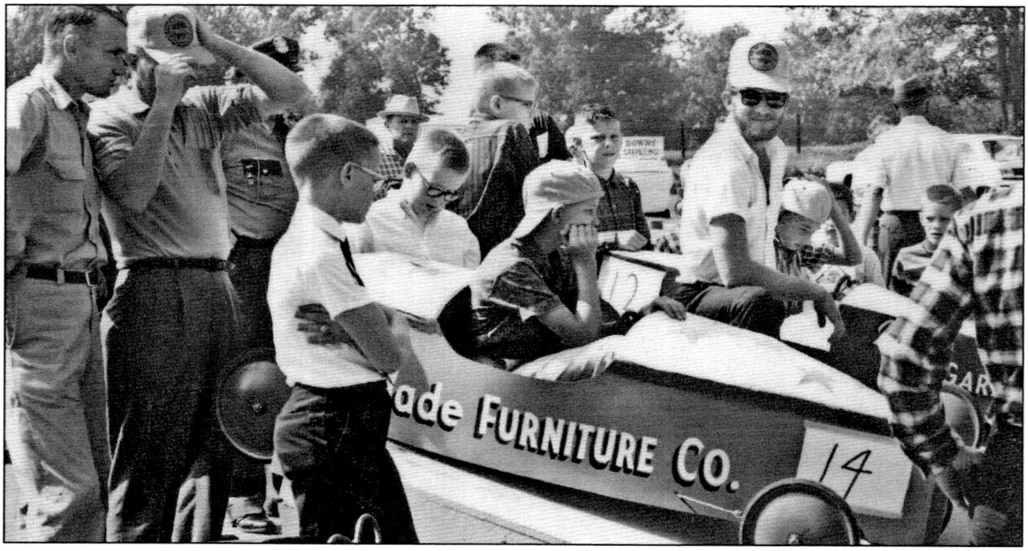

Typically held on youth day during Banana Festival week, the Banana Box Derby was grand entertainment. Boys in two age categories (11–12 and 13–15), with supervision, constructed derby cars of their own design. It was permissible for boys to have sponsors for their cars. The cars raced from a starting gate on a section of Highway 45 in elimination heats modeled after the American Soap Box Derby held annually in Akron, Ohio. Local winners then had a chance at the national event.

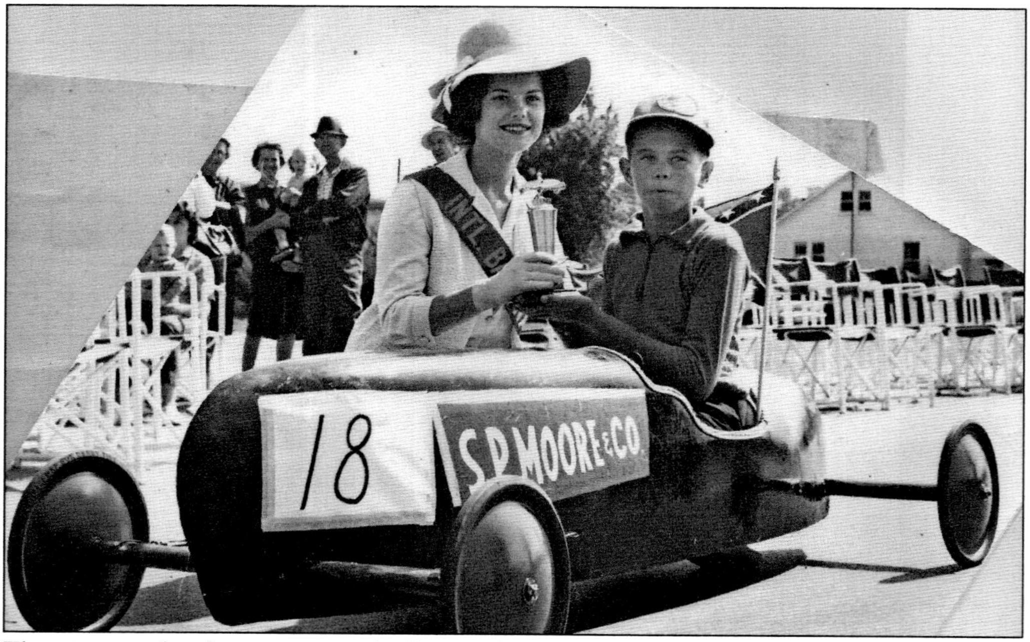

The winners of each age group in the Banana Box Derby competed for the grand championship at the end of the racing day. In addition to trophies, bonds were presented. There was also recognition for best brakes, best design, best construction, and best upholstery. David Hazelwood, pictured above, won a trophy as well as a kiss in this picture with the Banana Festival Princess of 1964, Miss Carol Glisson.

Two

PLACES OF THE PAST

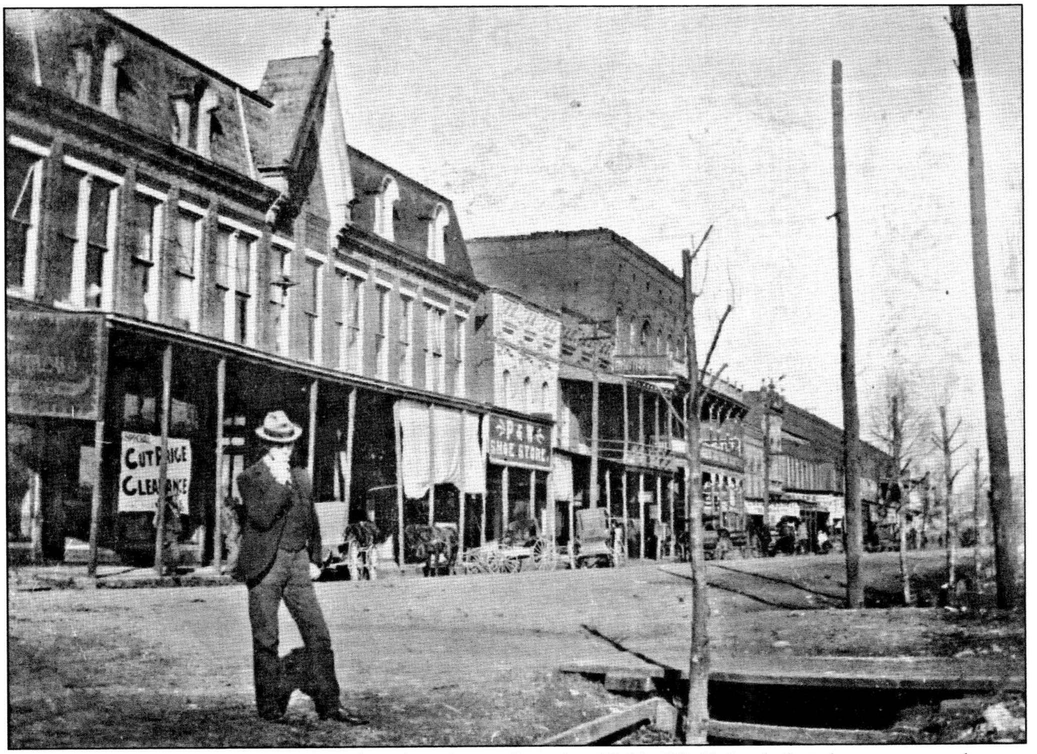

Lake Street in Fulton was already a bustling place by 1901. Well-built brick structures began to line the business thoroughfares, where all manner of merchandise was sold. The principle streets were Lake, Church, Main, Walnut, State (known as State Line), Commercial, and Plane. Sidewalks were wooden and the streets dirt. The Merchant and Business Men's Association brought famous drag road builder D. Ward King to Fulton in 1912. This was the beginning of road dragging in the county, which did much to improve the rutted condition of the main thoroughfares.

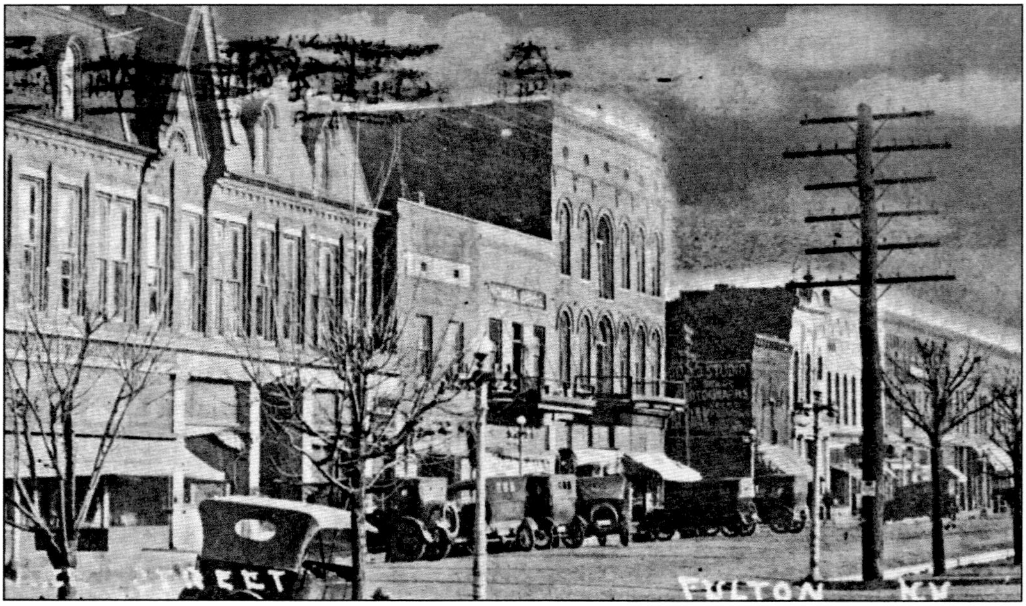

Lake Street got its name as the result of floods from the overflow of Harris Fork Creek. Flash floods have been numerous throughout the years, and many times Lake Street was accessible only by boat. At the turn of the 20th century, streets were gravel-paved and sidewalks were wood. By 1911, the city had four firms of automobile dealers and the "horseless carriage" was very popular, as evidenced by this scene.

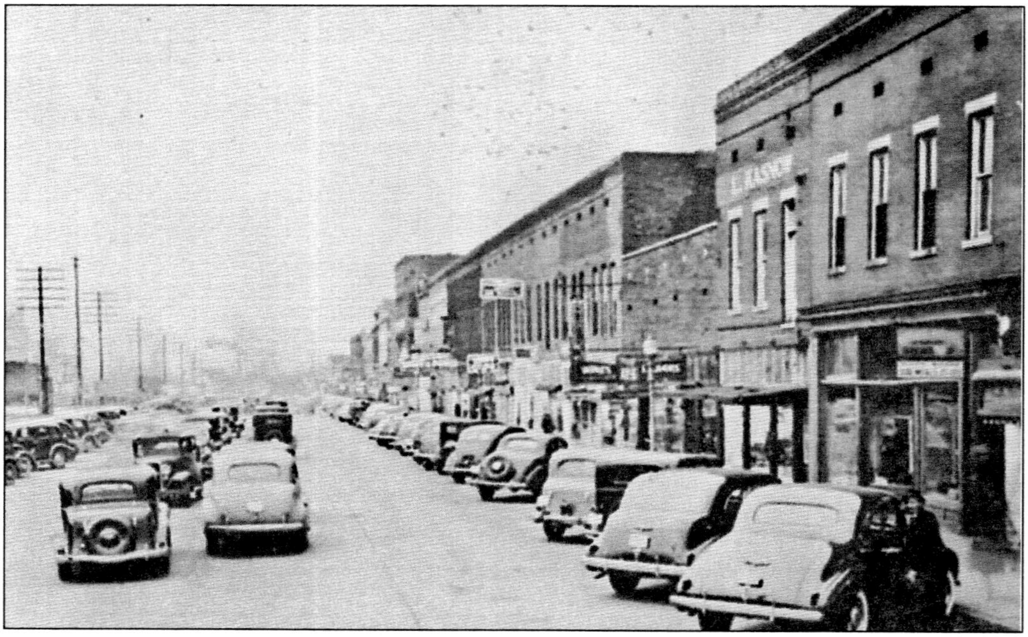

Progress is visible in this scene of downtown Fulton with the presence of electricity and telephone guide wires. Commerce was flourishing with many people about town. Note the cars parked vertically on each side of the street, as well as parked in double lanes in the center of the street.

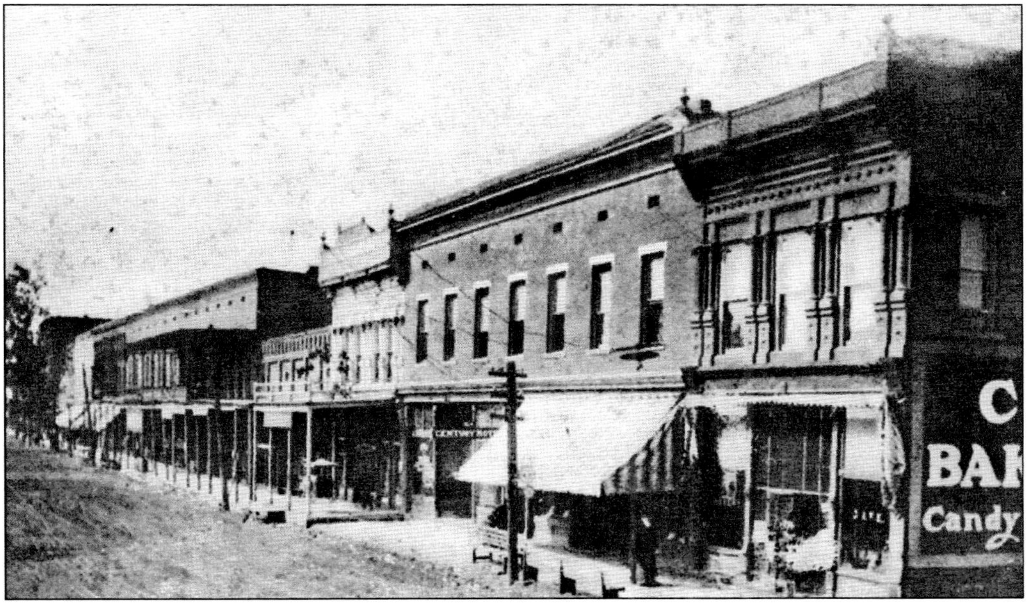

City Bakery was not only a bakery and confectionary extraordinaire; Mr. Guy Irby boasted a new, $1,500 soda fountain and heavily advertised the fact that he sold genuine Coca-Cola.

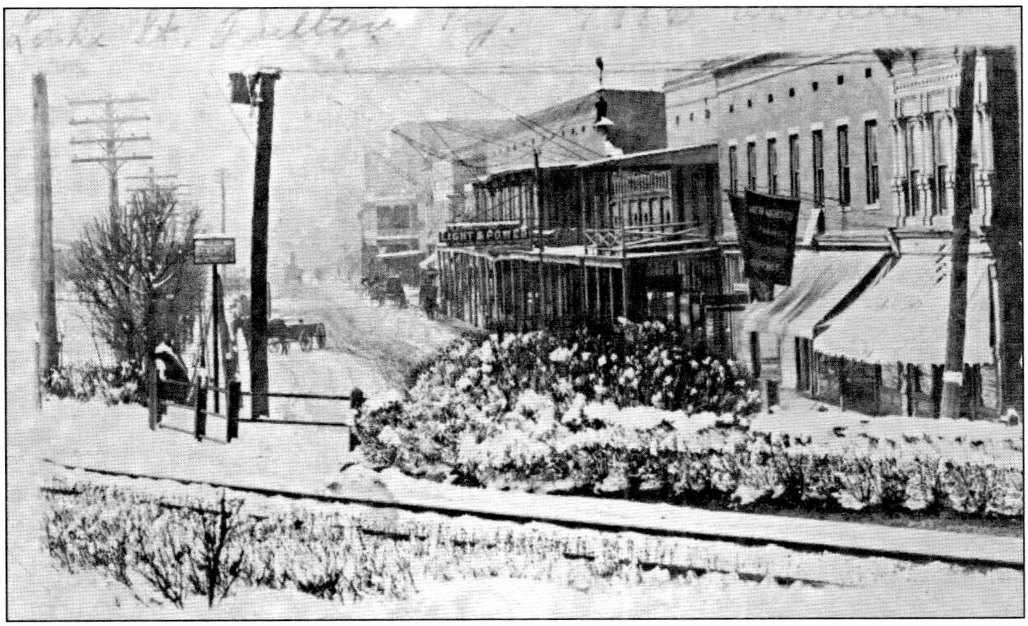

This 1916 scene of Lake Street was made into a picture-perfect postcard of Fulton. The view encompasses a western vantage of downtown, near where The Keg Restaurant stands now. The winters of 1916 and 1917 were particularly severe. A record snowfall on December 7, 1917, buried the town until March 1918. September 1918 saw the beginning of the world's great flu pandemic. Many in the Twin Cities succumbed to the dread disease, at times multiple members of the same household being lost.

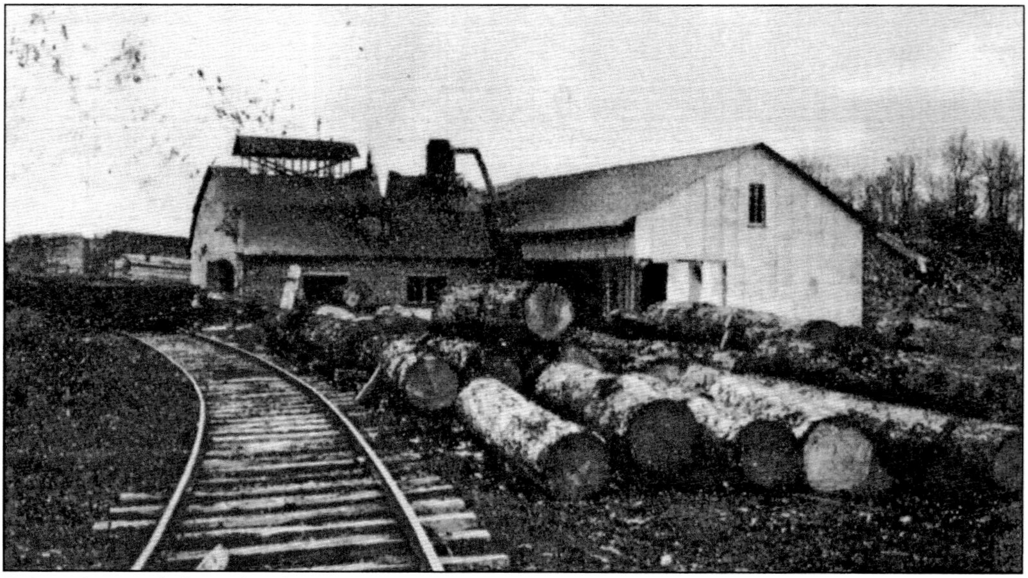

Fulton boasted three lumberyards and planing mills within its corporate limits by 1911. The yards sold paint, sash, and shingles as well. Seen above is the Swann Karmire Yard in 1909.

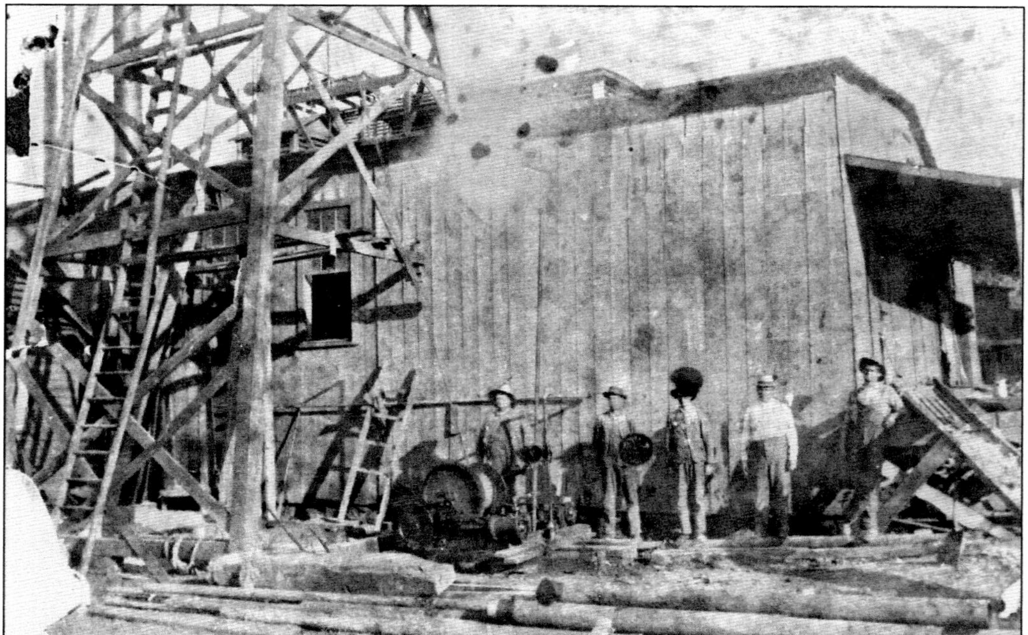

Building operations in Fulton were prospects of considerable activity because of the boom in both residential and commercial growth in the early 20th century. In addition to customary supplies, items such as doors, windows, sash, glass, inside finish, tiling, grates, mantels, firebrick, and shingles could be purchased at the local lumberyard. During World War I, lumber and building supplies were perhaps as low in price as they would ever be, and many property owners took advantage of the reduced price. Pictured again is the Swann Karmire Yard at the turn of the century.

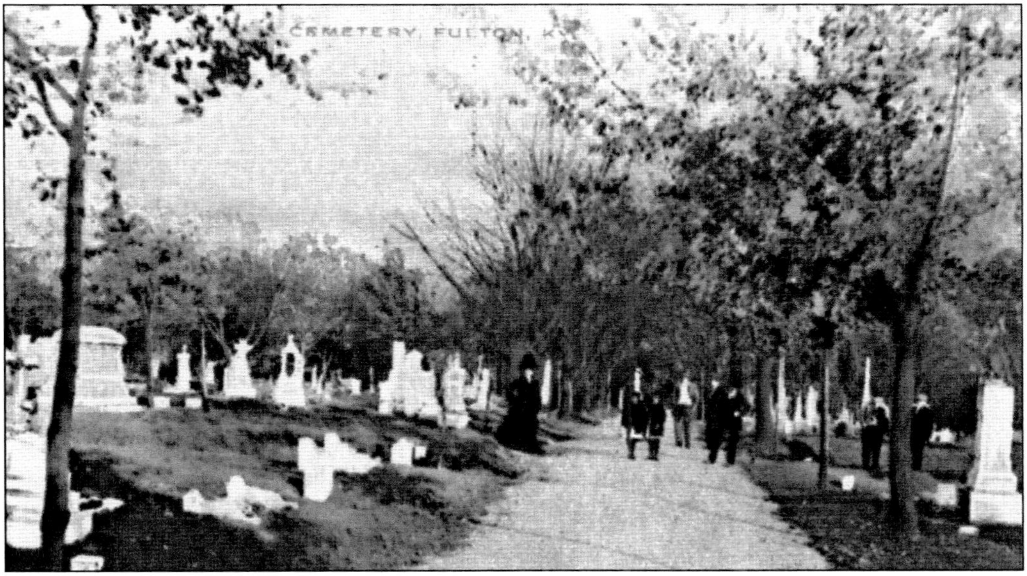

G.E. McFall and a Mr. McAdoo, two Fultonians, entered into a lively discussion one evening in the Knight Hotel (later known as the USONA). After talking into the wee hours of the morning, they went to B.F. Carr to purchase two acres of land for a cemetery named Fairview. The men gave several plots away and then sold the remaining plots for $10 each. The earliest date engraved in the cemetery is Usher, but Mr. McFall's death in 1881 was the first to be recorded.

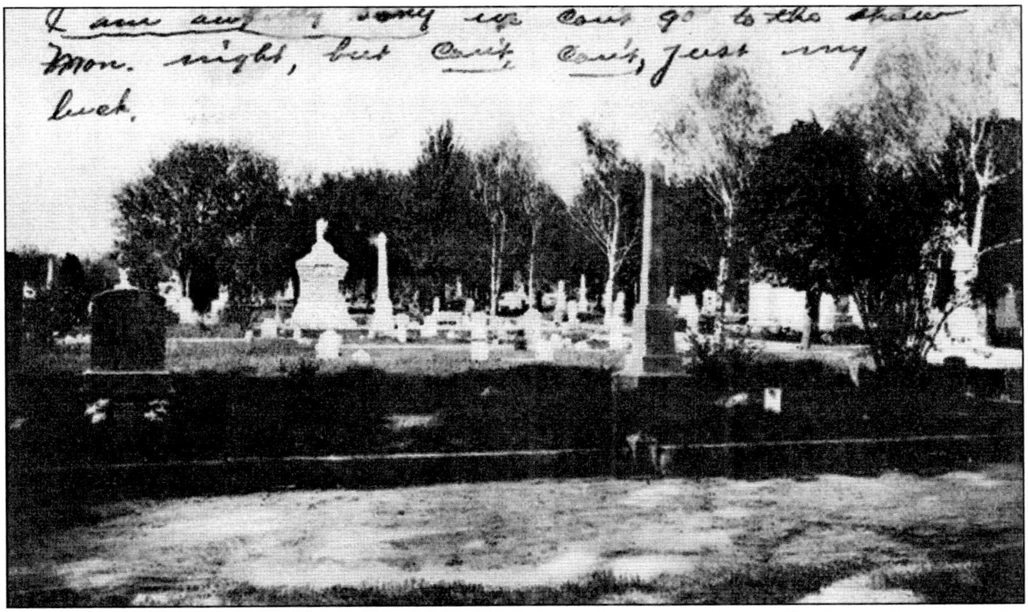

E.B. Eddings was responsible for surveying Fairview Cemetery. A small plot of land on the corner of Second and Carr Streets was the original resting place for Benjamin Franklin Carr, patriarch of the Carr family. His gravesite was moved during the first part of the 20th century, as his family members wished his remains to be included in the Carr family plot in Fairview Cemetery. W.W. Meadows, of the Meadows Hotel, built the only vault in Fairview Cemetery.

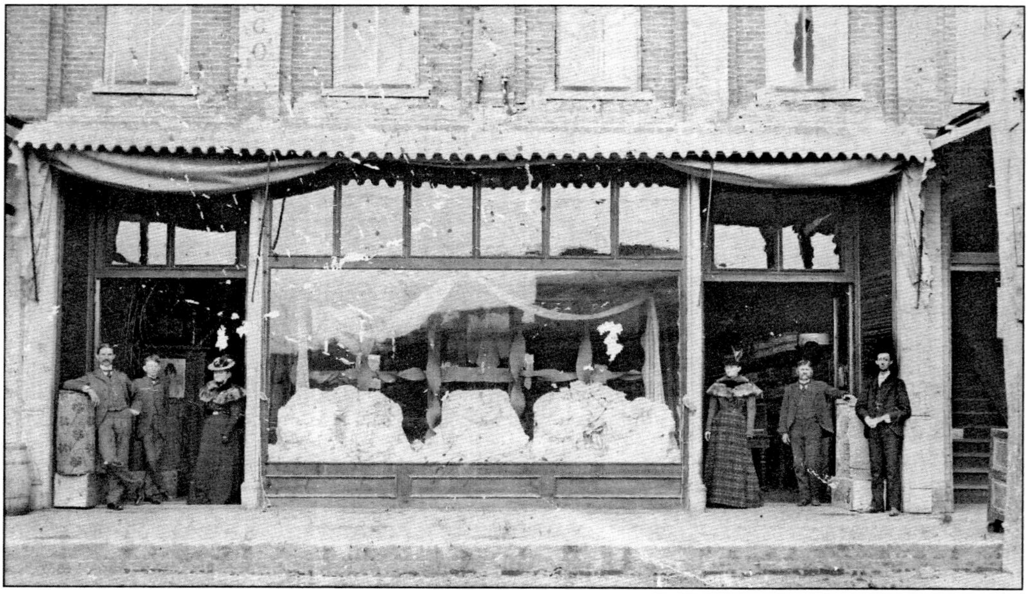

In the early days, there were many "combination" ventures between the founding fathers of Fulton. Stores were needed for the burgeoning population, and these entrepreneurial types not only had the vision for but also enjoyed the risk-taking involved with setting up a new enterprise. Recognized in this image are some "old" Fulton names such as Morris, McDade, Scott, and Noonan.

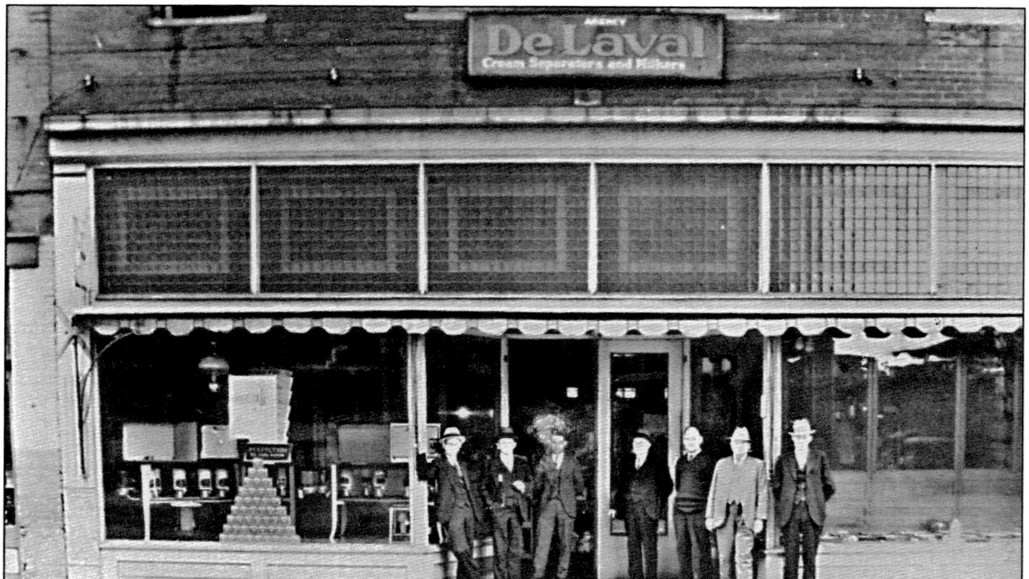

With the rise of several dairies by 1911, the prospect arose of producing butter and cheese in large quantities. De Laval cream separators and milkers were popular items sold at A. Huddleston's Hardware. De Laval capitalized on the opportunity to furnish a market for practically all the milk and cream that could be produced locally. At that point in time, the demand for "pure" milk and fresh, rich cream and butter far exceeded supply.

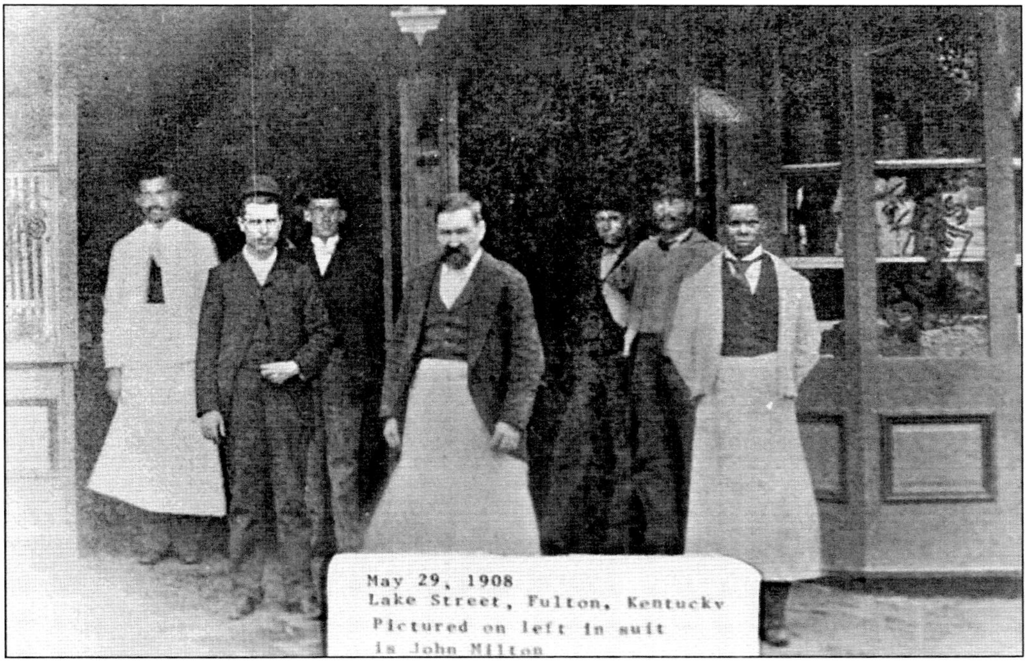

There were plenty of reasons to want to be a merchant on Lake Street by 1908. The Fulton Bank had opened in 1883, becoming First National by the turn of the century. Bennett Drug store opened in 1898, and by 1896, the Illinois Central owned two lines crossing north and south. Fulton, being so strategically located, had prosperity on its way.

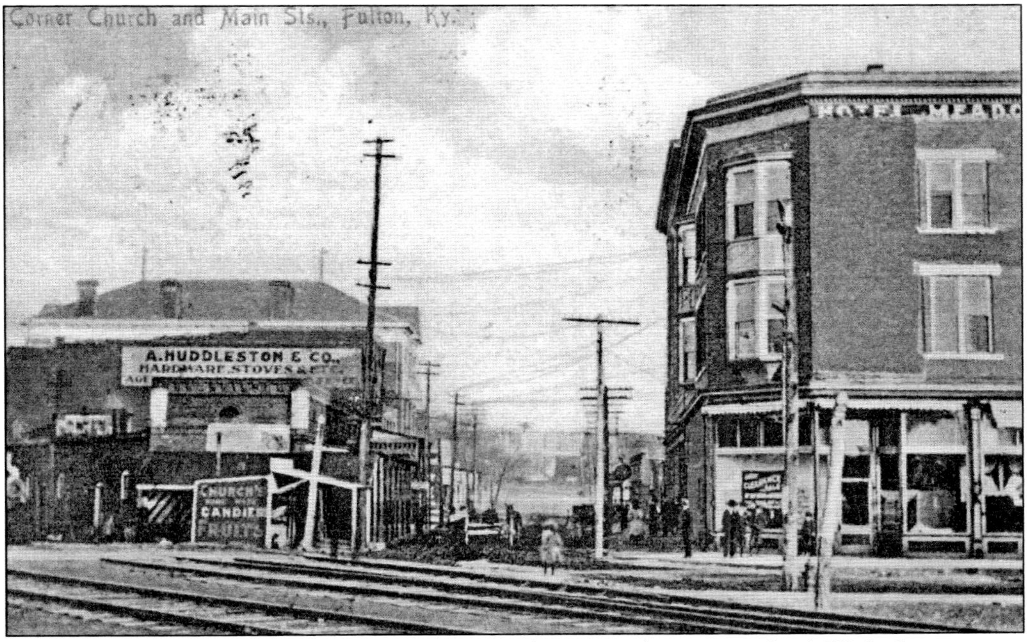

The corner of Church and Main in downtown Fulton was a busy one indeed. With the entrance of the Meadows Hotel on the corner of Church (Commercial) Street and Huddleston's Hardware just north on Main Street, traffic constantly flowed past.

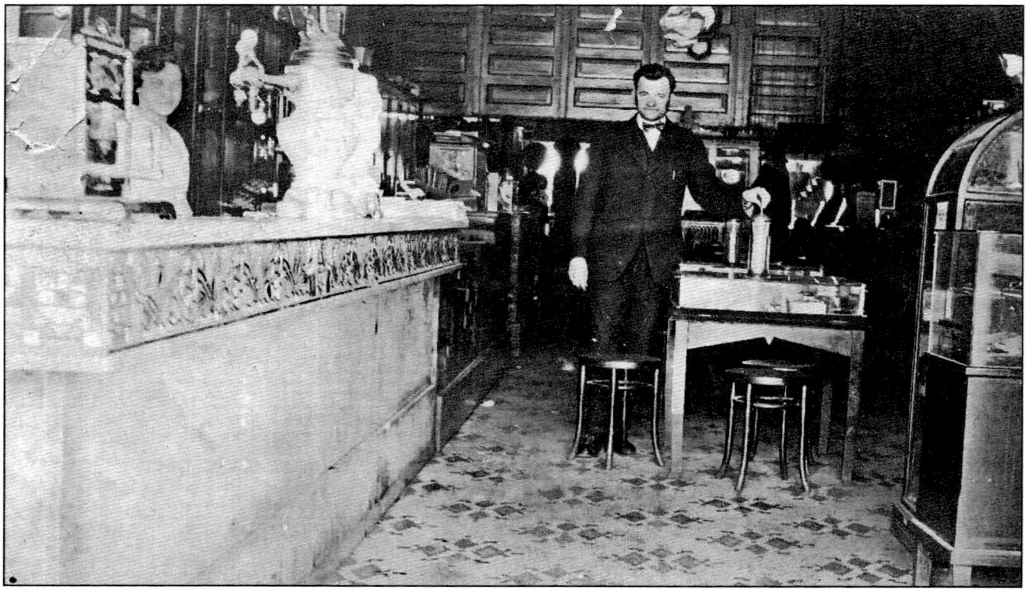

The Paschall Bros. Gem Pharmacy on Lake Street had a soda fountain and parlor beyond compare. In 1913, they boasted of the best ice cream, fresh lime, grape juice, and true fruit syrup. The soda fountain was considered by many to be the most delightful and attractive retreat in the city. Cigars, tobacco, and the purest of drugs were kept on hand for patrons. This image of the interior of the store showing the famed fountain is *c.* 1917.

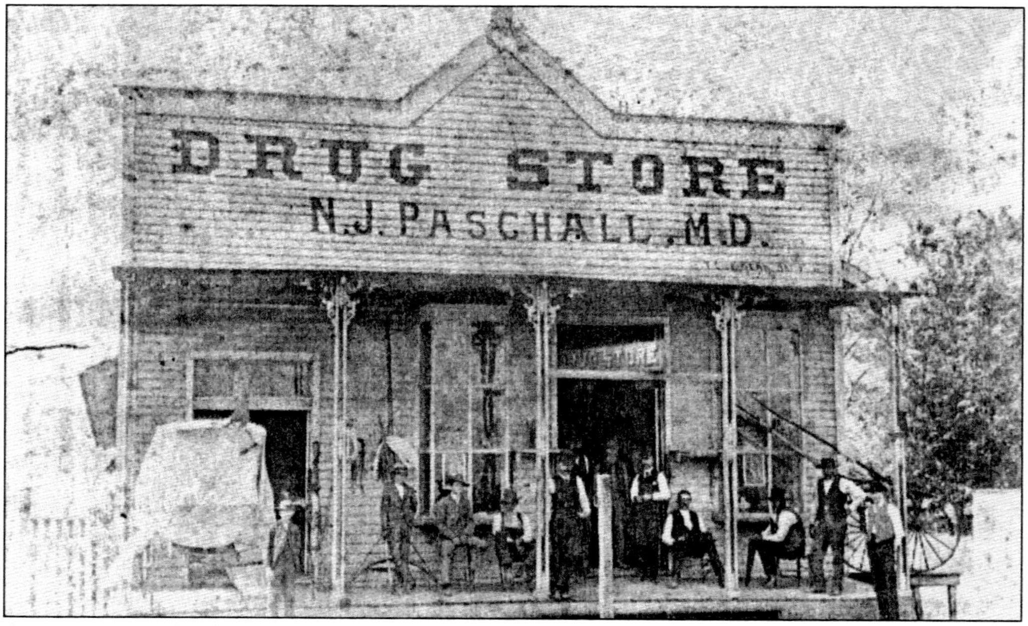

Among some of Fulton's first settlers was the Paschall family. They settled on the Tennessee side about the time B.F. Carr, F.G. Bard, and Noah Norman settled on the Kentucky side. Dr. Gideon (G.W.) Paschall was the first physician, practicing out of an old log house built on the State Line Road in the 1850s. He and his brother, Dr. Newton Julian (N.J.) Paschall, put up the first drug store for the community.

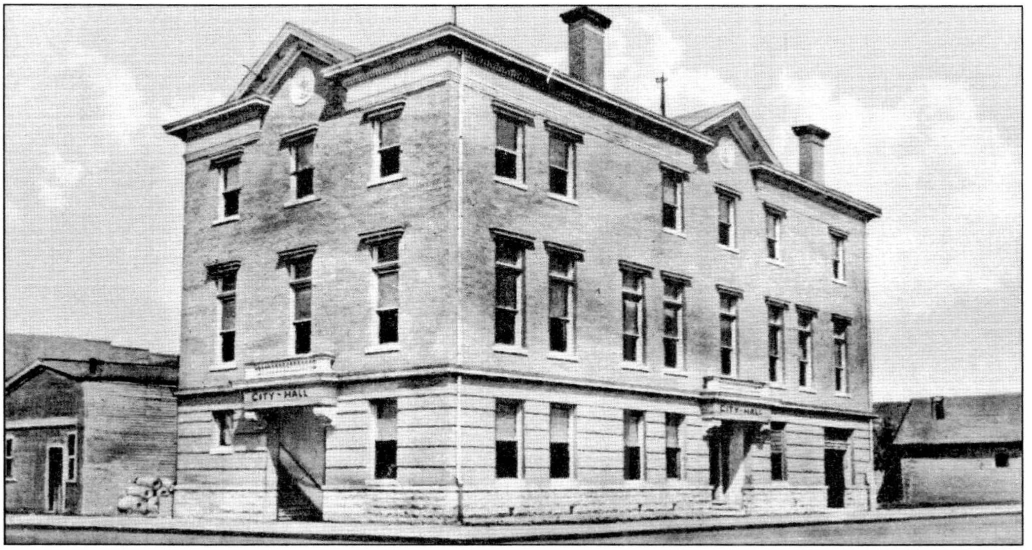

Pictured above is the three-story Fulton City Hall. Although the original building was razed, the current city hall occupies the same location. It served as home to all city administrative offices, police department, fire department, and city courtroom on the first floor, including a public drinking fountain located on the sidewalk outside the front doors. The second floor had another courtroom. Later, in 1904, the third floor was built and was occupied by two fraternal organizations, the Order of Odd Fellows and the Masons. The Masonic lodge, in existence near or around Fulton since 1847, remained in city hall until a new temple was built in 1955 at Washington and Walnut Streets, where it remains today.

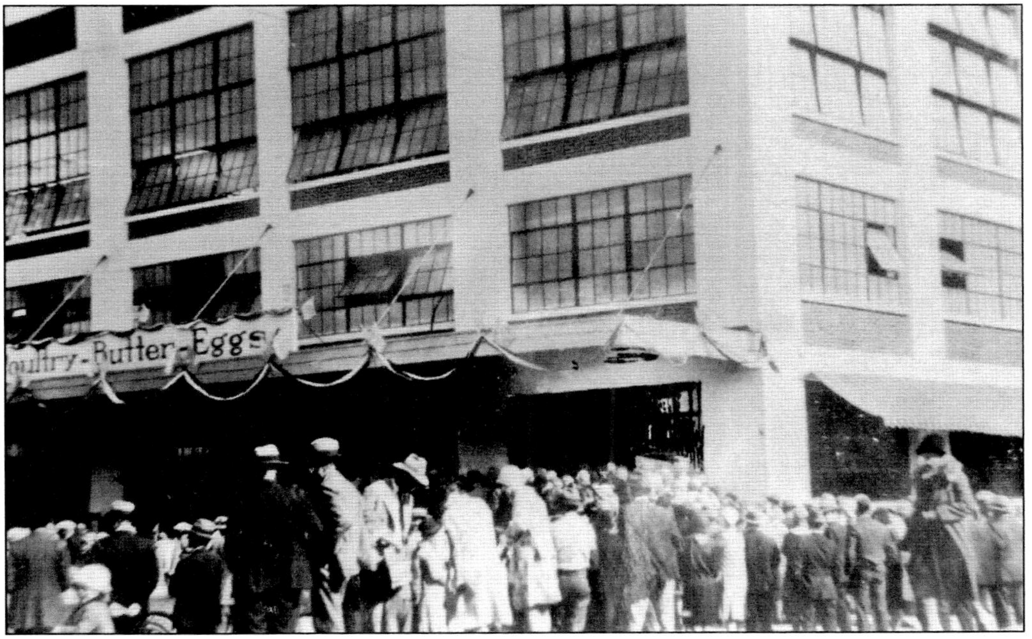

In September 1929, Swift and Company opened their local plant as a dairy and poultry processor on the Tennessee side of State Line Street. A large crowd was in attendance to tour the facility and sample its products.

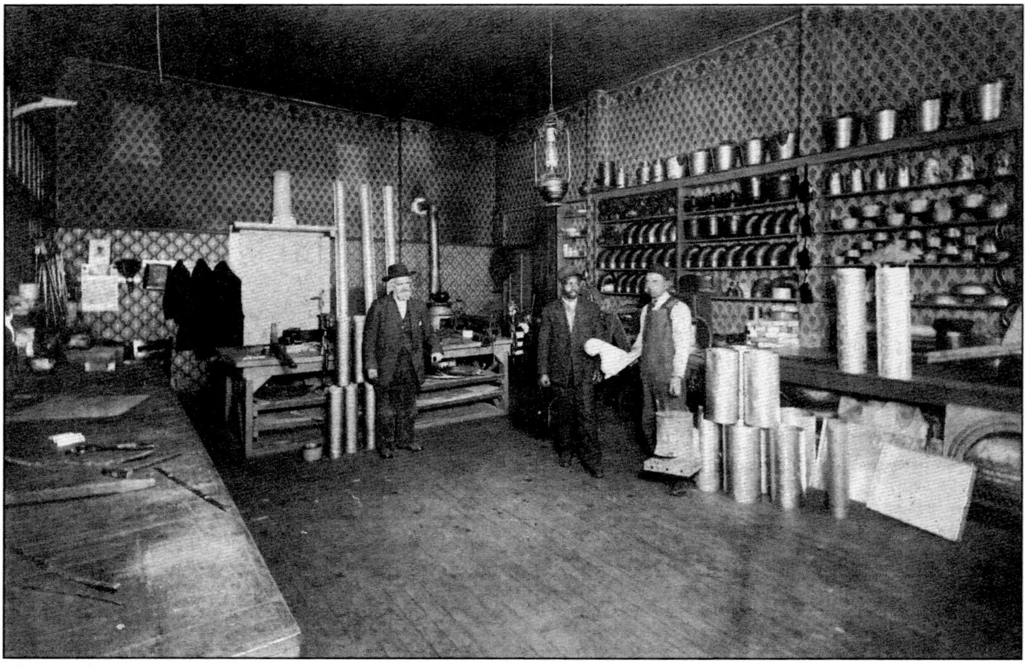

Shown here is a 1910 interior view of the A. Huddleston Hardware and Tin Shop on Main Street. Note the large display of stovepipes available to customers.

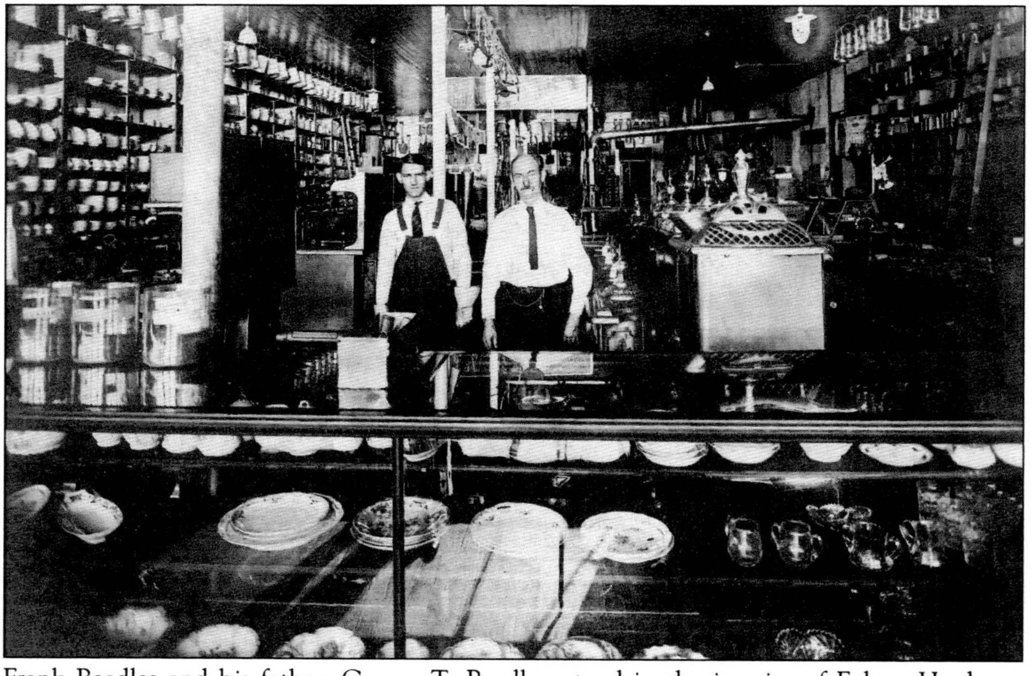

Frank Beadles and his father, George T. Beadles, stand in the interior of Fulton Hardware Company. In 1915, George Beadles and Arch Huddleston purchased the Shacklett-Thomas Hardware Co. and changed its name to the Fulton Hardware Company. In 1920, Beadles and his sons assumed sole ownership of the store, dissolving the partnership.

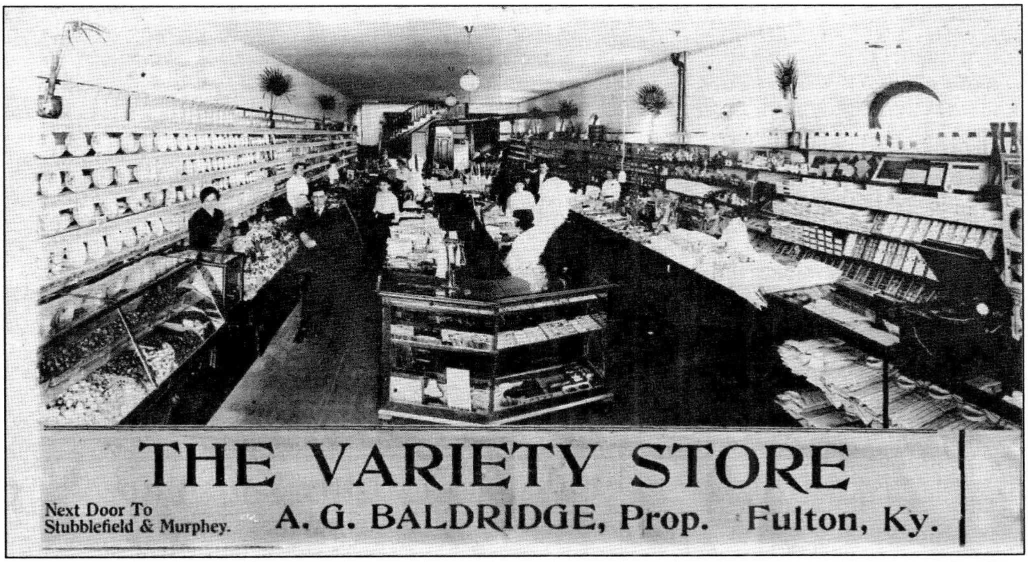

A.G. Baldridge founded the Baldridge Variety Store at 204 Lake Street in 1910. It was the first "dime store" in town and quickly became a Fulton institution. It was a particular favorite of the fair crowd. With display cases stuffed full of an enormous selection of goods, Mr. Baldridge traded in cash only and kept prices lower than his competitors. The store experienced a fire in 1948 and was rebuilt with a more modern façade in 1949.

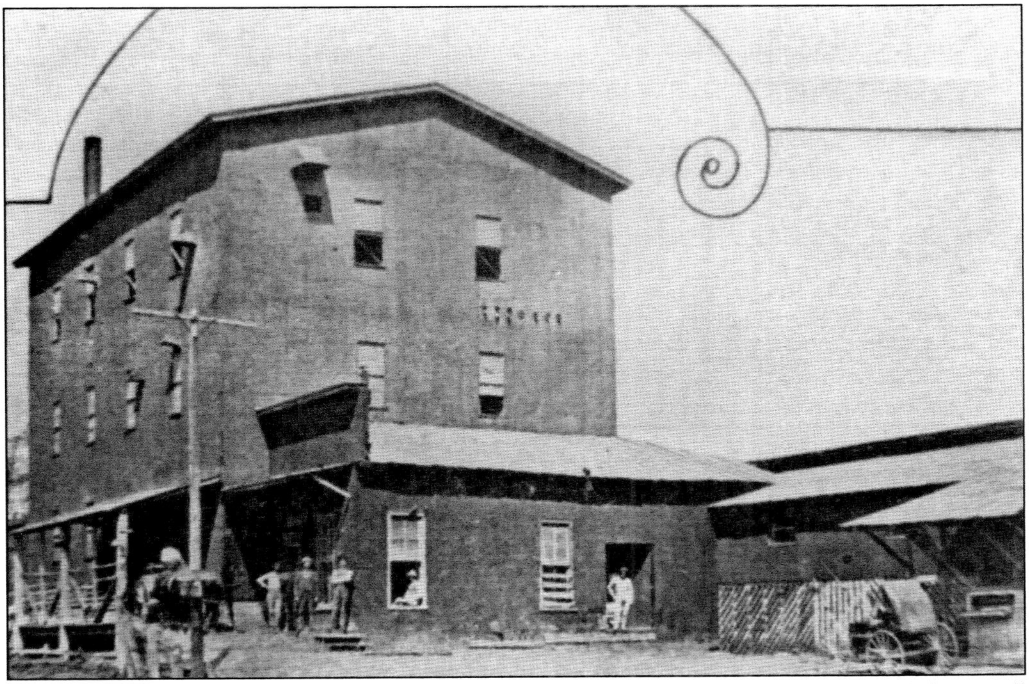

A pioneer of Weakley County, Tennessee, W.V. Brann operated a very successful flour mill along with farming tobacco and other mercantile ventures. He was in partnership with his son Joseph Commodore Brann, who built in 1910 the grand neoclassical home The Oaks, which still stands in Fulton as a private residence today.

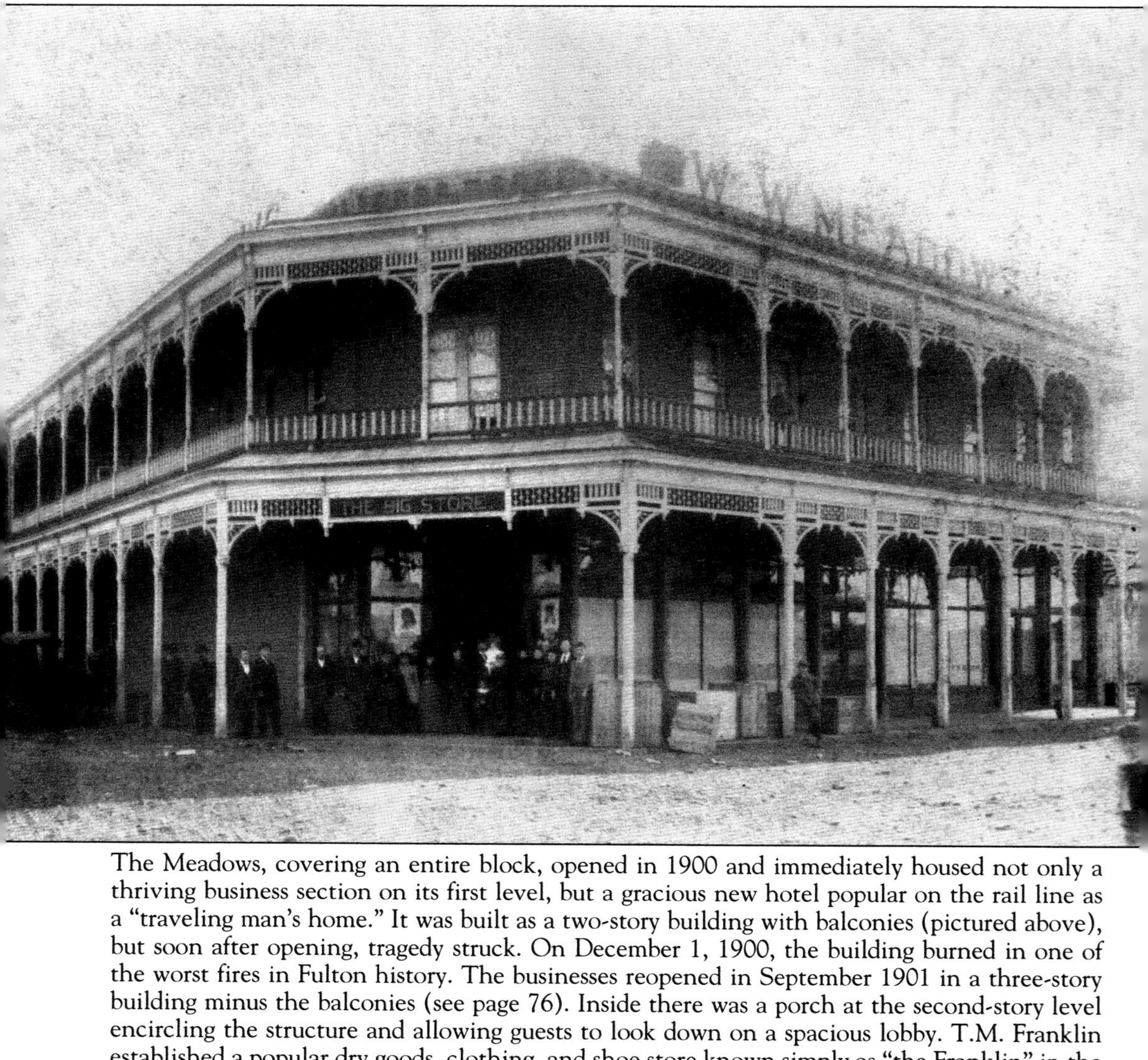

The Meadows, covering an entire block, opened in 1900 and immediately housed not only a thriving business section on its first level, but a gracious new hotel popular on the rail line as a "traveling man's home." It was built as a two-story building with balconies (pictured above), but soon after opening, tragedy struck. On December 1, 1900, the building burned in one of the worst fires in Fulton history. The businesses reopened in September 1901 in a three-story building minus the balconies (see page 76). Inside there was a porch at the second-story level encircling the structure and allowing guests to look down on a spacious lobby. T.M. Franklin established a popular dry goods, clothing, and shoe store known simply as "the Franklin" in the Meadows block.

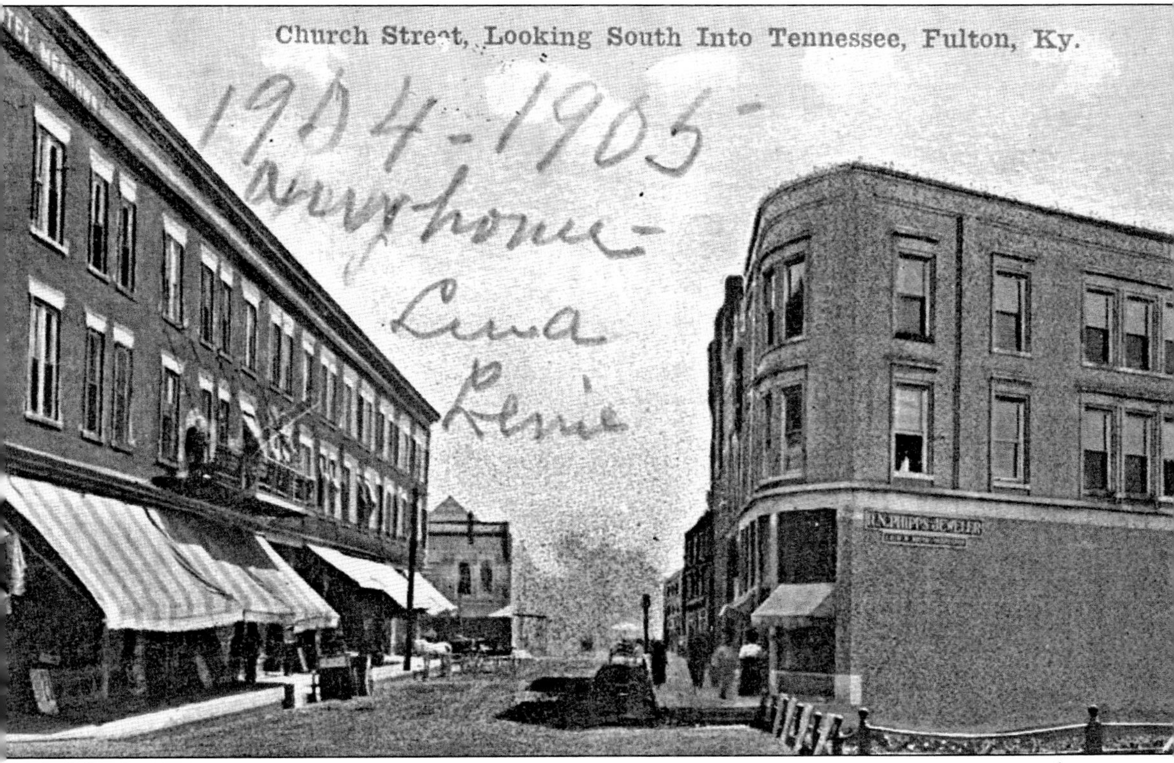

By 1904, Church Street (modern-day Commercial Avenue) had grown into quite a commercial prospect. This view is from Lake Street looking south into what was then called Fulton, Tennessee. The Meadows encompassed the entire left-hand side of the street, and on the right was the Flat Iron Building, occupying 226 Church. The Flat Iron Building was home to a variety of merchants, chiefly R.N. Phipps Jewelry Store. Dr. I.H. Read had a dental office on the second floor. In later years, the second and third floors were apartments.

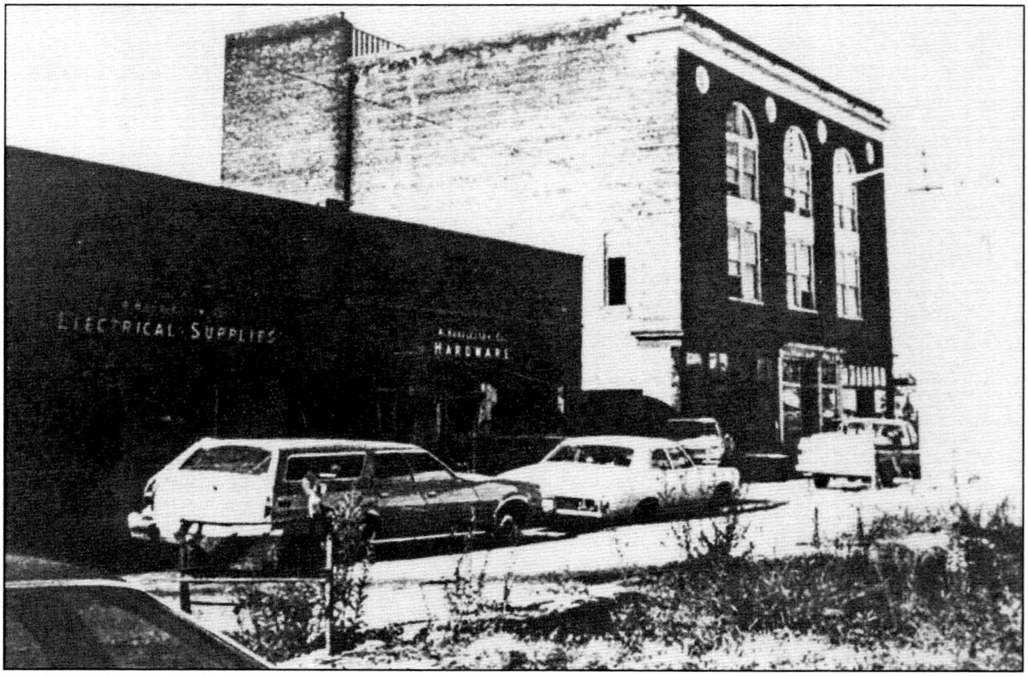

Looking for something to bring some culture to Fulton, Joe Bennett opened the Vendome on the corner of Main and Church (Commercial) Streets in 1896. Since Fulton was a stopover for passenger trains traveling from New Orleans to Chicago, and since it was also considered a prosperous and sophisticated town with several plush hotels and fine restaurants, it was not hard to attract big-name stars and shows passing through on their way to larger cities.

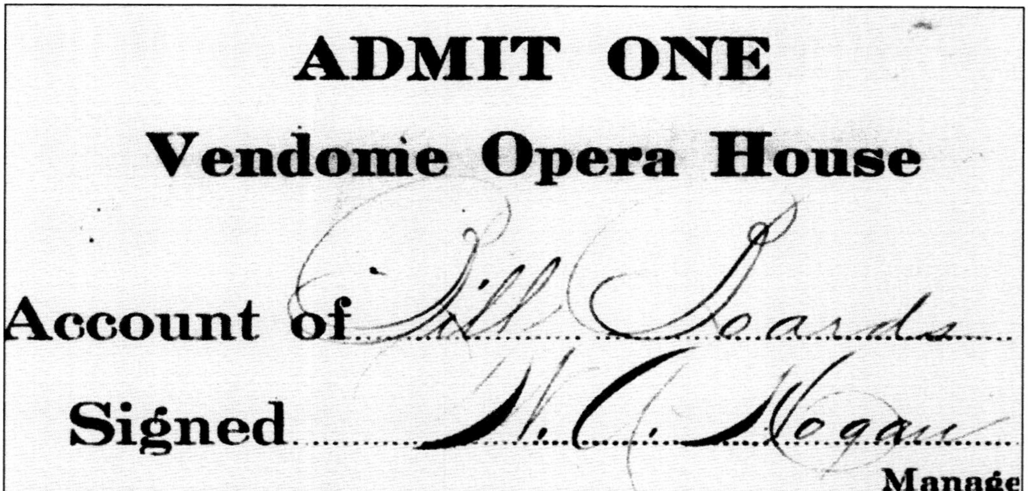

Town residents would dress in evening gowns, top hats, and coats and tails to attend a performance at the Vendome. Local jewelry stores advertised opticians able to fit patrons with opera glasses. Such acts as William Jennings Bryant, Jenny Lind, John Philip Sousa's band, and a number of vaudeville acts and Wild West shows were just a sampling of what a Vendome ticket could buy you.

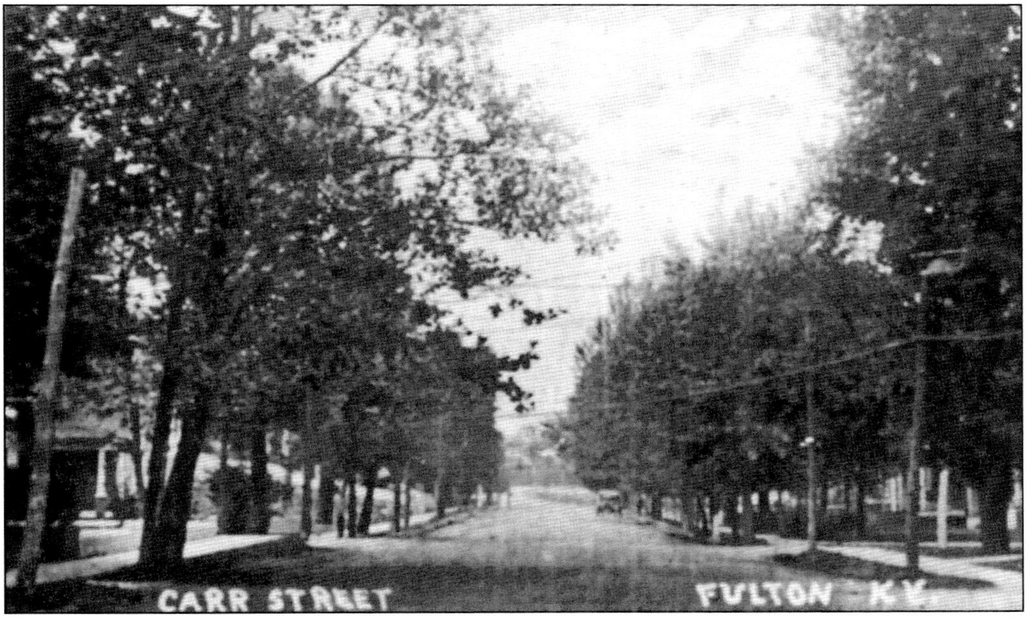

This is an early view of Carr Street. The principal residential streets were Carr, Eddings, Second, Third, and Fourth Streets on the east side of town and Walnut, Cedar, Jefferson, Jackson, and Vine on the west side. Homeowners paid to have the dirt streets sprinkled with water to keep down the dust.

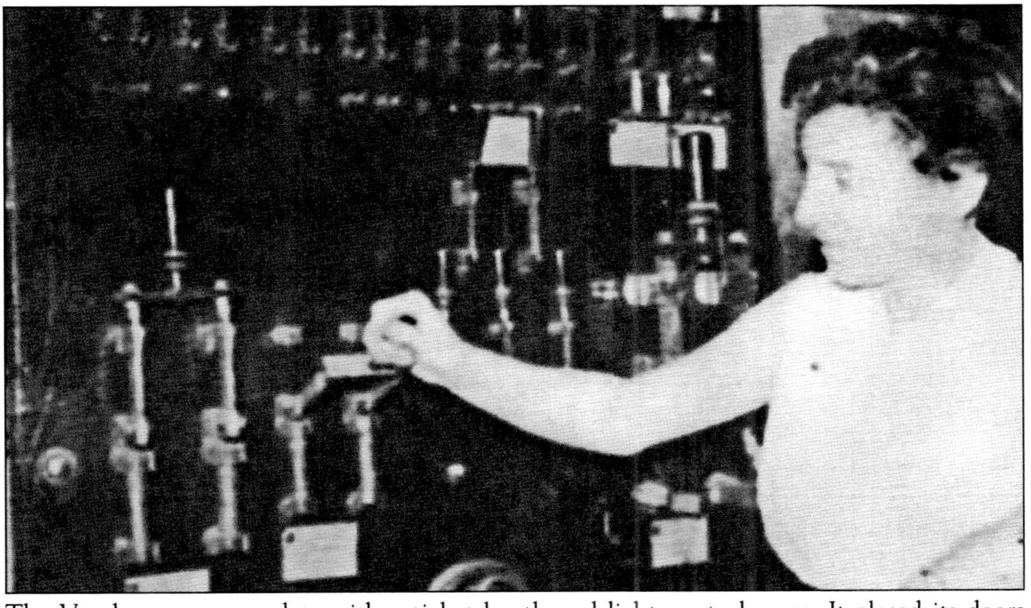

The Vendome was complete with a ticket booth and light control room. It closed its doors sometime around 1900 and never reopened. Between 1900 and 1912, the opera-house floor was leveled, and it reopened to hold dance recitals, aesthetic dancing lessons, and plays, but it closed completely in 1920. Ironically, on the day notification was received that the Vendome had been put on the National Register of Historic Places, the bricks from the top of the building were being removed. The building was razed in 1974.

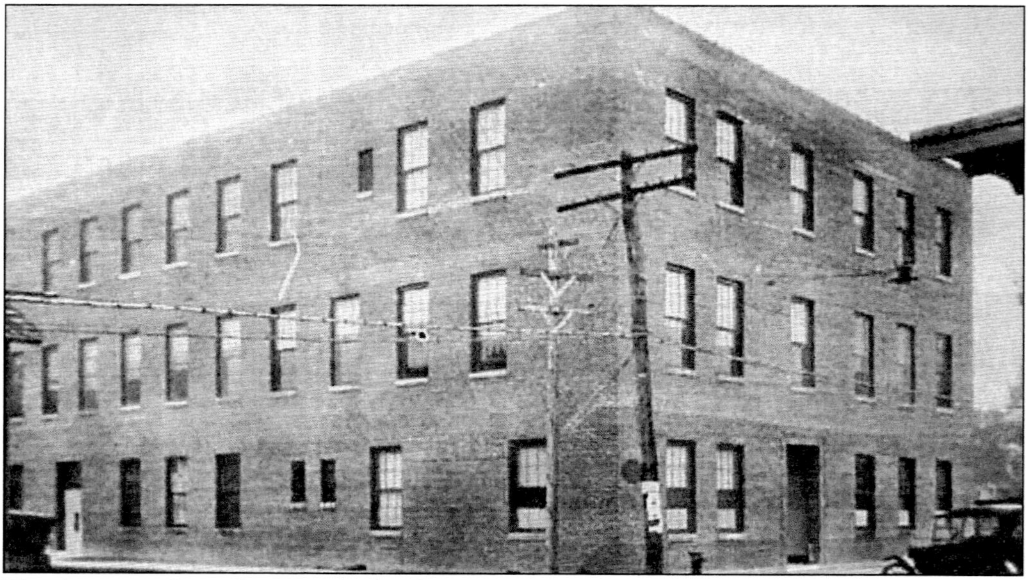

The American Cigar Company built a factory in Fulton in 1921 because of the town's prominent involvement in tobacco farming. It was located on the Fourth Street extension on the banks of Harris Fork Creek. The company vacated the imposing three-story brown brick structure in 1937, and the garment manufacturer Henry I. Siegel came to town from New York State around the same time looking for a place to establish a factory, remaining in the building until the 1950s.

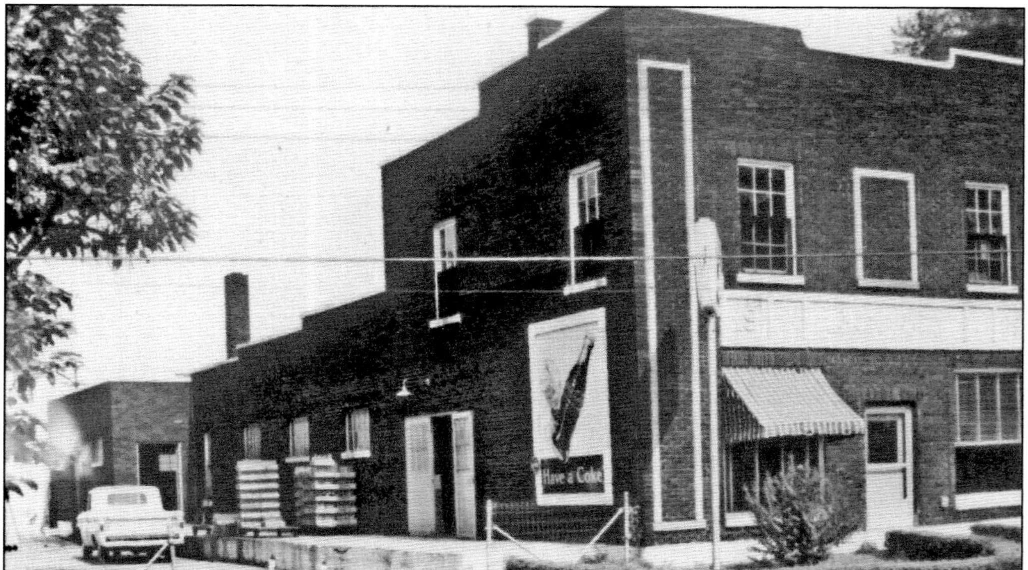

Coca-Cola has been in Fulton since the late 1800s. Many of the druggists sold it at their counters to patrons of all ages. In an advertisement for the fair in a 1913 circular, the Fulton Bottling Company manufactured "Coca Cola and all temperance drinks." During Prohibition, soft drinks became wildly popular. Seen here is the Coca-Cola plant that arrived in 1929. The 1929 building has had a variety of uses over the years thanks to its strategic location by the railroad viaduct.

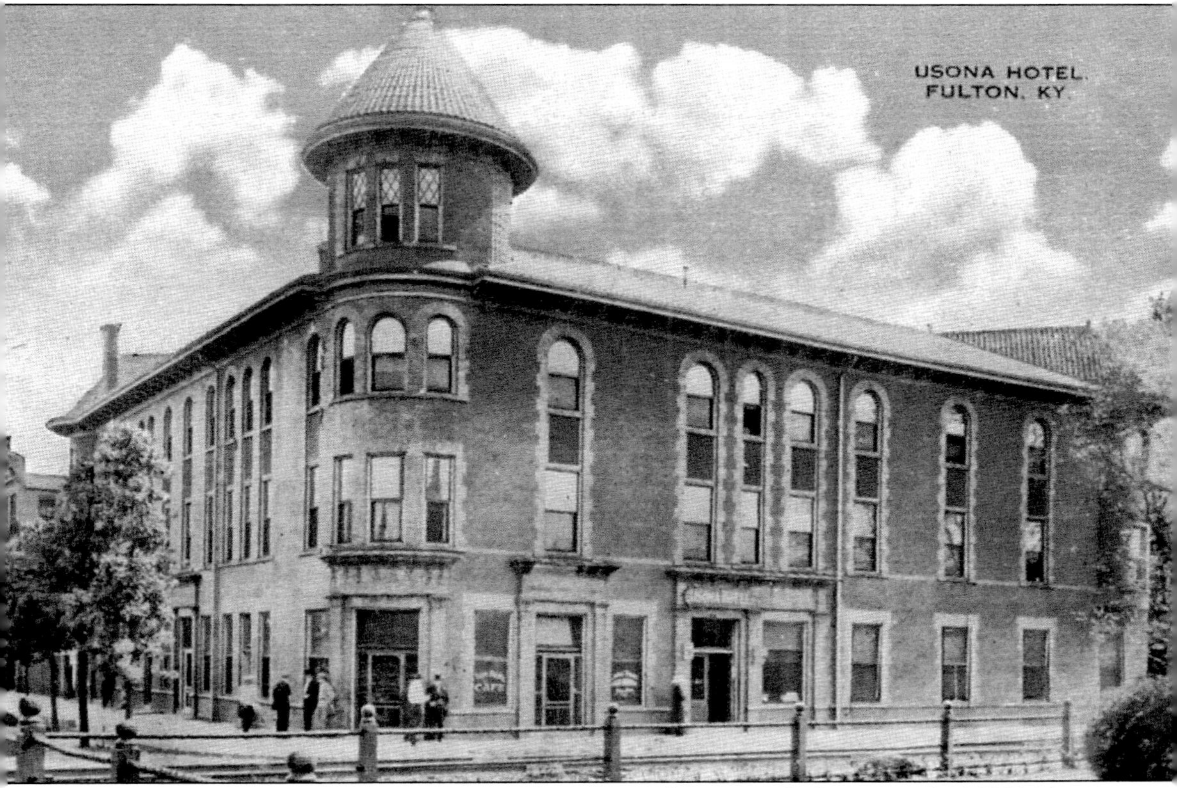

From the beginning, the impressive structure that eventually came to be known as the USONA Hotel had a cosmopolitan air. It was built in 1897 on Walnut Street on a lot costing $225. Of brick and four stories high (the fourth floor was a turret that later burned in a fire), it boasted a bathroom attached to each suite and a lobby with a magnificent spreading staircase and marble floors. The formal dining room was decorated in ornate red plush and gilt. The hotel was situated on a lovely, well-manicured lawn, with doors that opened to the passenger-train traffic on the north and the general public on the south. After Henry Knight took over management, the hotel truly began to flourish and was known simply as the Knight. Due to the connection with the railway, the hotel was a mecca not only for travelers but for those who lived in the community as well. It was rumored that Colonel Fall of Fall and Fall Insurance would leave his beautiful home on Vine Street in January and spend the entire winter at the Knight. In 1913, W.P. and J.M. Allen began to manage the establishment and the name was again changed to the USONA, an acronym for United States of North America. In its twilight, it became the Earle. Falling into a state of disrepair, the building was used for training by the Fulton Fire Department sometime in the late 1960s, when it was set on fire and razed. An era of fine dining and entertainment had come to a quiet close.

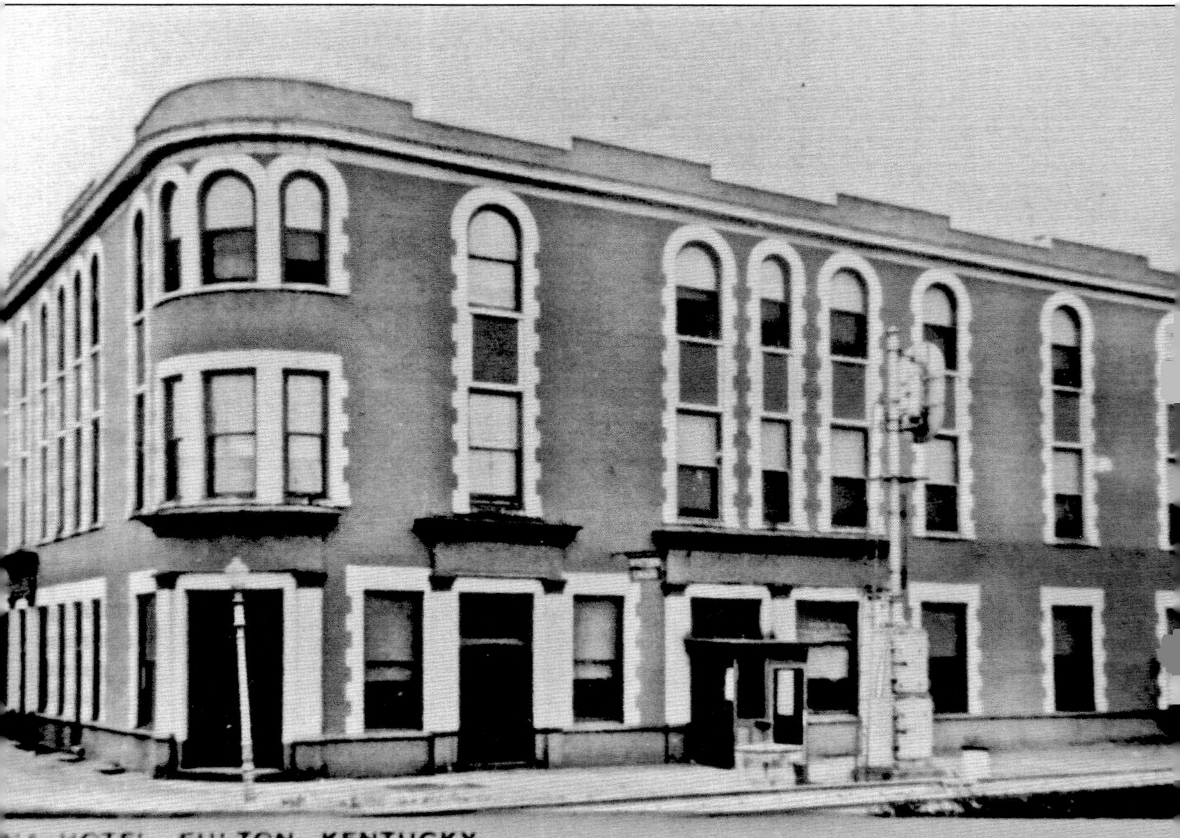

The USONA Hotel was listed as having 80 guest rooms (many were double and family rooms), several parlors, a sample room, dining room, electric lights and fans, hot and cold baths, steam heat in cold weather, and even a barber shop. It operated on European plans with rates at 75¢ per day and up, according to chosen location and furnishings of the room. Meals were served "á la Carte" in the 40-by-20-foot dining room. Club breakfasts were also featured. Churchgoers flocked to the USONA for their Sunday noon meal, and many holiday meals were served as well. The dining room doubled as a dance hall when big bands stopped on their travels between Chicago and Memphis. It is documented by the local newspaper of the day that the Illinois Central line arranged its schedule so its trains could arrive from Paducah, Kentucky, about seven in the evening, bringing drummers (the term used for peddlers) and "socially minded people" from neighboring trains. It made a return run to Paducah on the same evening with few to no passengers, everyone choosing to remain for the fun at the hotel. The image above shows the USONA after the fire, with the façade slightly remodeled to accommodate the missing turret.

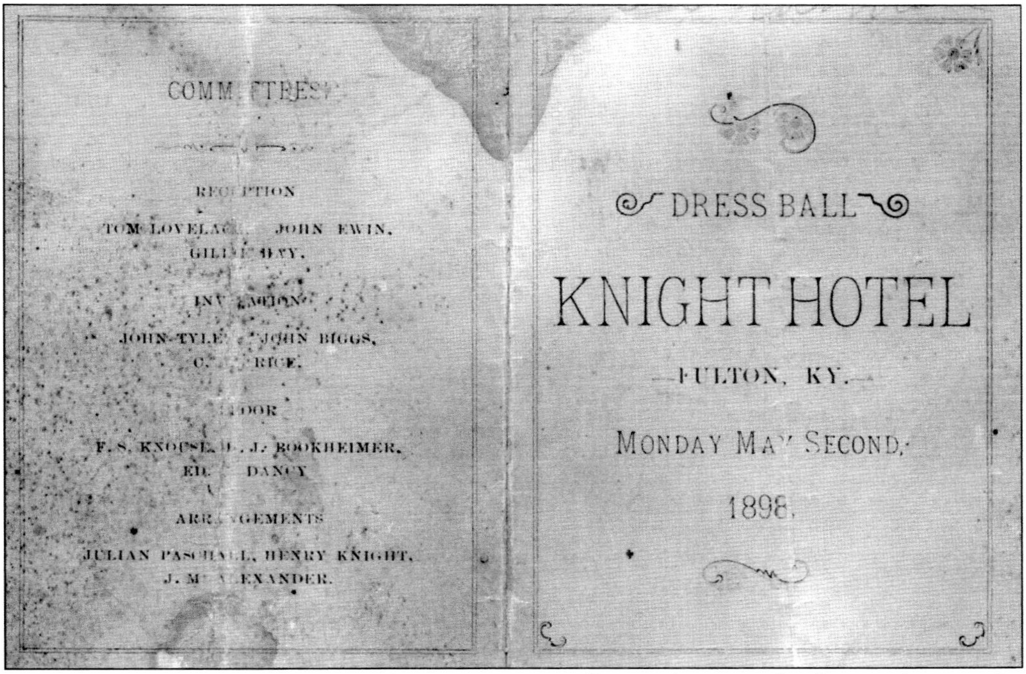

COMMITTEES

RECEPTION

TOM LOVELACE, JOHN EWIN,
GILL DAY.

INVITATION

JOHN TYLER, JOHN BIGGS,
C. RICE.

FLOOR

F. S. KNOPSE, J. BOOKHEIMER,
ED. DANCY

ARRANGEMENTS

JULIAN PASCHALL, HENRY KNIGHT,
J. M. ALEXANDER.

DRESS BALL

KNIGHT HOTEL

FULTON, KY.

MONDAY MAY SECOND,

1898.

Each dress ball had a program of dance music as well as a dance card. The gentleman who escorted the lady to the event would take the first and last dance and keep a watchful eye on any potential suitors that might fill the dances in between.

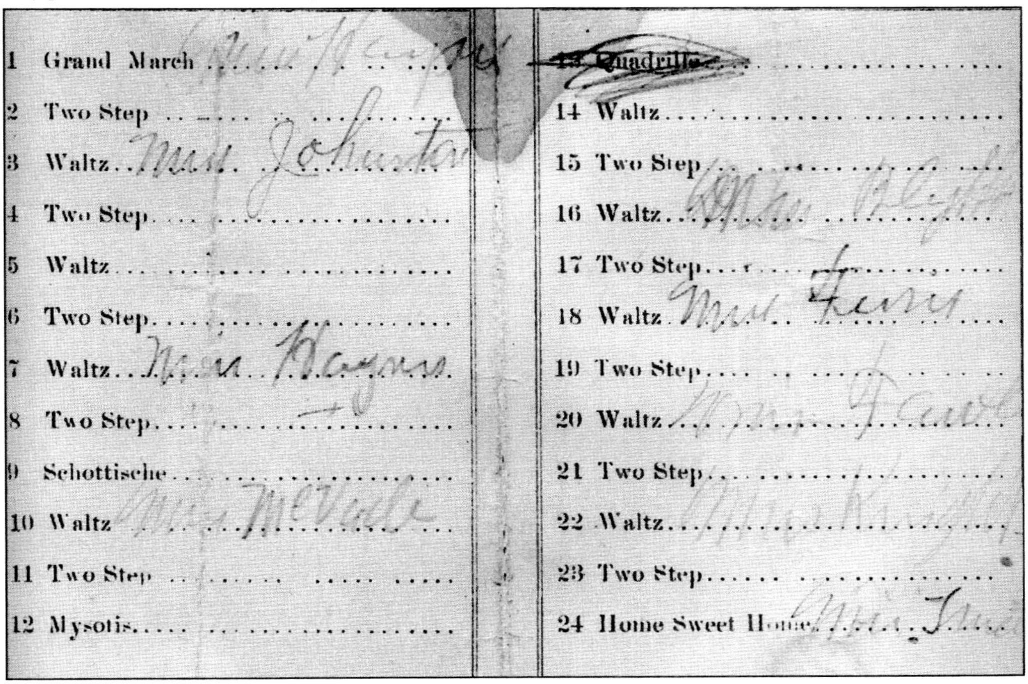

1 Grand March
2 Two Step
3 Waltz
4 Two Step
5 Waltz
6 Two Step
7 Waltz
8 Two Step
9 Schottische
10 Waltz
11 Two Step
12 Mysotis
13 Quadrille
14 Waltz
15 Two Step
16 Waltz
17 Two Step
18 Waltz
19 Two Step
20 Waltz
21 Two Step
22 Waltz
23 Two Step
24 Home Sweet Home

Everyone looked forward to a formal occasion at the Knight. Seen here is a dance card for a cotillion in the hotel *c.* 1900.

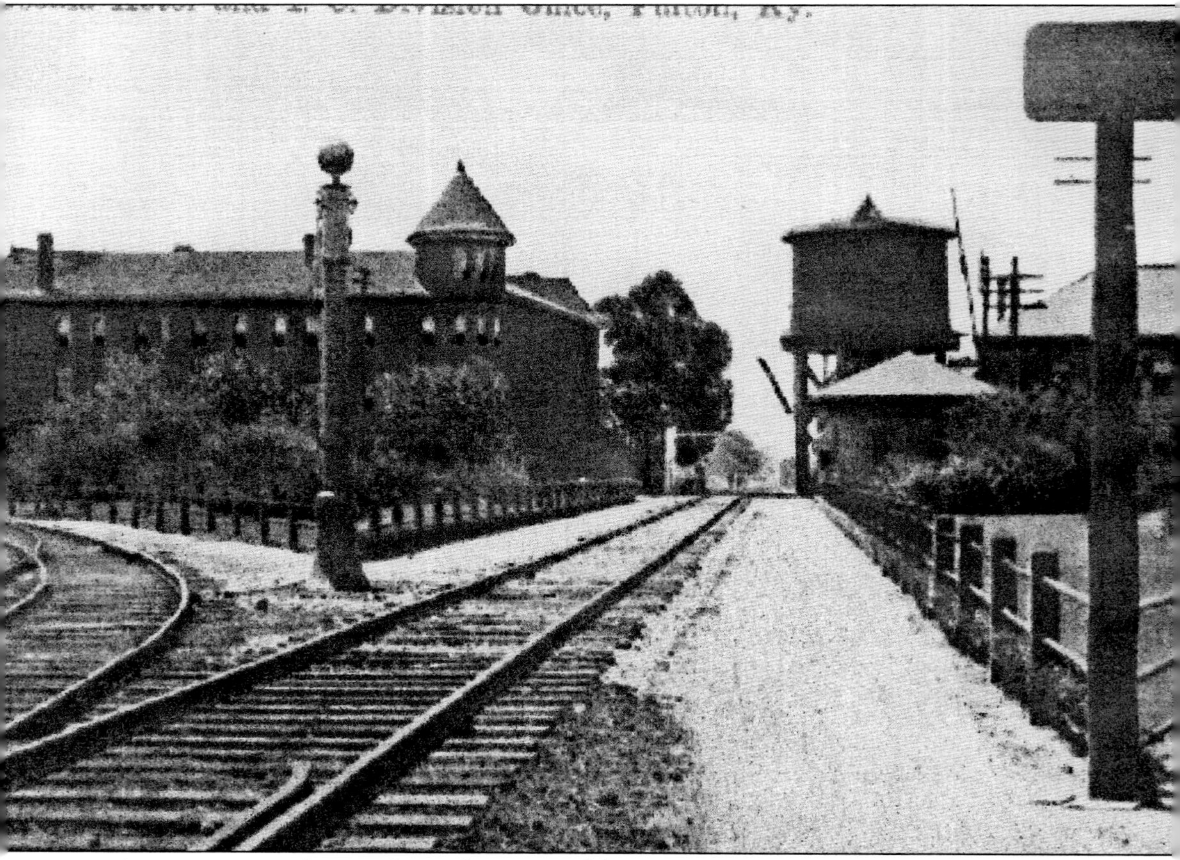

As a movement for city beautification and better parks came about in the early 1900s, the Illinois Central took the initiative in Fulton, having the lofty goal of turning the waylands from Chicago to New Orleans into a "Roadway of Flowers" along 900 miles of right-of-way. The lawn space in the USONA Park contained 4 acres of ground with 375 shade trees and 2,550 ornamental and blooming shrubs, including 4,500 feet of hedge. Perhaps the most outstanding feature of the park was an ornate concrete rose arbor, which hosted an enormous variety of roses. H.M. Moulder was employed as the landscape gardener by the railroad and had a staff of many assistants to keep the park well tended.

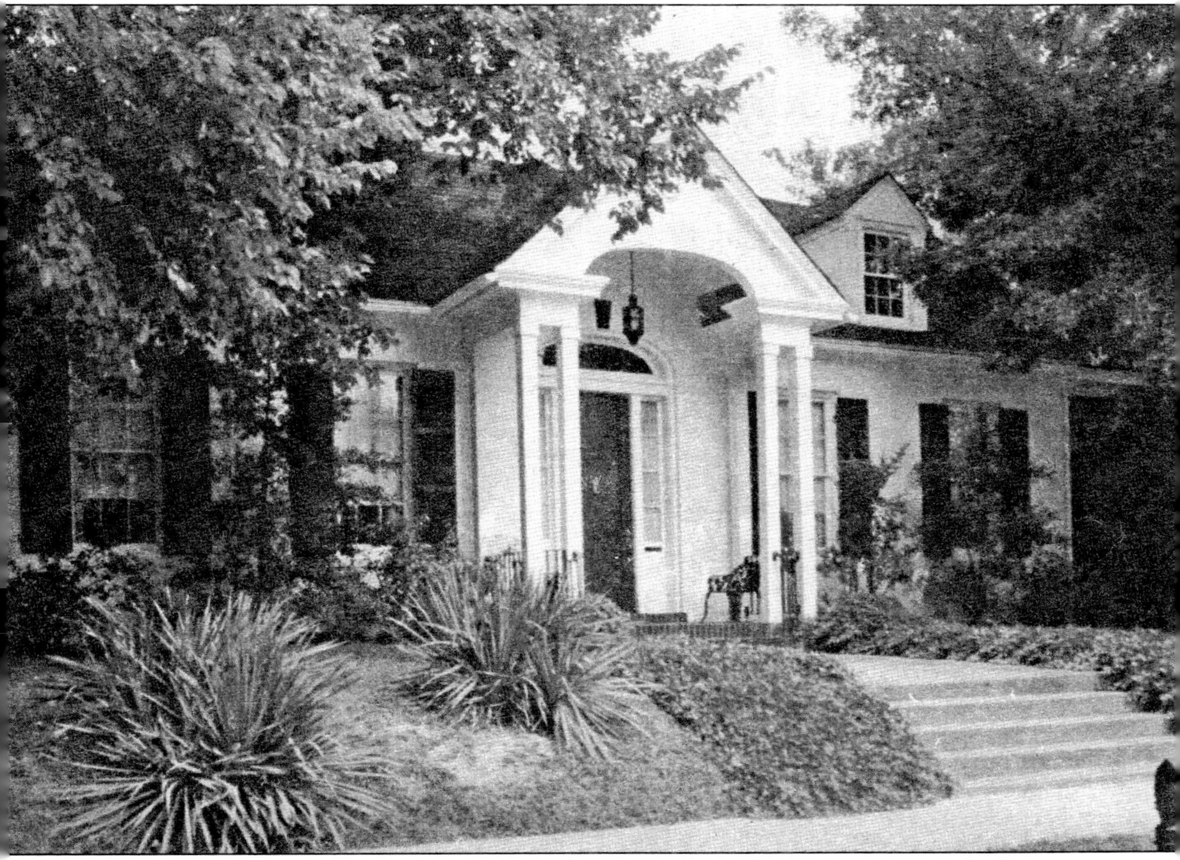

The A.J. Mitchell home at 301 Eddings Street began as a log cabin in 1880, was rebuilt as a frame house, and was finally remodeled in brick in 1940. It has been greatly enlarged from its original two stories with a central hall. In Colonial revival style, it sits at two stories with the date of construction in the keystone over the entrance. Also above the door is a Masonic emblem. There is a hitching post still standing where the front walk intersects the street. The owner of the home was the president and founder of Bank of Fulton. He failed in the venture and was forced to sell the home. A.J. Mitchell's only daughter married W.W. Meadows, of Meadows Hotel fame.

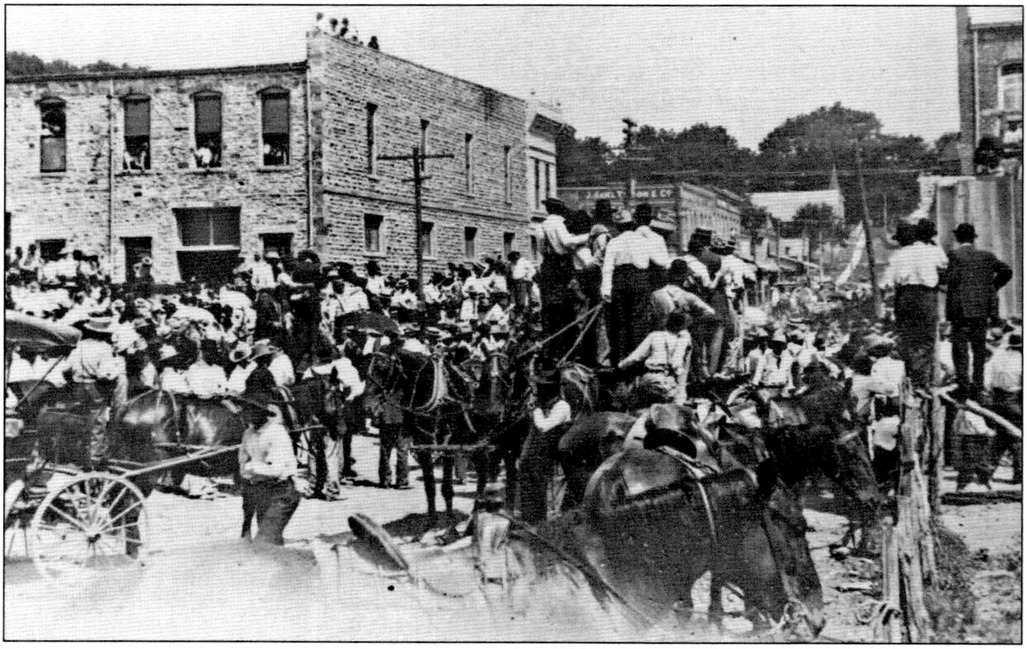

Downtown Fulton was a lively place. Due to the area's production of grain and tobacco, the streets were crowded with people, livestock, and wagons. All manner of goods were brought into town, and there was often much confusion. It was no uncommon sight to see a wagon mired down, with extra mules or horses required to pull it out. The merchants paid to have the street sprinkled in front of their stores to keep dust and dirt to a minimum during the summer.

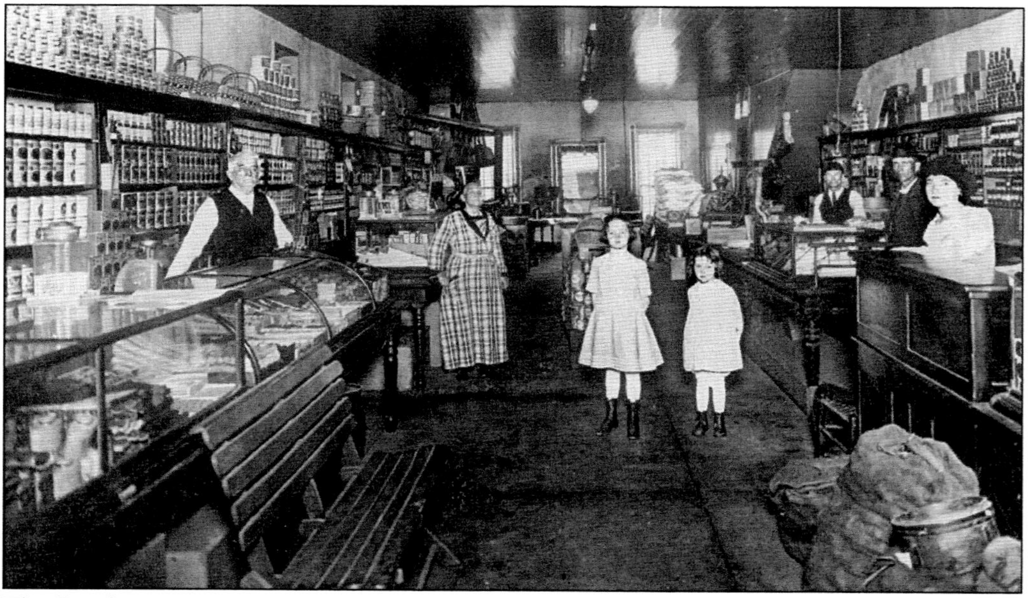

The Bondurant Grocery Store was established in 1898 at 201 State Street and the corner of Church (Commercial) Street. The shelves were always stocked with the "best of everything to eat," and free delivery to the home was offered. With this kind of service there were rarely any complaints. To the left behind the counter is D.R. Bondurant with his wife and grandchildren.

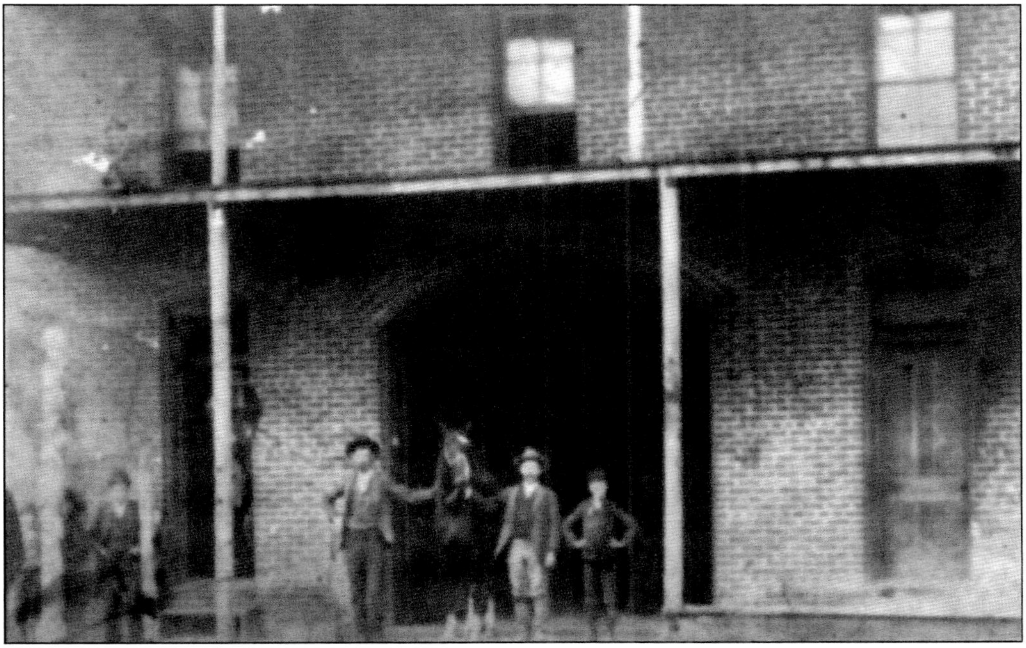

The first livery and stable man for Fulton was T.T. Twigg. Many others followed suit, providing care for the livestock of those coming to town on trade or travel. Featured above is a typical livery, feed, and sale stable located downtown. The people are unidentified.

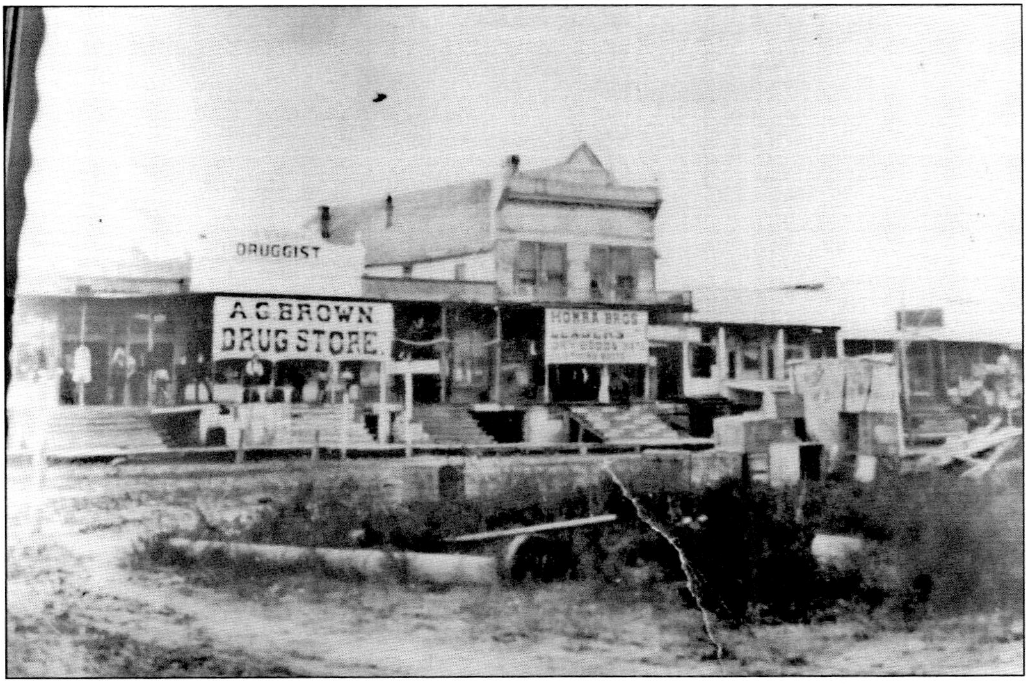

The founders of the Homra Brothers store on Lake Street were born and reared in Syria, coming to America to flee Turkish tyranny. They started selling men's and women's attire in a dry-goods store, and descendants of the family remain in retail business on Lake Street today.

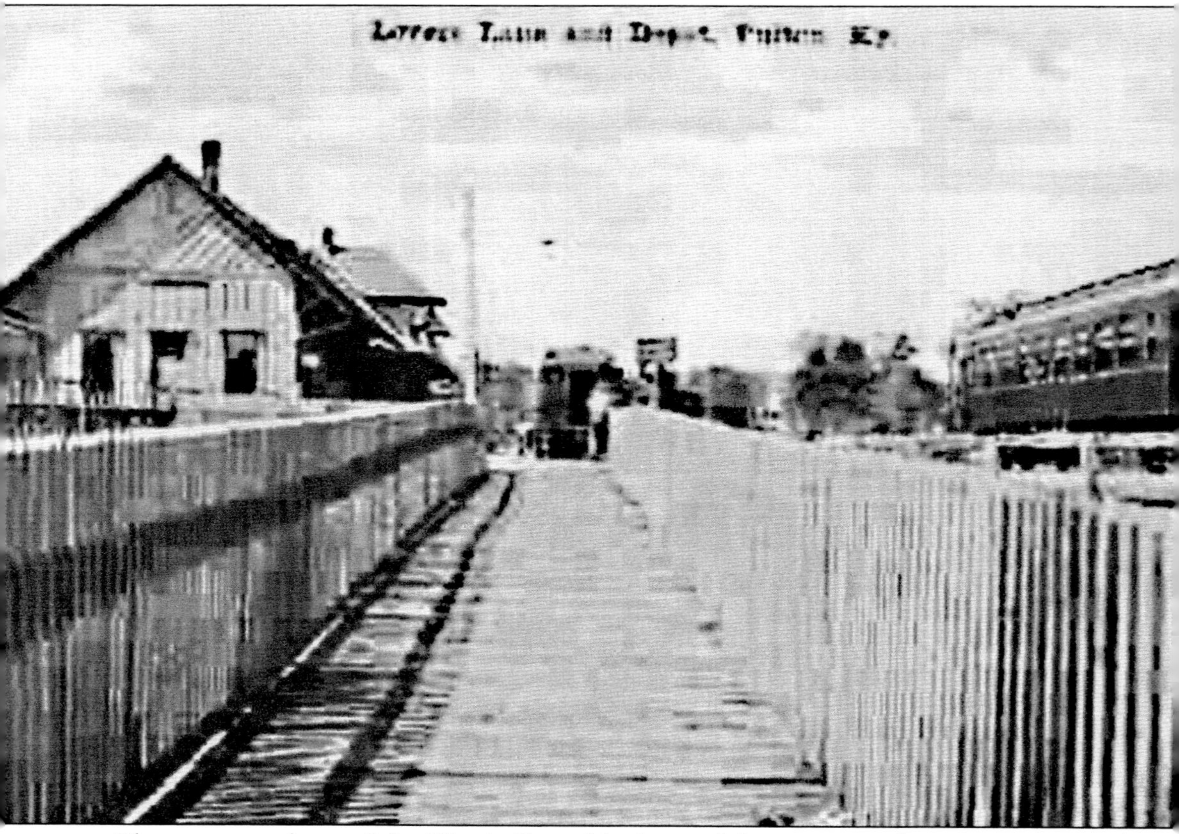

The passenger depot of the Illinois Central had one of the neatest and most attractive park systems along the southern track of the Illinois Central. The plank-lined walkway known as "Lover's Lane," pictured here, was a popular stroll for young courting couples. It connected the USONA Hotel to the depot, providing a "dry" walking to the trains.

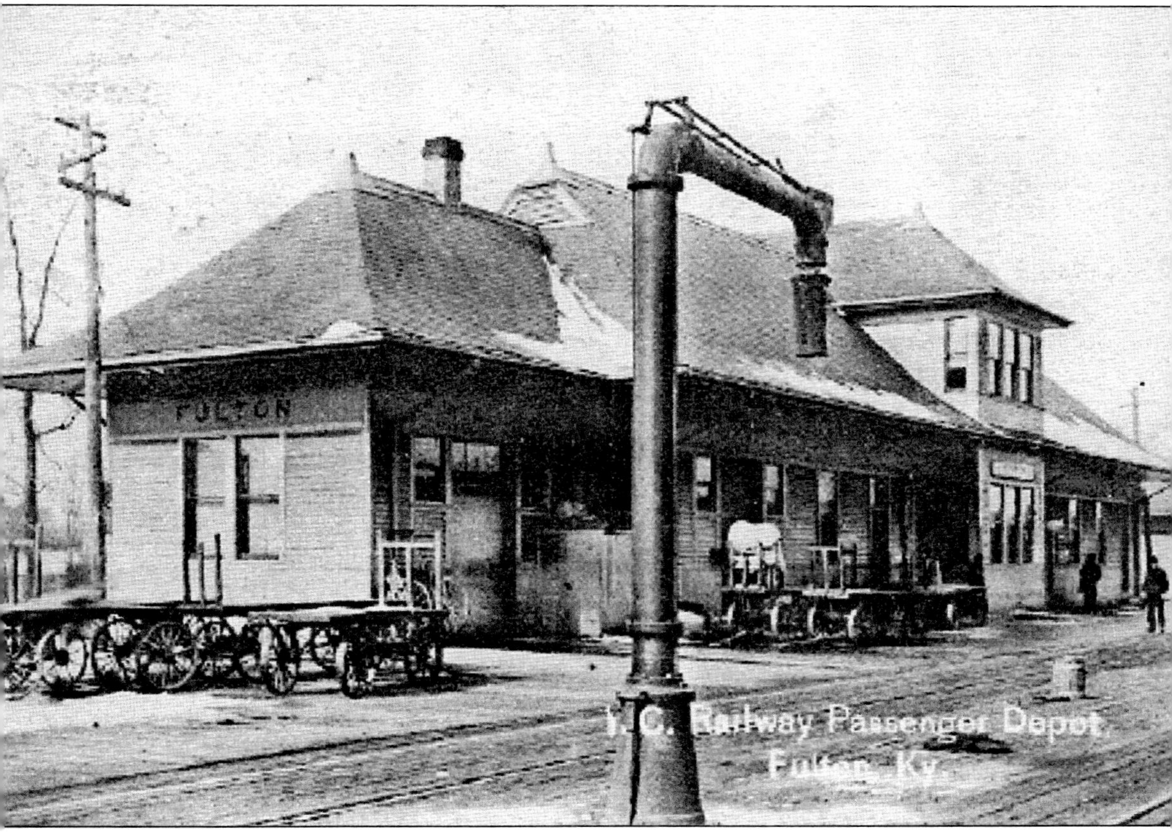

A total of 30 passenger trains were coming and going in all directions 24 hours a day by 1913. About 3,000 freight cars picked up or delivered cargo at the express office on Depot Street and at a freight depot in South Fulton. Bananas and other perishables were iced down along the tracks at area ice plants. Often, every seat would be occupied on the passenger lines, and "standing room only" was common on trains going south on Saturday afternoons. Meeting the trains was a favorite pastime of the population at large, especially on Sundays after church and lunch at the USONA. The ICRR Passenger Depot, a Fulton landmark, unfortunately was not preserved.

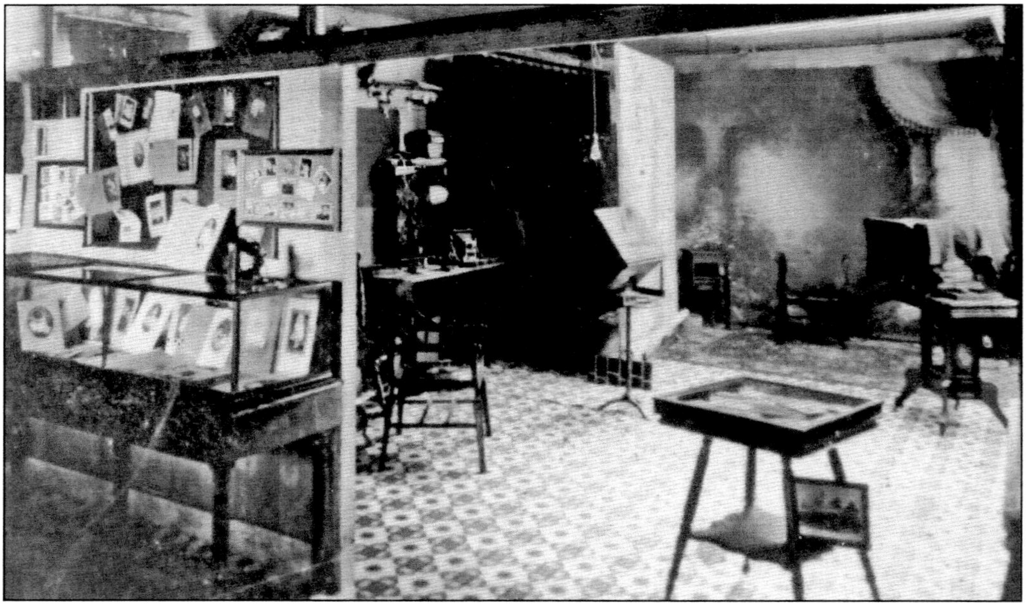

Many of the photographs in this book were taken by C.L. Gardner, proprietor of the Park Studio at 220 Commercial Avenue. The interior of Park Studio is pictured above c. 1908. In addition to traditional portraiture of people, he recorded innumerable residences, churches, schools, and public buildings in the area during his career. His studio was purportedly busiest when photographing babies and children during fair week.

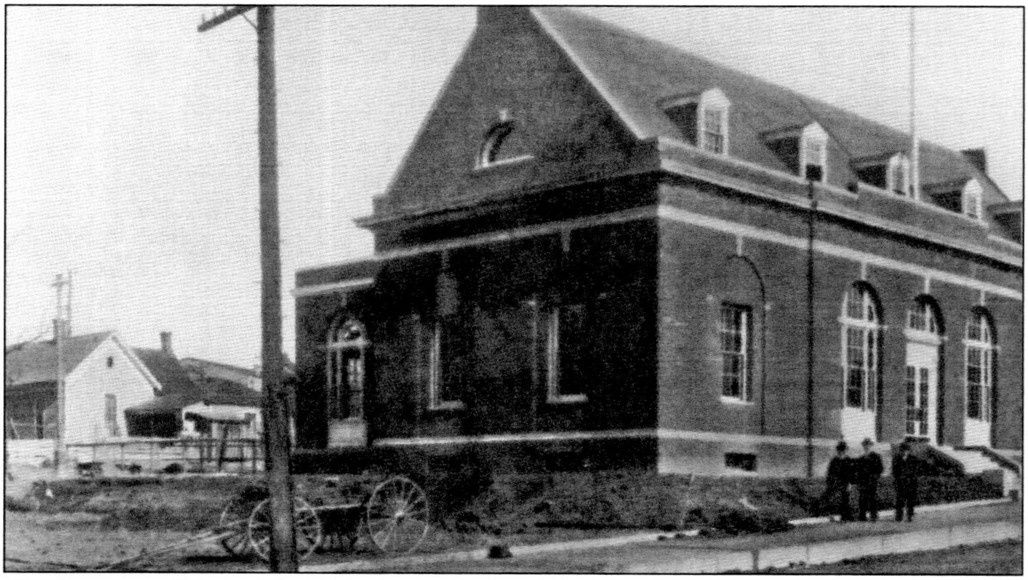

The first post office in Fulton, then named Pontotoc, was established in 1862 by B.F. Carr, in a cabin located in front of the Carr home. Dr. V.A. Hawkins, a pioneer physician, was the first postmaster. The post office then moved to the Meadows block in 1911. A new federal building was commissioned at 312 Main Street in 1914 for $50,000. The Fulton Public Library is now housed in the old post office building. In 1964, a more modern facility for postal service was erected on Walnut Street, where it remains today.

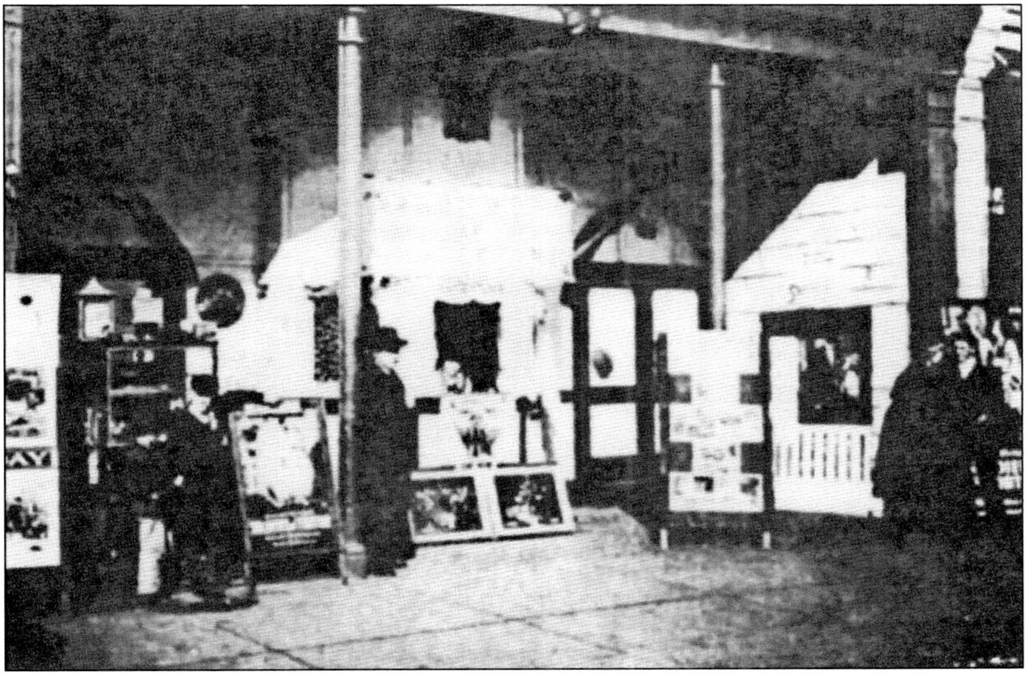

In 1907, W. Levi Chisholm brought movies to town. The original establishment was known as the Theatorium, but it was later called the Rex, the Strand, and the Grand. It was built in the early 1920s. Going to the movie house on a Saturday afternoon was the thing to do. A pianist provided accompaniment to the silent films. The theater was bought in 1949 by the owners of Smith's Café and converted into a dining room called the Rose Room.

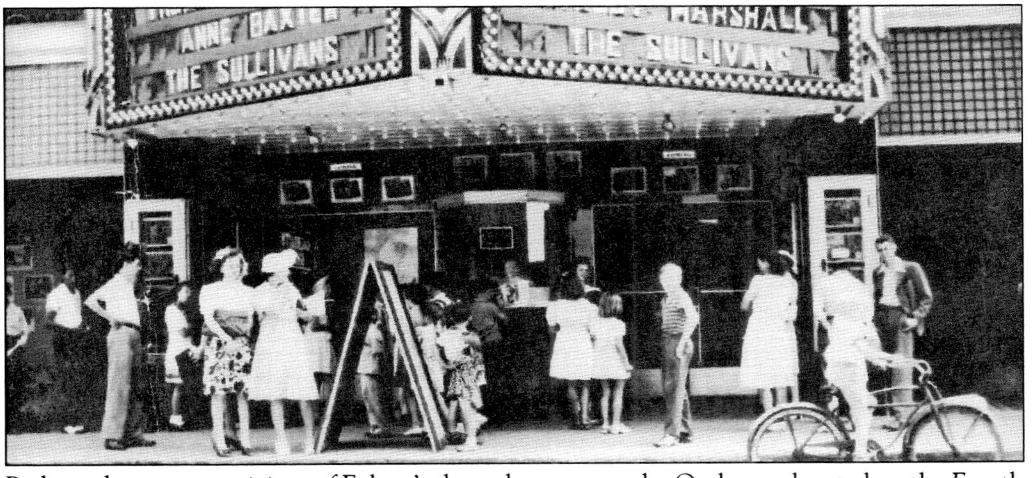

Perhaps the most prestigious of Fulton's three theaters was the Orpheum, located on the Fourth Street extension. It was the first movie house in town to have talking films. There were stories about the ghost of owner Levi Chisolm haunting the establishment. This image depicts the Orpheum after it was sold to Malco Enterprises around 1950. It was extensively renovated, and business boomed again for a period of time.

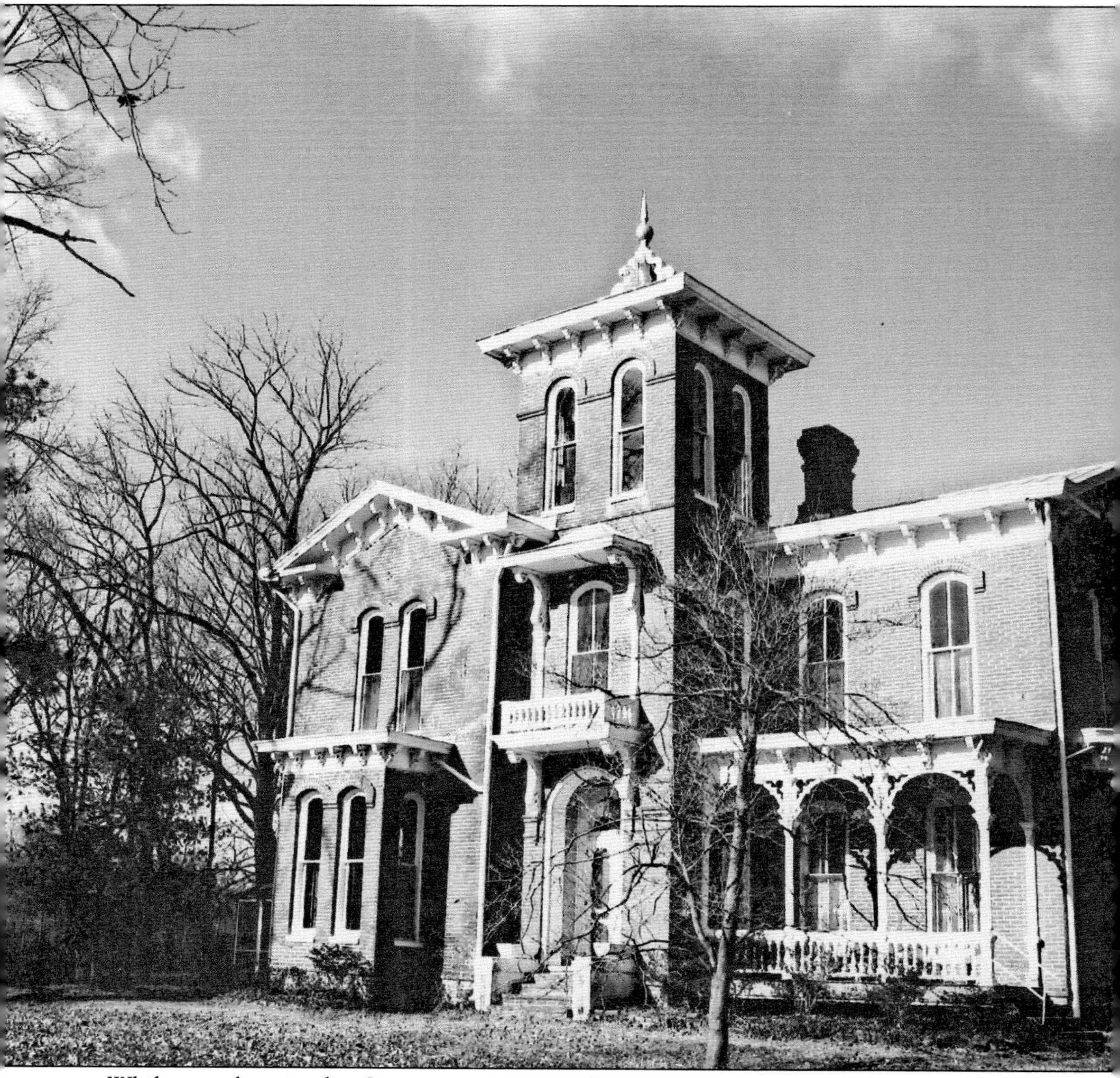

While traveling in the Cincinnati area to sell tobacco, Jesse Whitesell saw a house under construction that caught his fancy. He hired the carpenter to come to Fulton and build him a house in the same style. It is a two-and-a-half-story structure built of home-burned brick; the ceilings are 13 feet high, and there is a ladder in the upstairs hall giving access to the attic tower. In the late 1860s, one of the children died in the lower southwest-corner room of complications from a tonsillectomy, helping to place the date of the home construction sometime between 1865 and 1870. The home typifies late 1800s architecture, with its gingerbread fretwork and narrow porches on the front façade. Descendants of the Jesse Whitesell family reside in the home today.

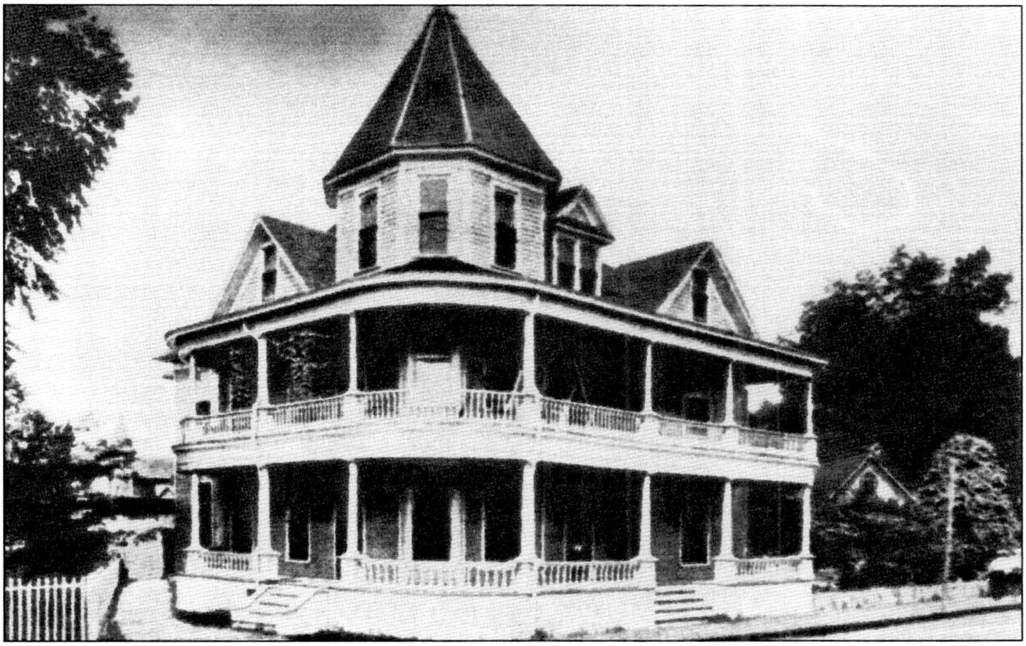

Rudd's Eclectic Sanitarium opened for business in 1905. Dr. R.T. Rudd specialized in the treatment of chronic nervous diseases. The sanitarium derived its name from the Eclectic line of modern medical equipment installed there. Items such as x-ray machines, static machines, wall plates and vibrators, electric baths, and private patient rooms made it a sought-after clinic. The upstairs of the 17-room building also served as the family home.

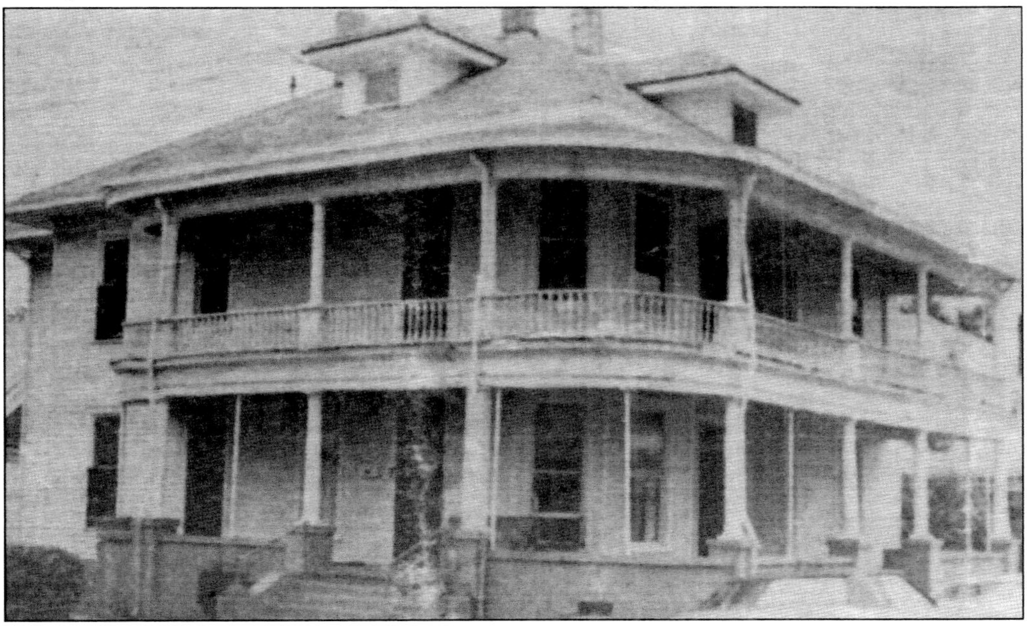

The third floor of the Rudd Eclectic Sanitarium burned in 1913, and the home was remodeled. R.T.'s only son, Dr. Russell Rudd, continued to practice medicine out of the downtown office through the 1970s. The home stands today as a private residence.

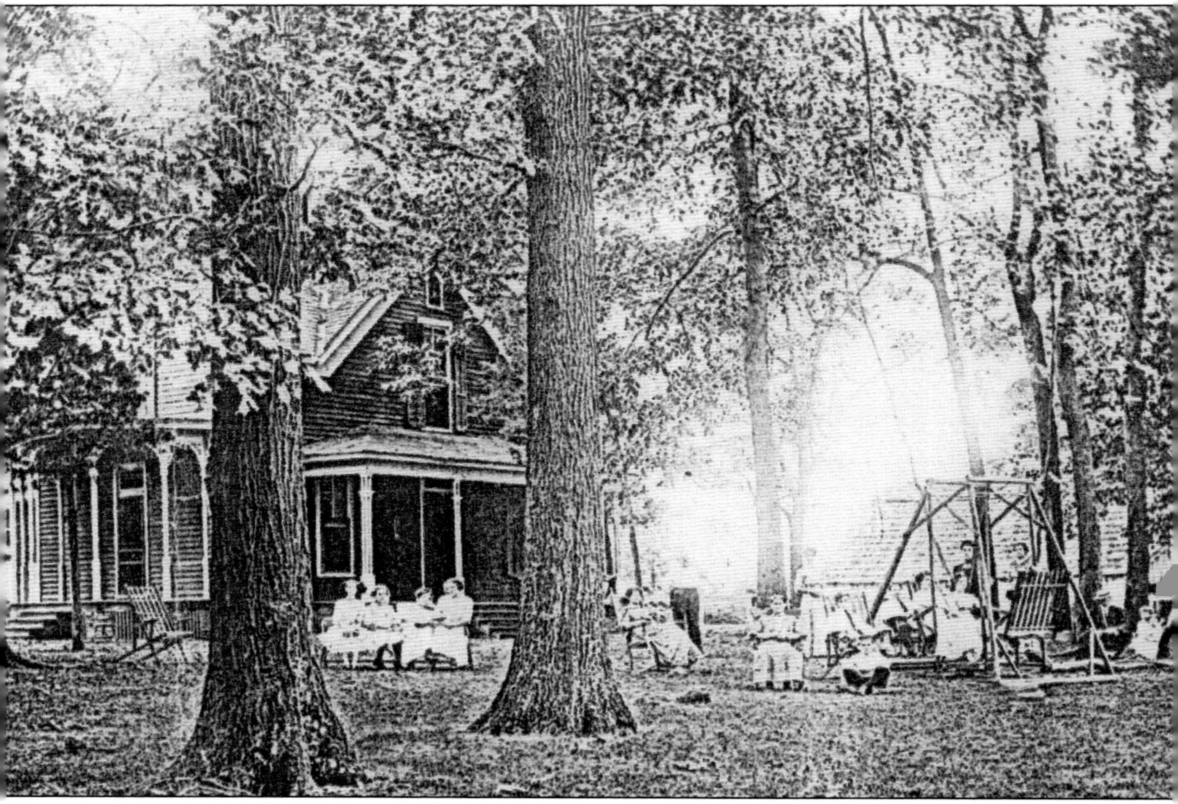

Enjoying an afternoon on the lawn is the Dr. N.J. Paschall family at their home, Forest Dale. The Paschalls were one of the first families to come to Fulton, with Dr. Gideon Paschall choosing the Kentucky side of the state line for his residence, and Dr. N.J. building in Tennessee. The home was located near where the Smith Street Church of Christ in South Fulton is now located. A story is told about the strange "white box" that hung in Dr. N.J.'s drug store on the state line (see page 44). Many curious customers watched in amazement as the doctor rang his house on the top of the hill (present-day Forestdale Avenue) and spoke to his wife over the telephone. This is the first known record of a telephone in the community, sometime around 1928. Dr. N.J. Paschall died in 1937, and the ancestral home eventually moved out of family hands and gave way to other development interests.

In 1893, the South Fulton Normal School and Business College opened at College and Bates Street in South Fulton. The name "normal school" indicated its primary purpose was training teachers. It was one of the few boarding schools in the area and had dormitories next to the school for the students. In 1897, the building was sold to the City of South Fulton for a public institution called the South Fulton School.

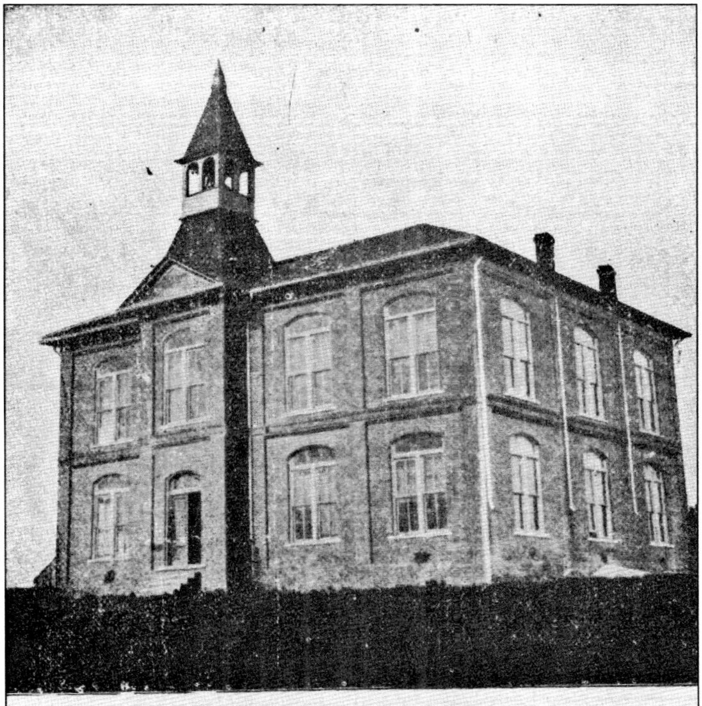

SOUTH FULTON COLLEGE.

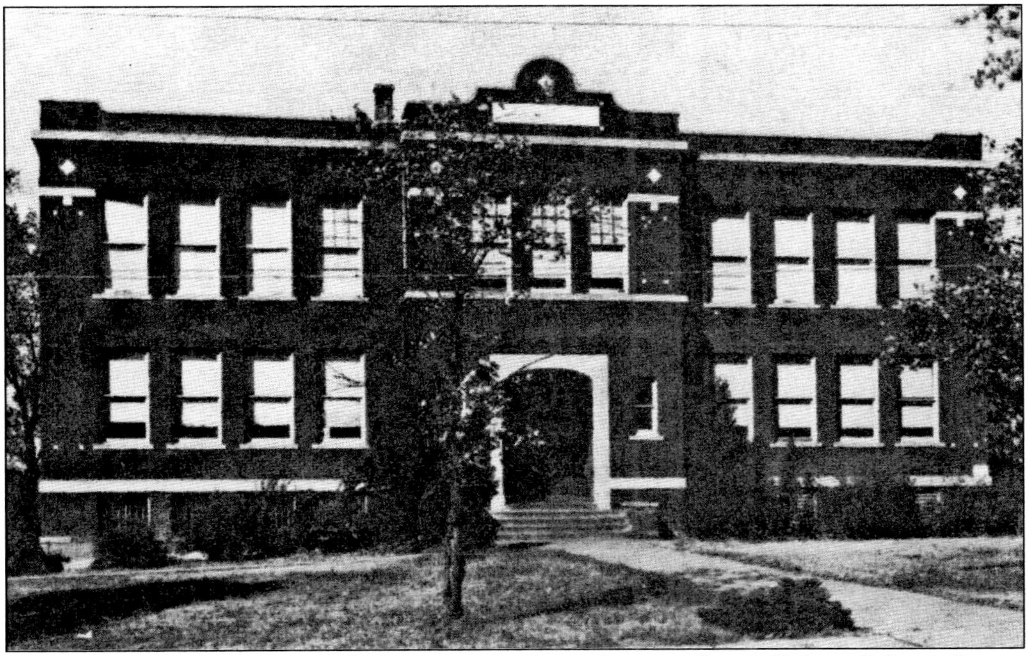

In 1917, the building pictured above was built as the new South Fulton School. It was incorporated into the Obion County School System in 1940 and has changed buildings twice since.

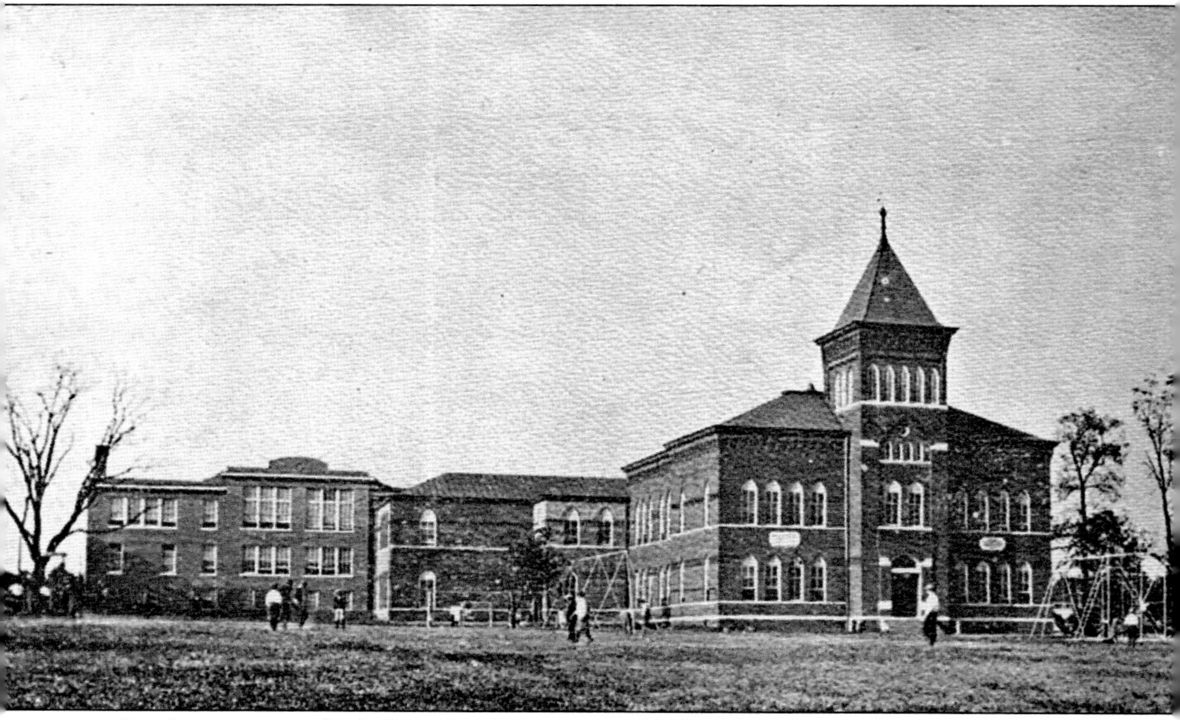

Carr Institute was deeded to school trustees in 1884 by W.T. Carr and wife. In this same year, there was a $15,000 building constructed that included a bell tower housing the bell that called all the children to school. By 1904, the school taught grades 1 through 12. Prior to 1904, a student needed to attend a prep school to get 12th grade work. J.C. Cheek was elected superintendent in 1901 and served 20 years in that capacity. In 1941, the Gothic structure, designed by architects John L. Smith and H. Cibel, was razed and a more modern facility was built on the Carr Institute site. By order of the state Department of Education the name was changed to Carr Elementary.

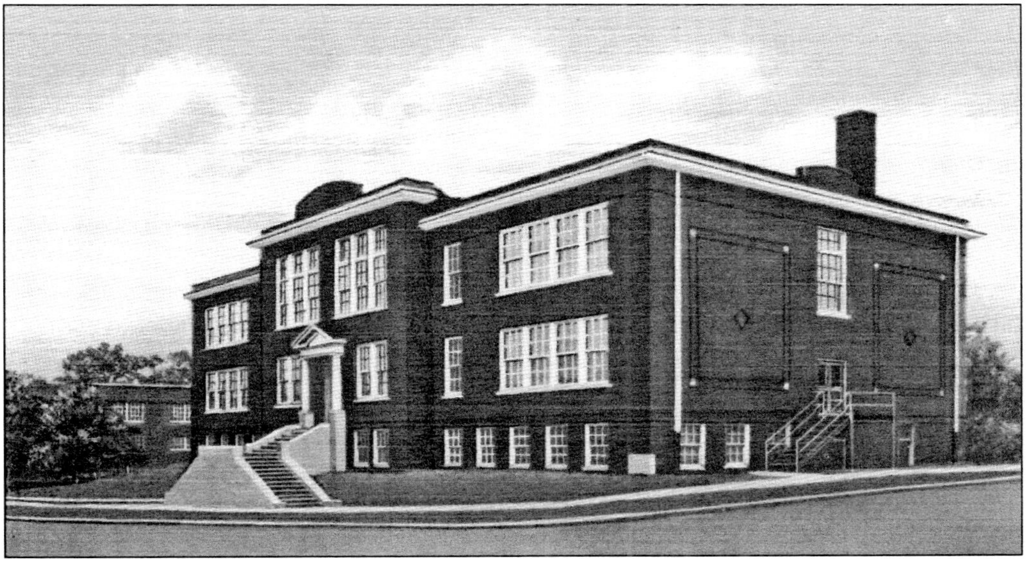

A Fulton High School building was built on part of the land donated by the Carrs. It was completed in 1922 for $65,000. A science hall was added in 1928, burned in 1953, and was rebuilt in 1954. The present high school resides on Stephen Beale Drive, having been located there in the early 1980s. The old high school was razed, but kindergarten through sixth grade remains at the original school site.

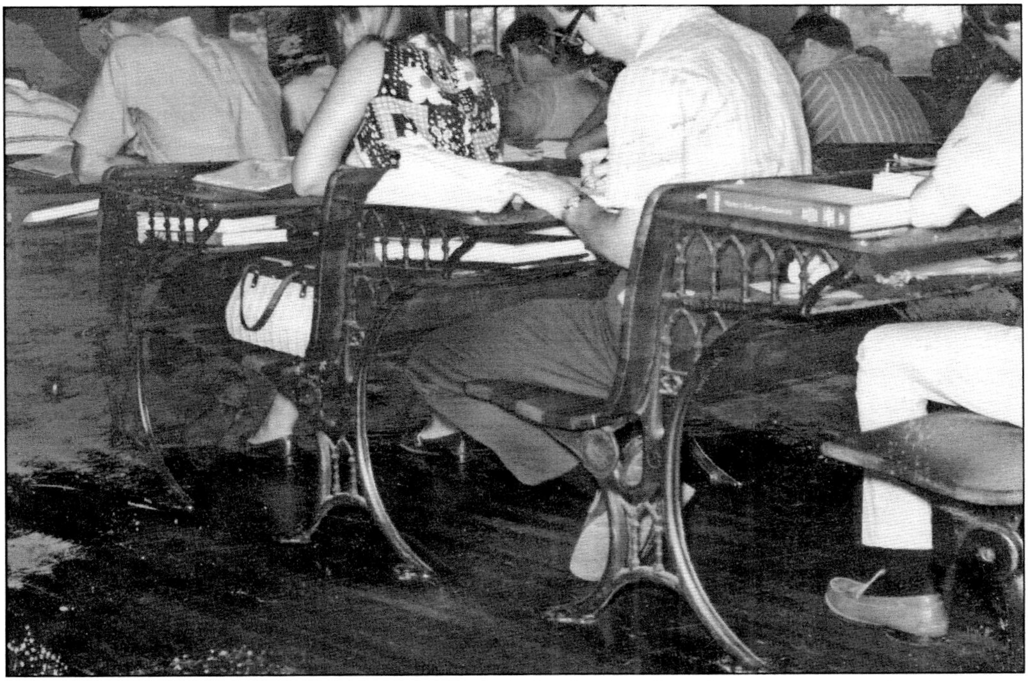

After 47 years, the original desks and some of the high school's infrastructure were beginning to show major signs of wear and tear. This image ran in the local paper to alert the public to the condition of the school. In 1971, the doors to a modern Fulton City High School opened on Stephen Beale Drive. Classes continue in this building in 2004.

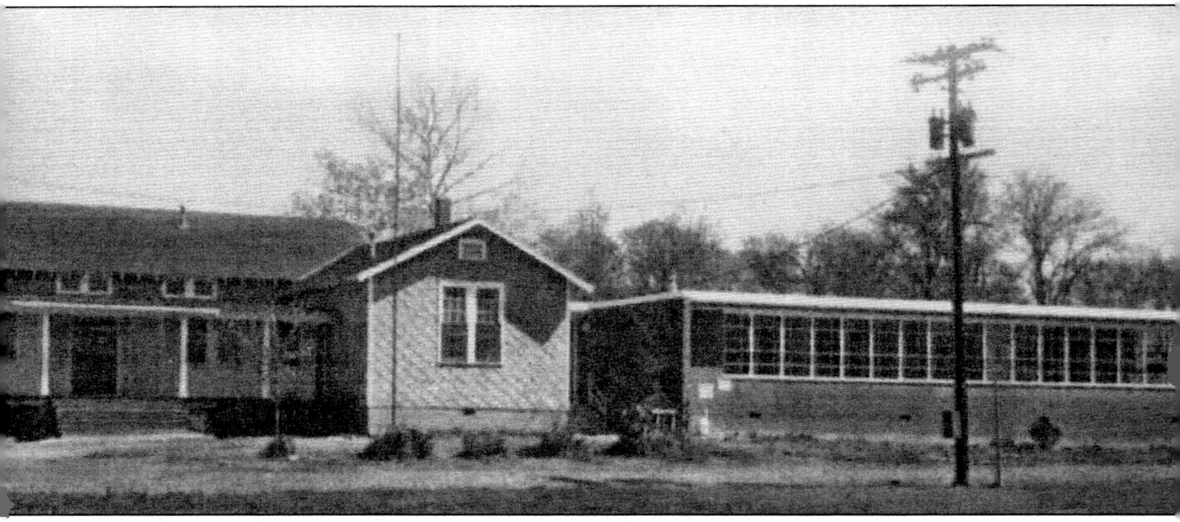

On his 50th birthday in 1912, Julius Rosenwald, president of Sears, Roebuck, and Company, presented Booker T. Washington a check for $25,000 to aid African-American colleges and preparatory academies based on the Tuskegee Institute model. Like several other Northern philanthropists, Rosenwald was attracted to Washington's belief of "self-help" and Tuskegee's education system. With $2,100 left over in 1913, Washington persuaded Rosenwald to take the money and help rural America build elementary schools for the African-American community. Rosenwald agreed but stipulated that each community receiving the gift would have to match his contribution with one of their own—hopefully derived of a joint community effort. It was during this period the Rosenwald School in South Fulton, Tennessee, was built. All that remains of the original site is a gymnasium and science building built in the 1950s and 1960s. These buildings are currently in use as a community center.

The Terry Norman School was located on a three-acre lot on the east side of Fulton donated to the city by Will Terry and the Noah Norman estate. It was built at the turn of the century to help provide education for the rapidly growing school-age population; it taught grades one through six. When the school closed its doors in 1972, the playground was bought by the city park system for $3,000, and $2,500 was paid for the equipment. This image shows a *c.* 1958 recess at Terry Norman.

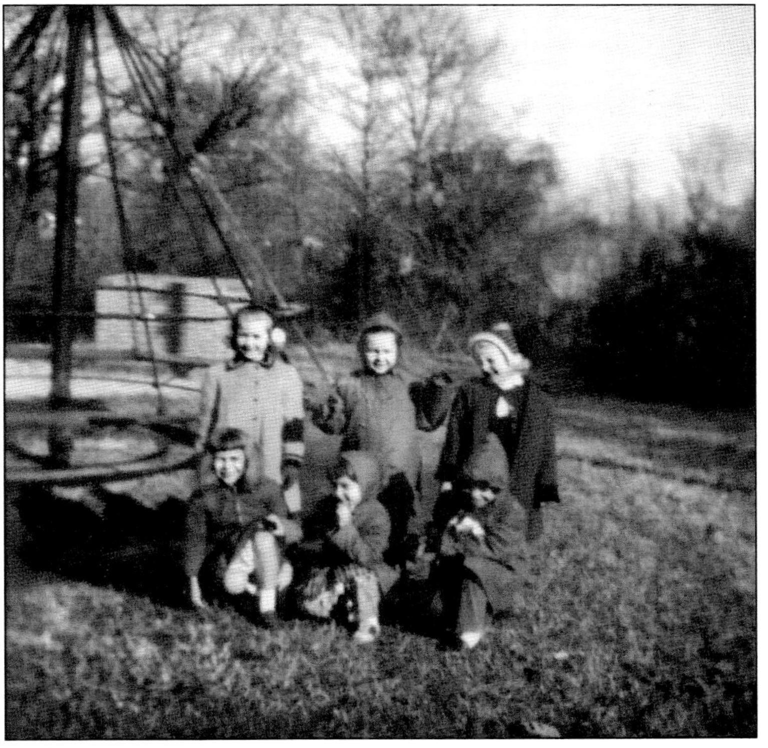

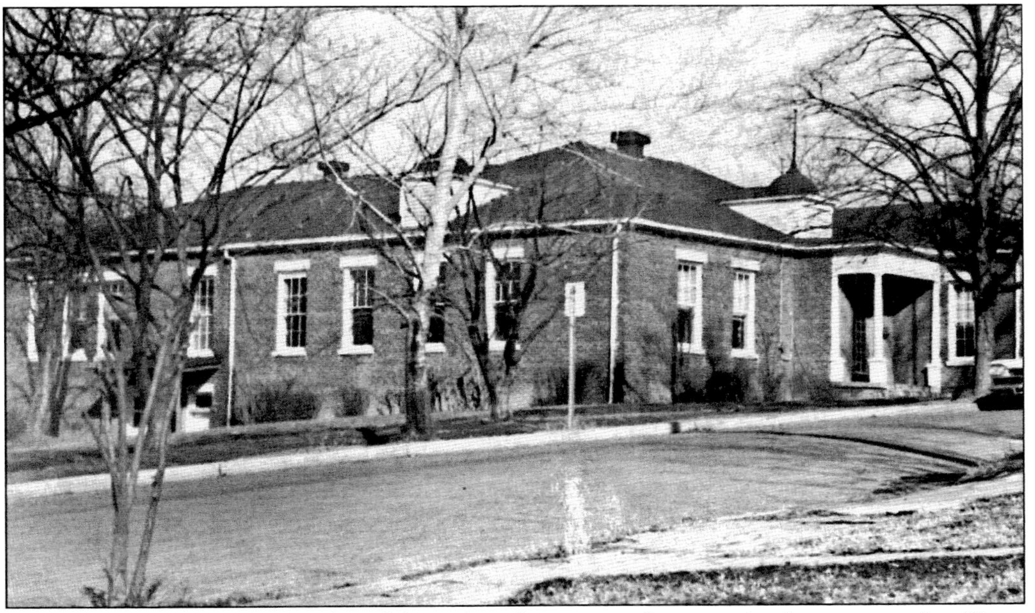

Mrs. Hettie Collins was transferred from Carr Institute to become the first principal at Terry Norman School (1905), and she received a raise from $40 to $50 per month. The school continued its close-knit family tradition for 50 years. The children of East Fulton walked to school, often with family pets tagging along, and on snowy days in the winter, they brought sleds to use at recess. It was a well-beloved part of the school system.

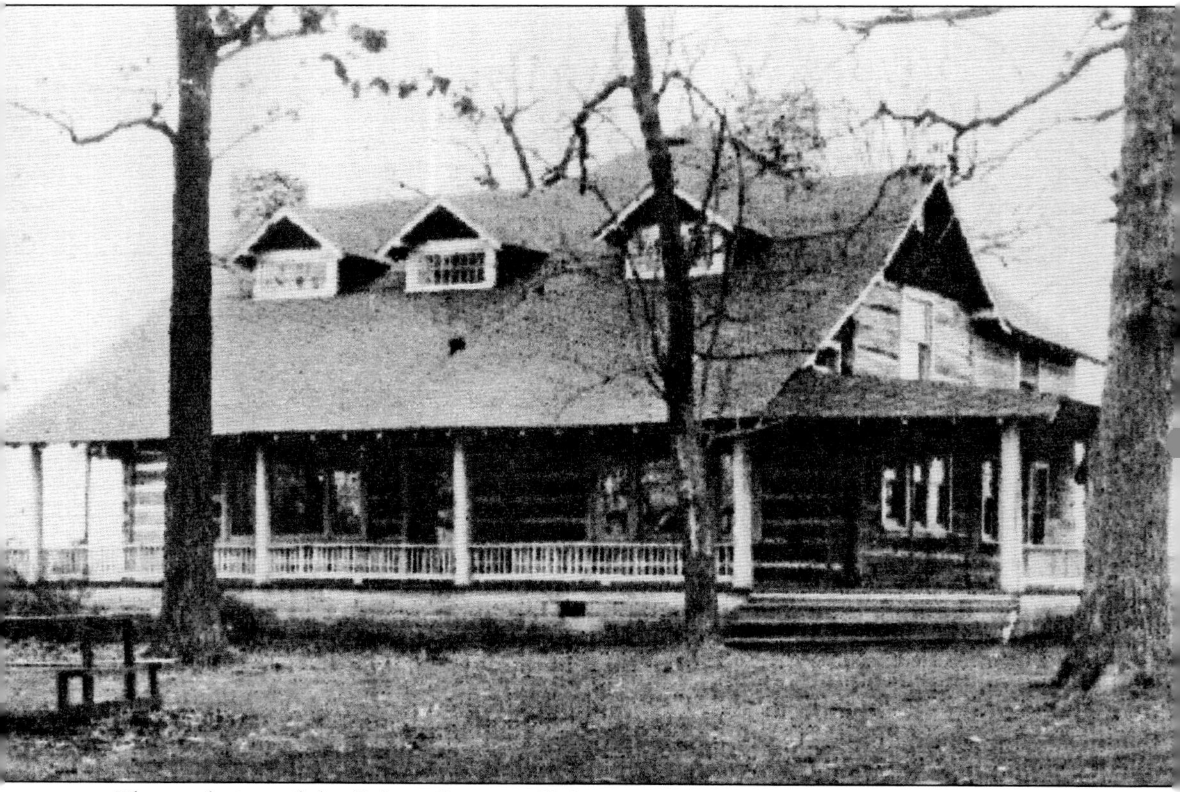

The evolution of the Fulton Country Club is an interesting one. From its initial days in East Fulton on the Thomas property to the formation of the Woodlawn Land Company—the stockholding company for this voluntary, unincorporated association—the citizens of the Twin Cities were determined to play golf. Eighty acres of land in Obion County were purchased from Ed Thomas, including a log home to be used for the clubhouse seen in the photograph above. A nine-hole golf course was built in 1925 under the direction of golf professional Bob Brown. In 1927, the course was opened, the clubhouse furnished and remodeled, and a locker room added for members. In 1941, the beloved log cabin clubhouse caught fire and burned to the ground. The present "all-in-one" clubhouse opened in 1944 with modern conveniences. There was a reported crowd of 500 to attend the open house, featuring the novelty of locker rooms and clubroom all under one roof, a pool, and basketball and tennis courts. At present the course has been extended to 18 holes and is still owned and operated by the Woodlawn Land Company.

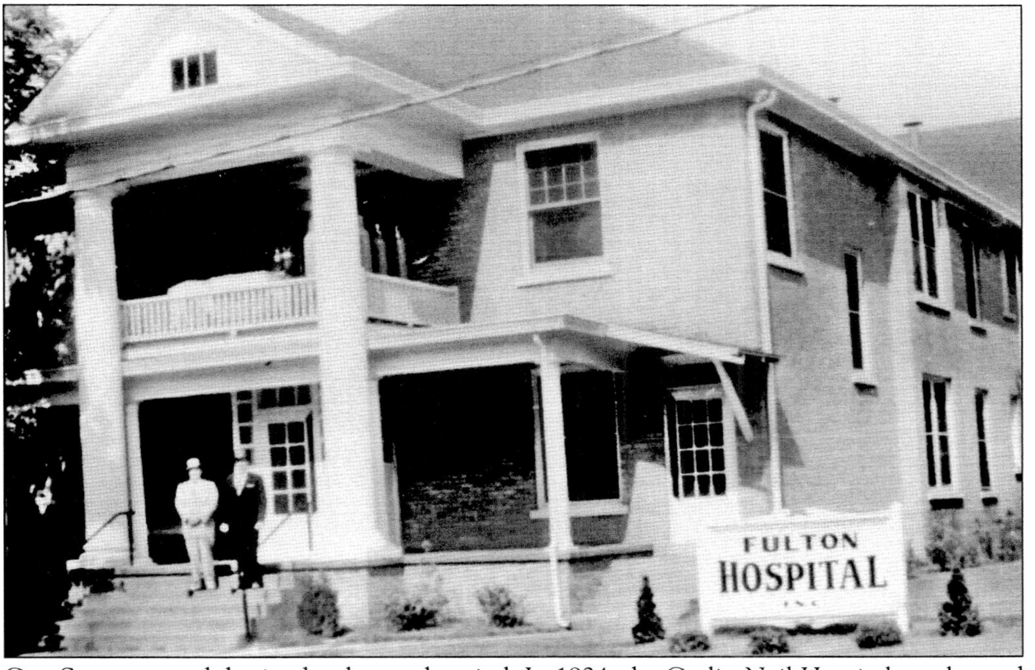

Carr Street seemed destined to have a hospital. In 1924, the Curlin-Neil Hospital was located there. In May 1937, Dr. R.L. Bushart and his sons Dr. G.F. and Dr. R.W. Bushart purchased and moved Fulton Hospital to Dr. Whitehead's home at 223 Carr Street, seen above.

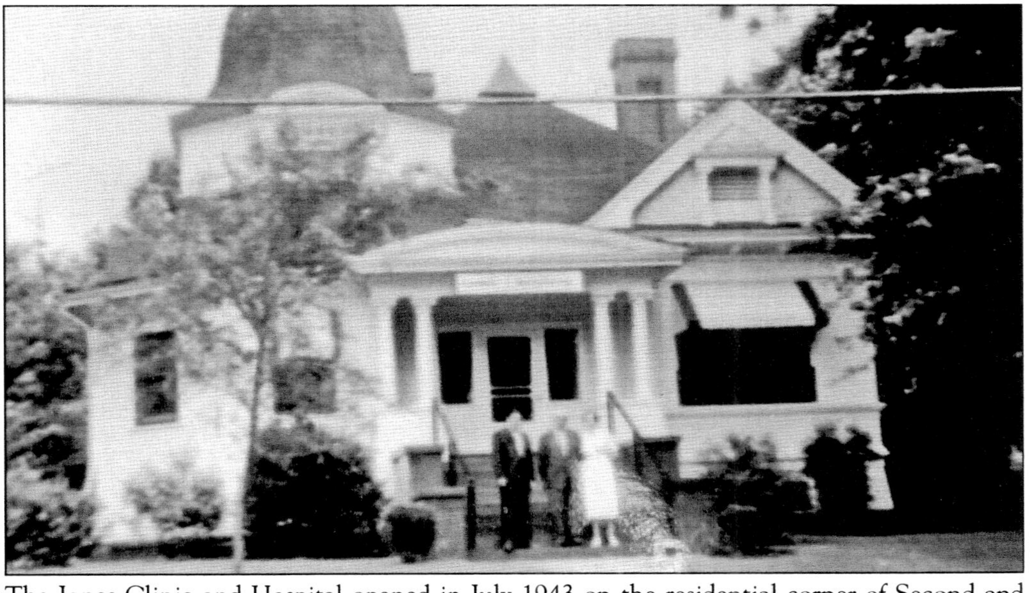

The Jones Clinic and Hospital opened in July 1943 on the residential corner of Second and Park Streets. It was formerly the Lewis Fields House. Fields sold the property in 1908 to J.P. Joyner, who sold to the Winstead and Jones Funeral Company in 1927. The house wound up in the hands of Dr. D.L. Jones in 1943, and it was known as Jones Hospital for the next 26 years. D.L. Jones's brother, W.W. Jones, had bought the home in partnership for use as a funeral parlor in 1927. His other brother, Dr. J.L. Jones, ran a private dental practice in Fulton.

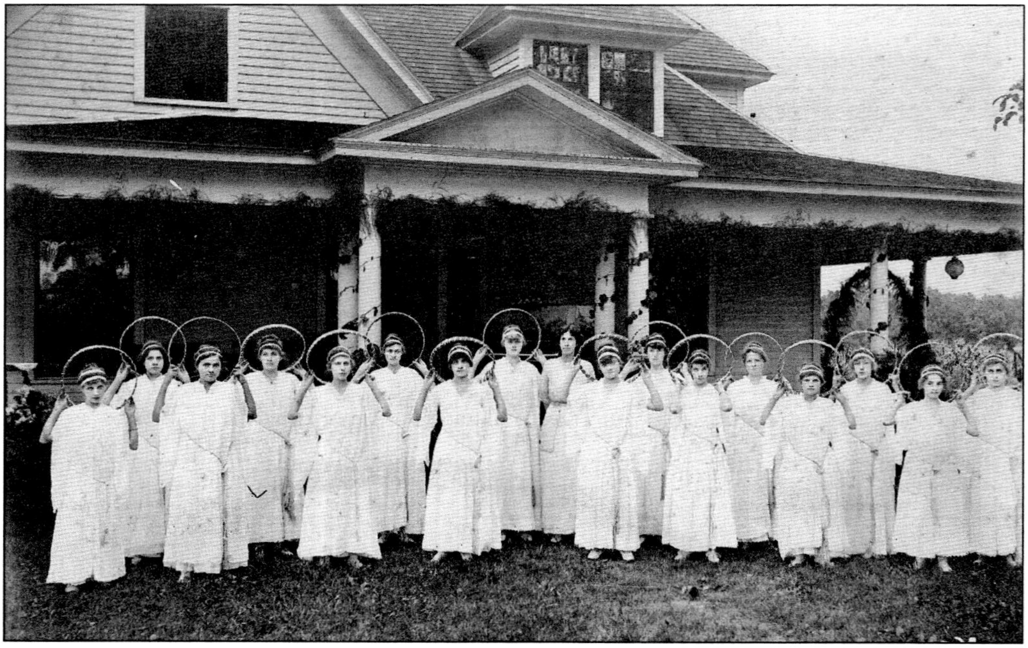

This interesting group of young women appears to be performing some type of exercise or dance with hoops. With similar attire and signs that the weather was moderate, it is possible some type of spring festival celebration or church program was underway. The women are unidentified.

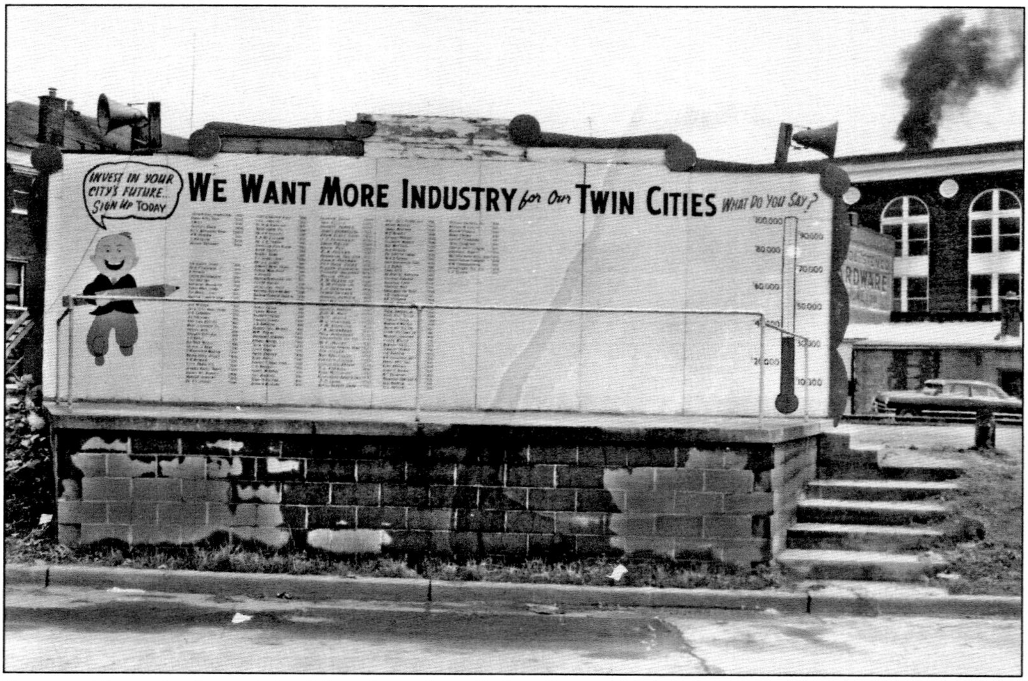

Featured here is the original bandstand on Lake Street. It was often used to post community notices and for parades and award ceremonies. It has been replaced by a larger structure in the same general area.

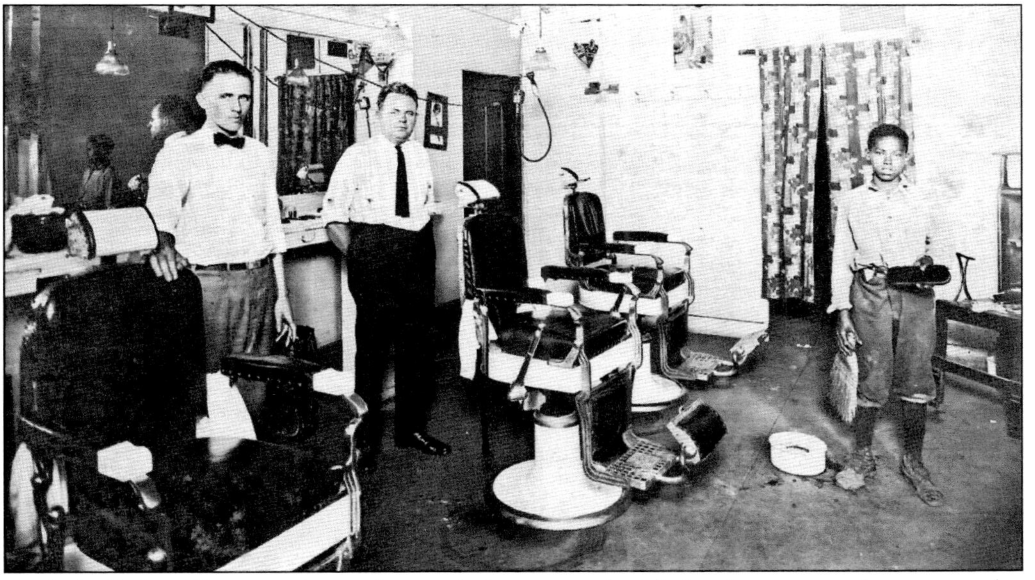

Neeley's Barber Shop was located toward the east end of Lake Street near the present-day location of The Keg Restaurant. On the left is Leonard Brown; the others are unidentified. Barber shops have been on Lake Street since 1908, beginning with the Palace, and have served as community gathering places as well as providing personal grooming services for generations of customers.

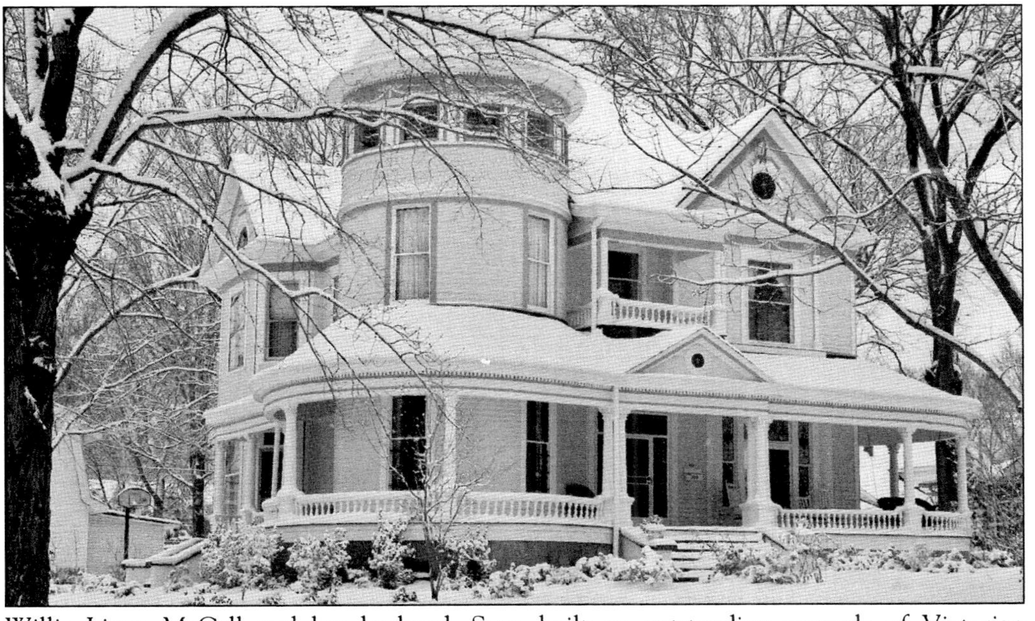

Willie Ligon McCall and her husband, Sam, built an outstanding example of Victorian architecture on the corner of Eddings and Green Streets. The home has exceptional millwork, parquet floors, and 13-foot ceilings. The library has curved, built-in bookcases, and originally there were seven coal-burning fireplaces. An Italian fresco artist painted the rooms of 300 Eddings in the highest fashion of the day. Cherubs were on the parlor ceiling, and flower garlands and hunting scenes were scattered in other living areas. It remains a private residence today.

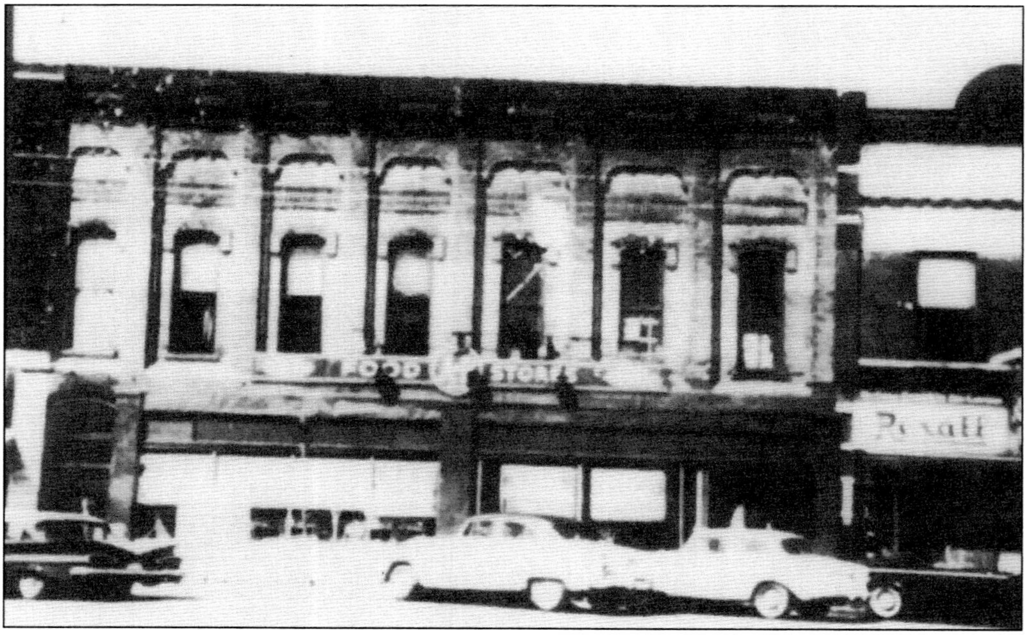

The original A&P grocery storefront on Lake Street is displayed here. The grocery later moved to Mears Street. Note Paschall Drug Store, with the Rexall sign, to the right of the A&P.

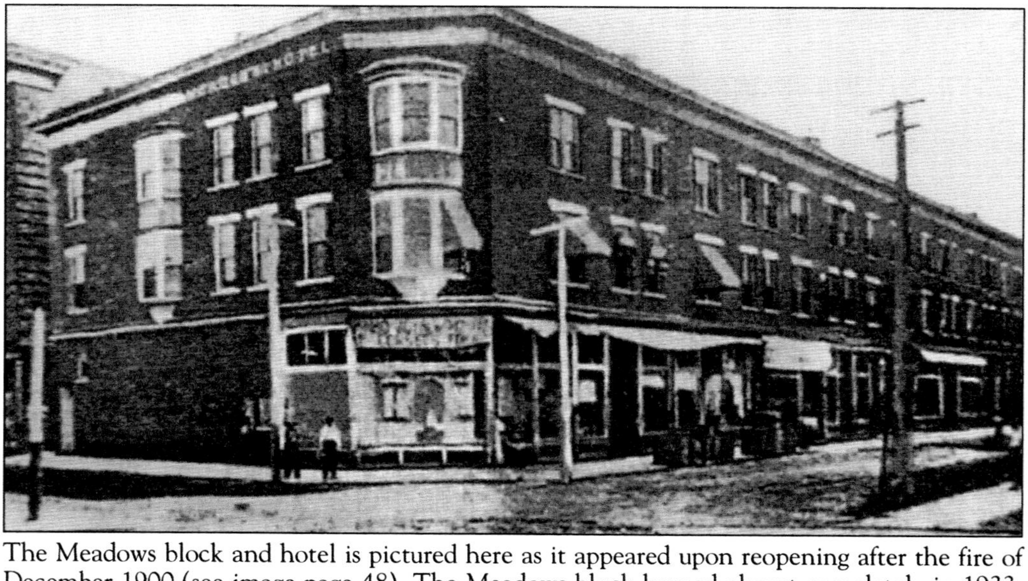

The Meadows block and hotel is pictured here as it appeared upon reopening after the fire of December 1900 (see image page 48). The Meadows block burned almost completely in 1933. However, a portion was restored and now houses an auto parts store.

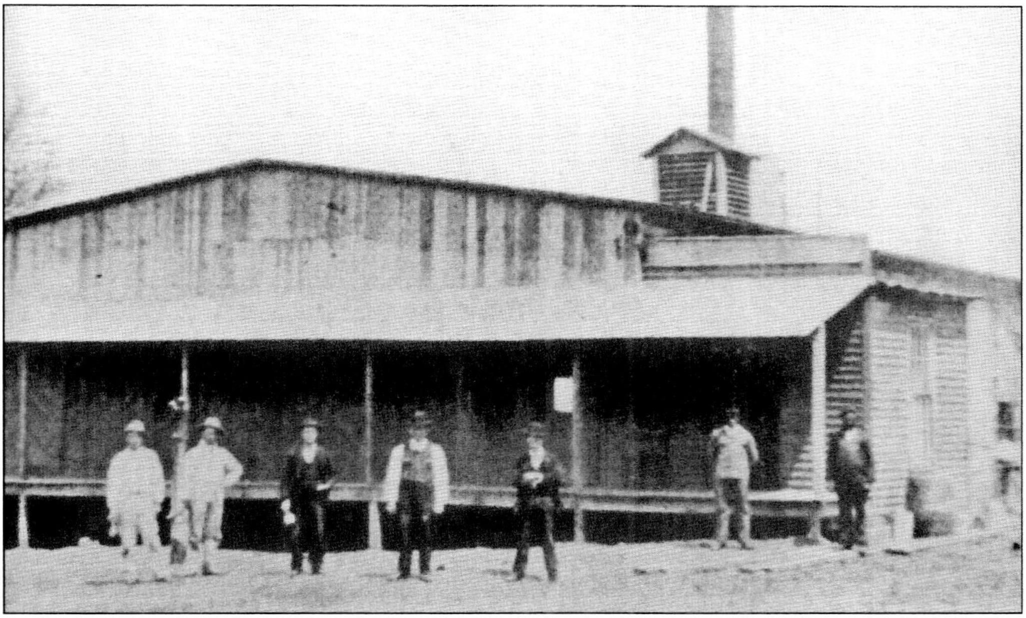

The Fulton Ice Company, established in 1898, was one of Fulton's leading industries. Known as the R.H. Wade Ice Plant when the Wade brothers took control, it had four delivery wagons that made calls for ice in the morning and evening at area homes lucky enough to own galvanized iceboxes. The going rate for ice was 40¢ per 100 pounds. Ice was also shipped COD. Being near the railroad tracks, the company serviced all northbound refrigerator cars. In time, the plant expanded to a five-story brick building that also supplied water for a community swimming pool, known as the Sunny Dip.

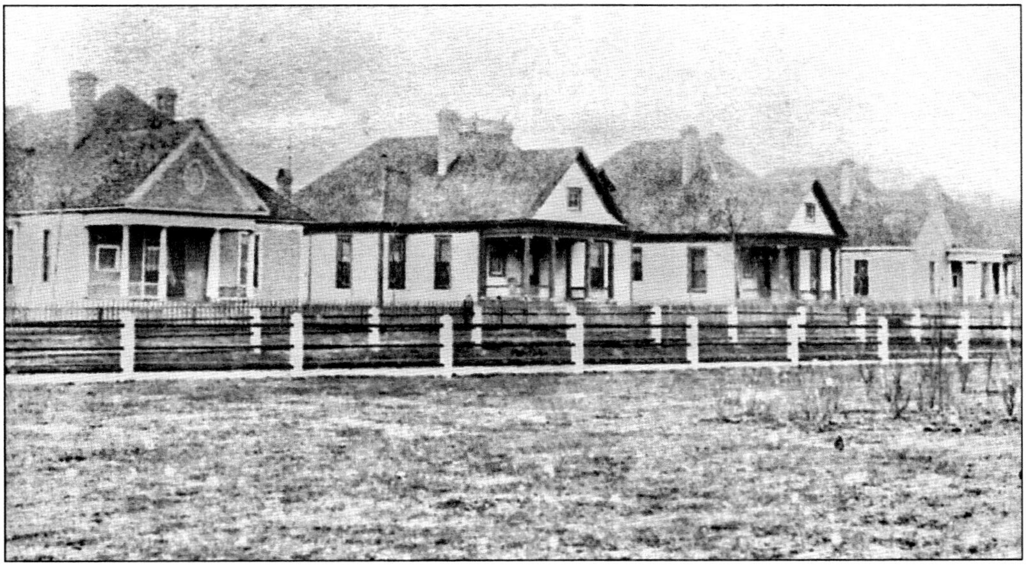

Pearl's Village was a row of houses facing the railway on Burton Row, looking north from the Viaduct on Mears Street. This area reportedly gained its name in honor of the daughter of the property owner. Burton Row is no longer in existence. It was closed to through traffic when the houses were razed and the rail pulled up on this section of the track.

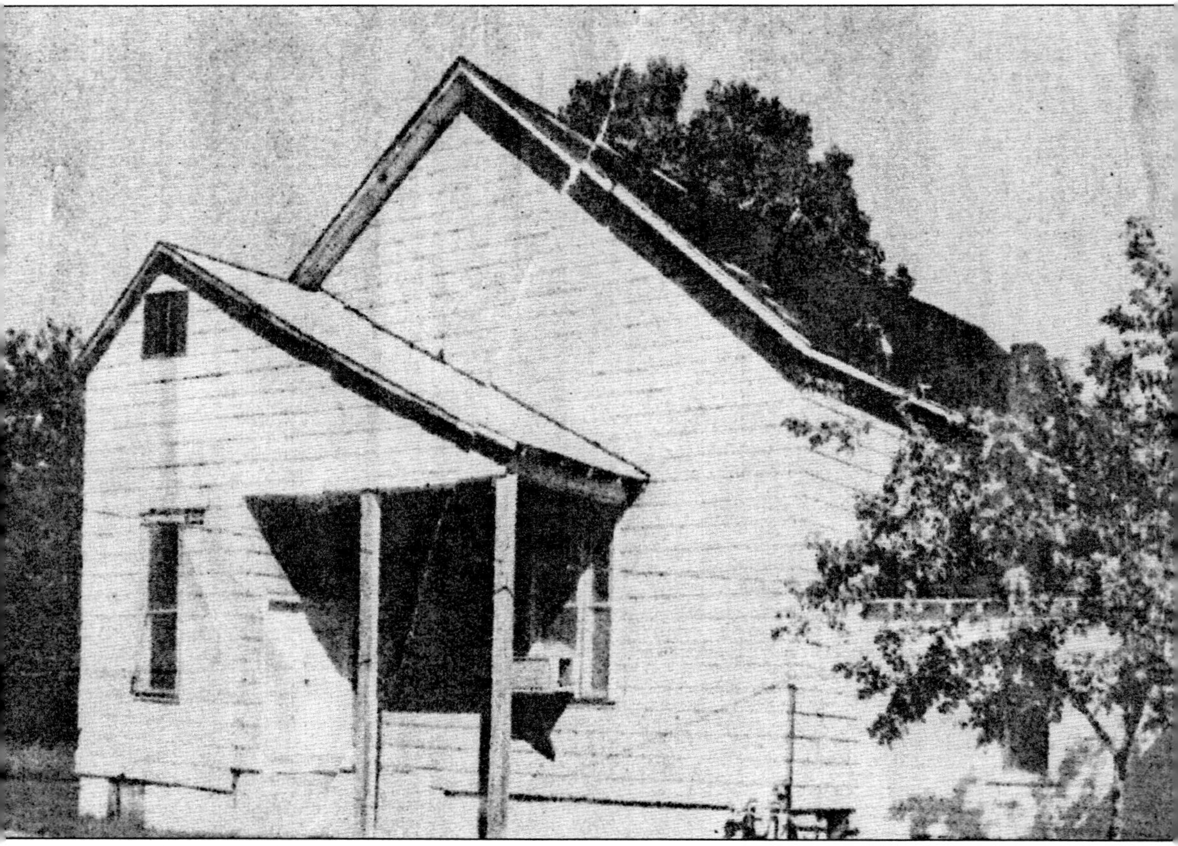

On Harris in South Fulton, Tennessee, is the Jacksonville Freewill Baptist Church, which is reported to be the oldest African-American church in the state of Tennessee, dating from 1881. An early school was established here. It is in close proximity to the Jacksonville Freemasons Society on College Street, which claims to be the oldest black Freemasons society in the state of Tennessee.

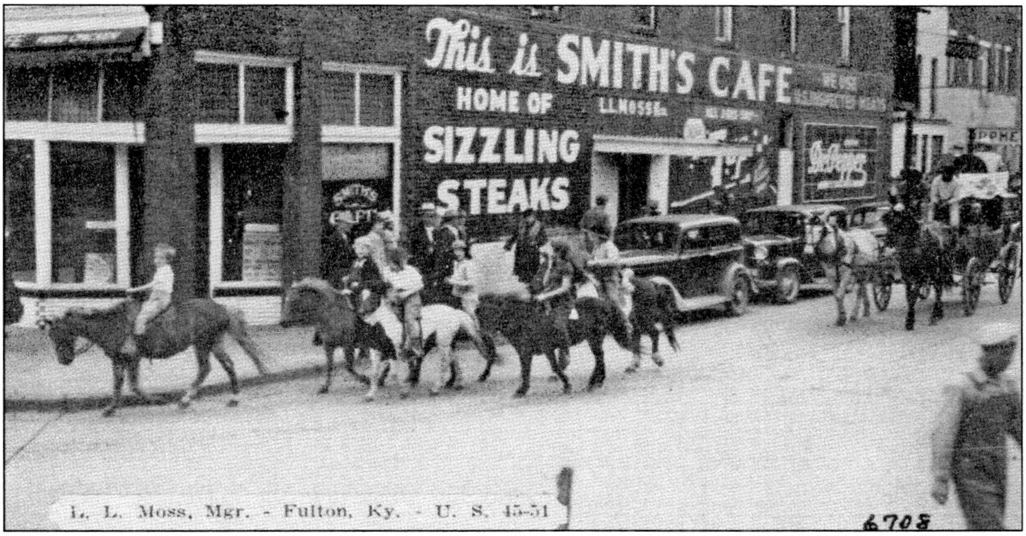

Known originally as the American Café, Smith's catered to the railroad employees but fast became a favorite of the local citizens as well. Steaks were the specialty, but many other items were served from an á la carte menu. A full meal cost as little as 25¢ and was available 24 hours a day. Around the corner can be glimpsed the Fulton Bottling Company and the Orpheum Theater.

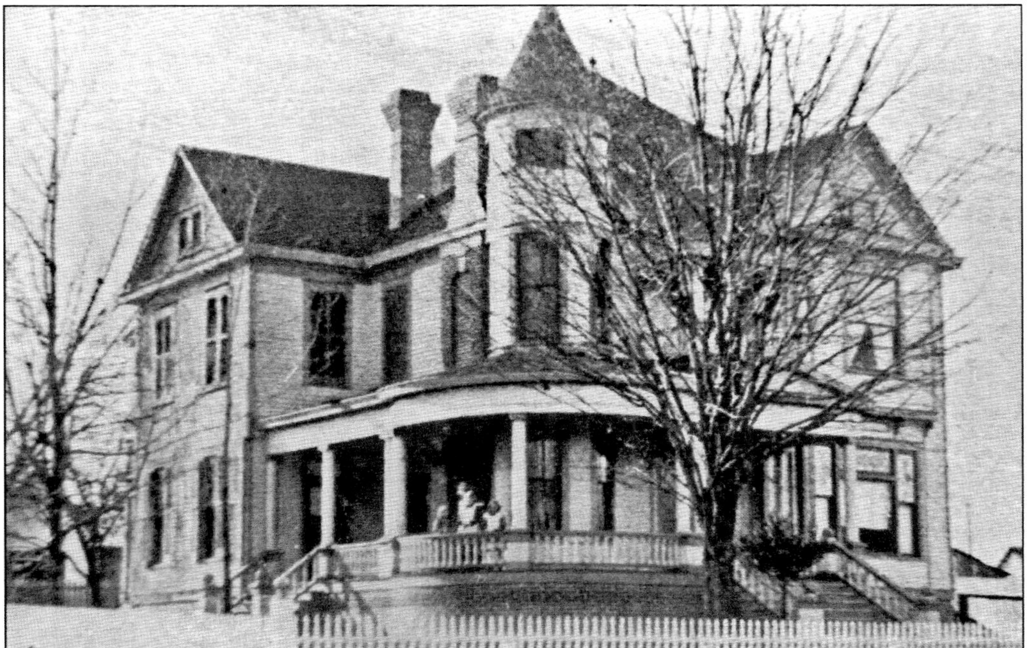

This impressive home is the Smith-Fields House at 200 Eddings Street c. 1890s. Mr. Fields was the first president of City National Bank. He and his wife, Hattie Binford Smith, had three daughters, Lillian, Clara, and Virginia. Due to Mr. Fields suffering from tuberculosis, the family moved to North Carolina and sold the home. However, the Fields family eventually returned to Fulton and bought back their original home when it was determined that Mr. Fields would not recover. He died at age 42.

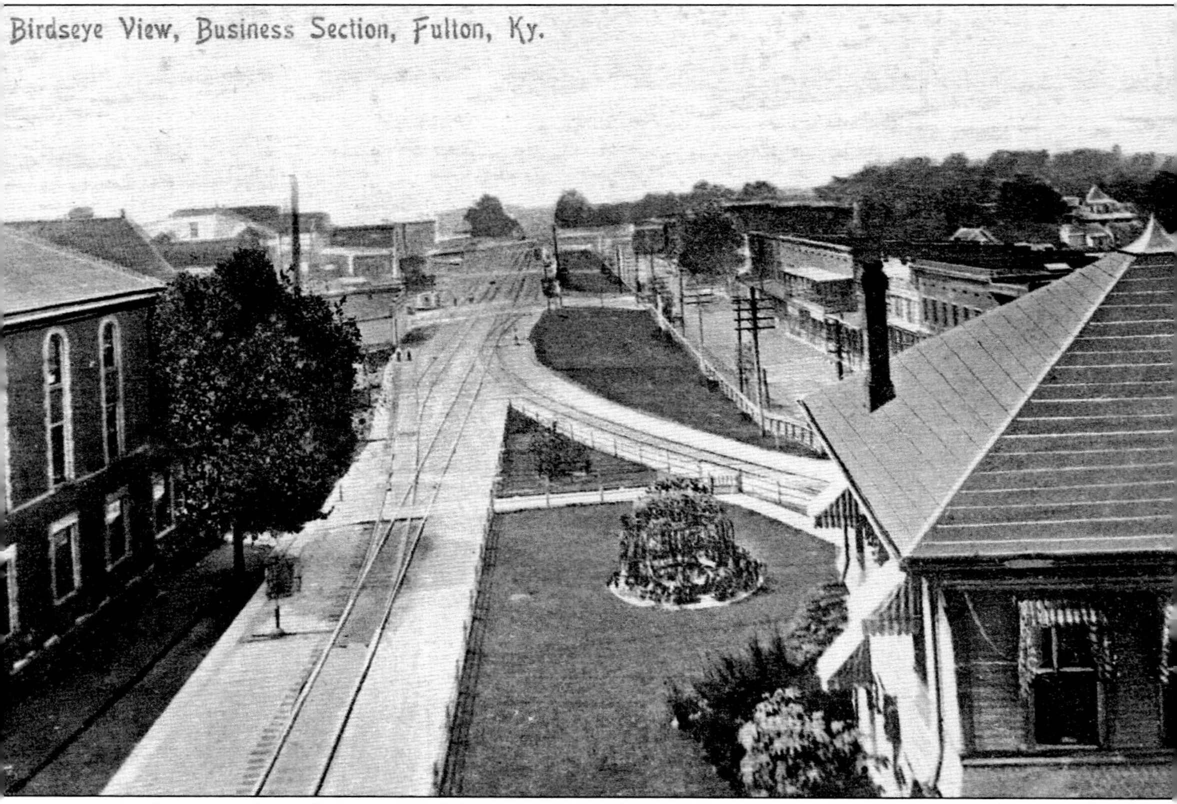

Looking southward down the ICRR tracks to Lake Street, this picture is an aerial view of the Tennessee Division Office of the Illinois Central on the right and the USONA Hotel on the left. Note the rose arbor in the yard, with manicured lawns and other landscaped frontage unsurpassed in its day. The wooden storefronts of downtown can be seen in the distance.

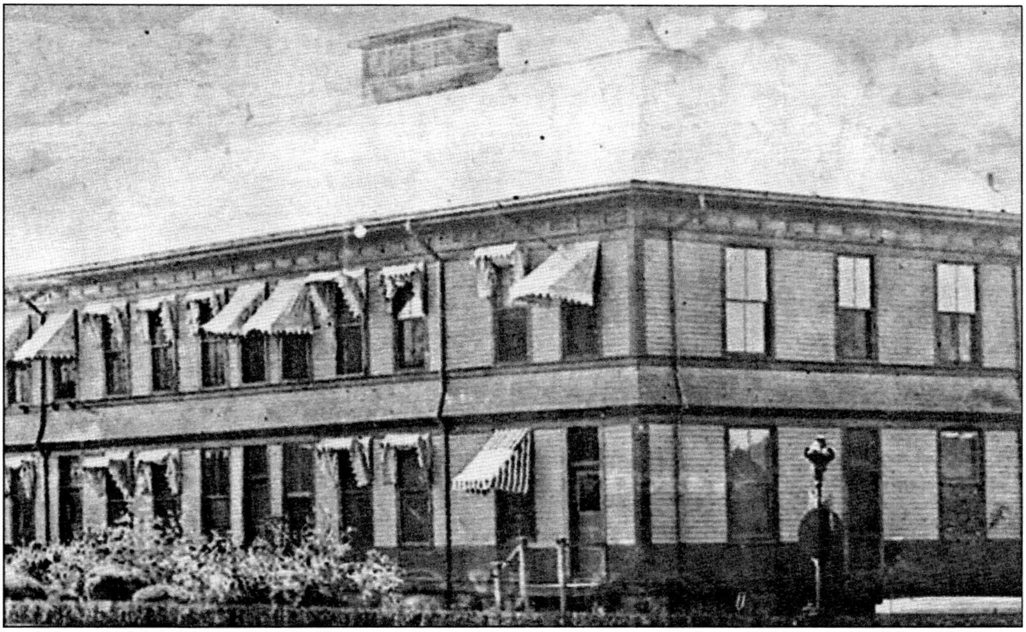

The railroad has been the foundation and backbone of the community since about 1874. Due to Fulton's strategic location, the Illinois Central established their Tennessee Division Office here and employed a large number of office workers. In addition, the city has served as the headquarters for division officials, many of whom made Fulton their home.

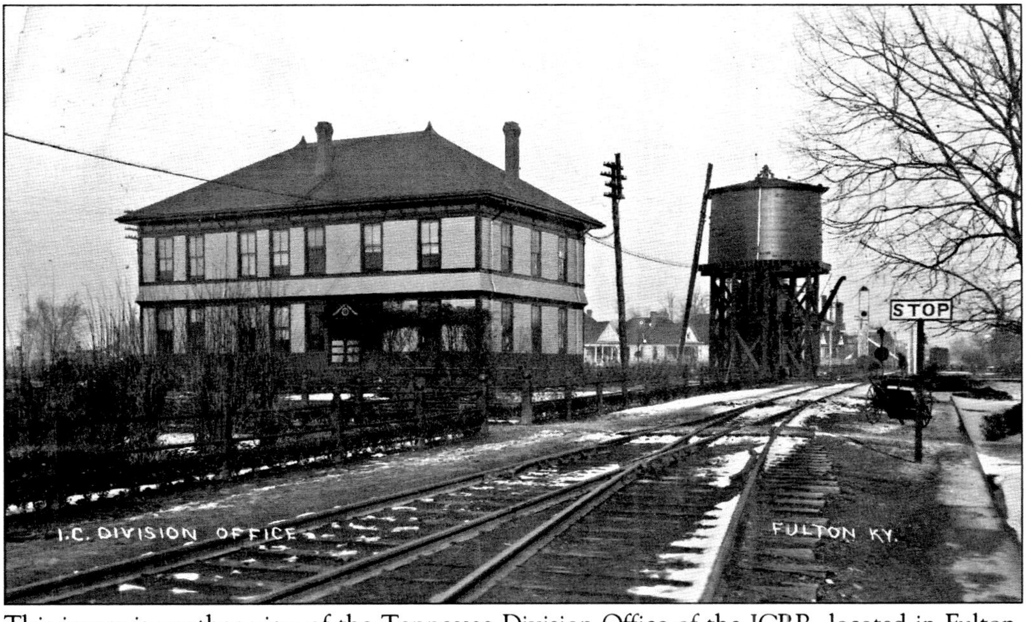

This image is another view of the Tennessee Division Office of the ICRR, located in Fulton, Kentucky. In the background, Pearl's Village can be seen along the railway.

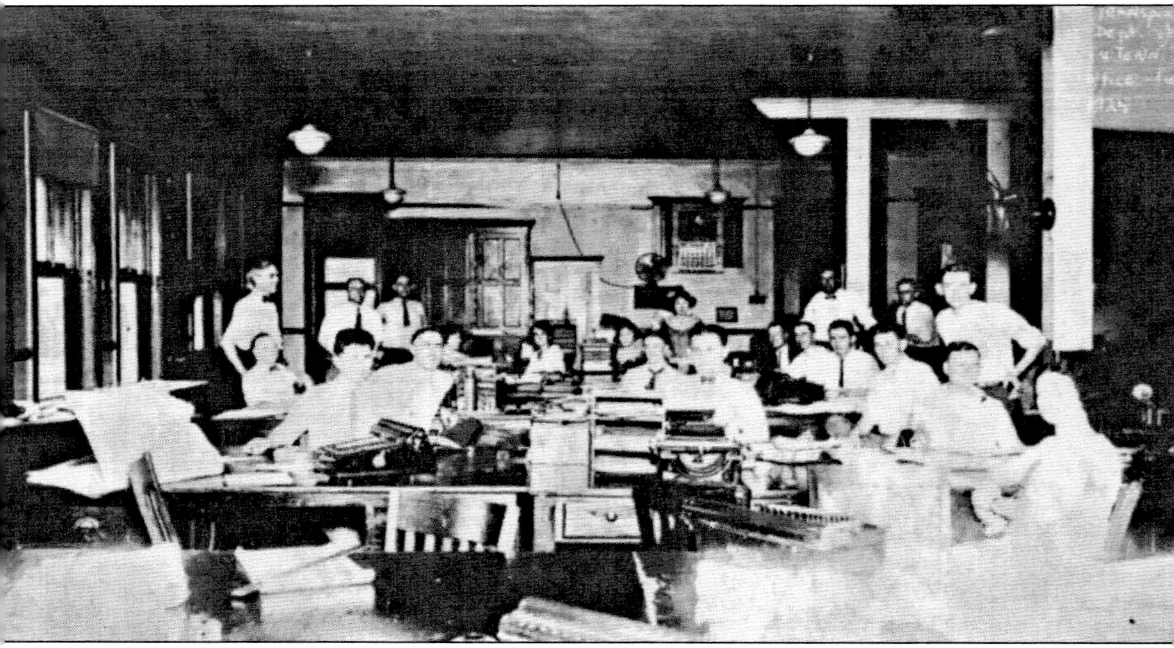

This image was captured inside the transportation department of the Tennessee Division Office of the ICRR around 1925. As evidenced by the number of employees, the railroad was a major provider in the work force of the community and a welcome addition to the economy of the day.

Three

Traces of the Past

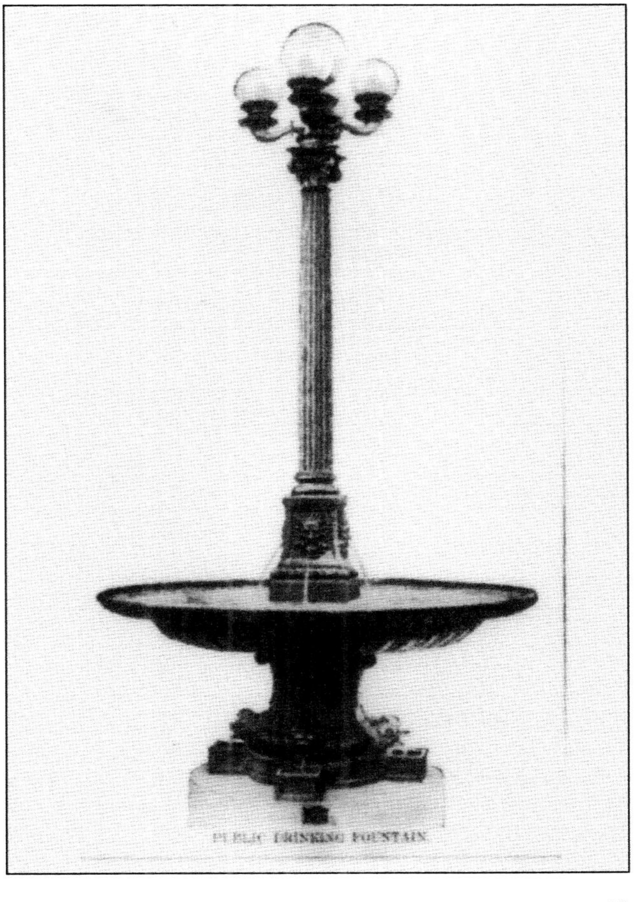

Mayor Chowning was the impetus behind a pubic drinking fountain on Lake Street sometime between 1910 and 1915. The fountain was funded in part by the city council and the remainder by private donation; it was to be erected in the business section of town. The iron fountain with a bronze coating was purchased from Mott Iron Works of New York City and erected in the middle of Lake Street at the intersection of Walnut Street. Water flowed from the lips of four gargoyles into a basin almost three feet deep and six feet in diameter. The basin included four troughs for dogs. Five electric globe lights illuminated the fountain at dark. The fountain stood 11 feet, 3 inches tall and was operated by a ball and cock water supply, preventing waste.

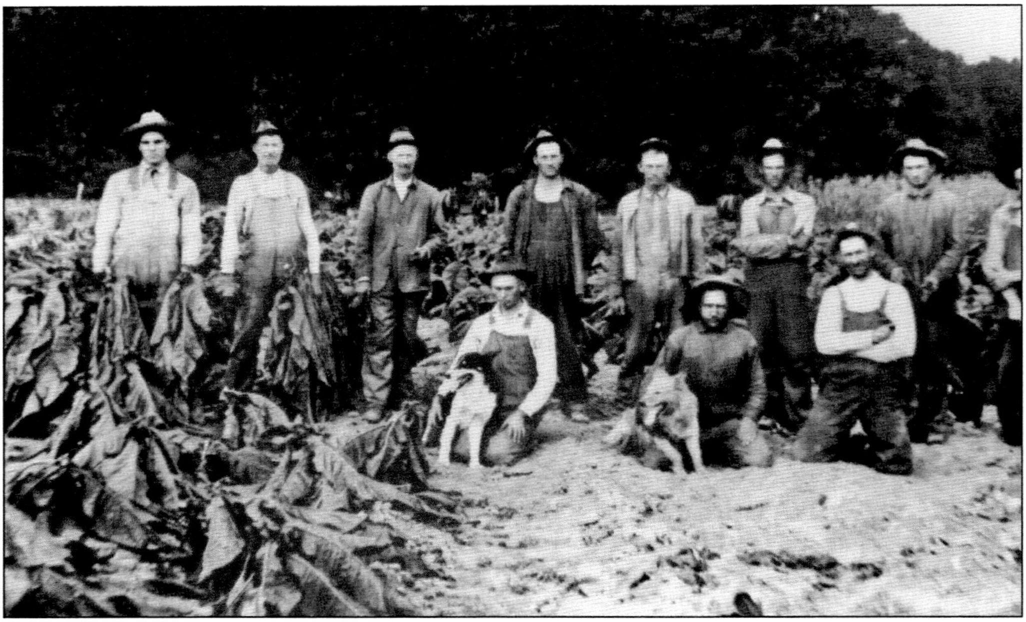

Tradition has it that the first settlers came into western Kentucky to grow a special type of tobacco known as "black patch." In the late 1800s, the tobacco industry was booming in Fulton. About 12 percent of cultivated land was planted in tobacco. After the mature plants were gathered, as seen in the above image, it was necessary to hang and cure the leaves with wood fire.

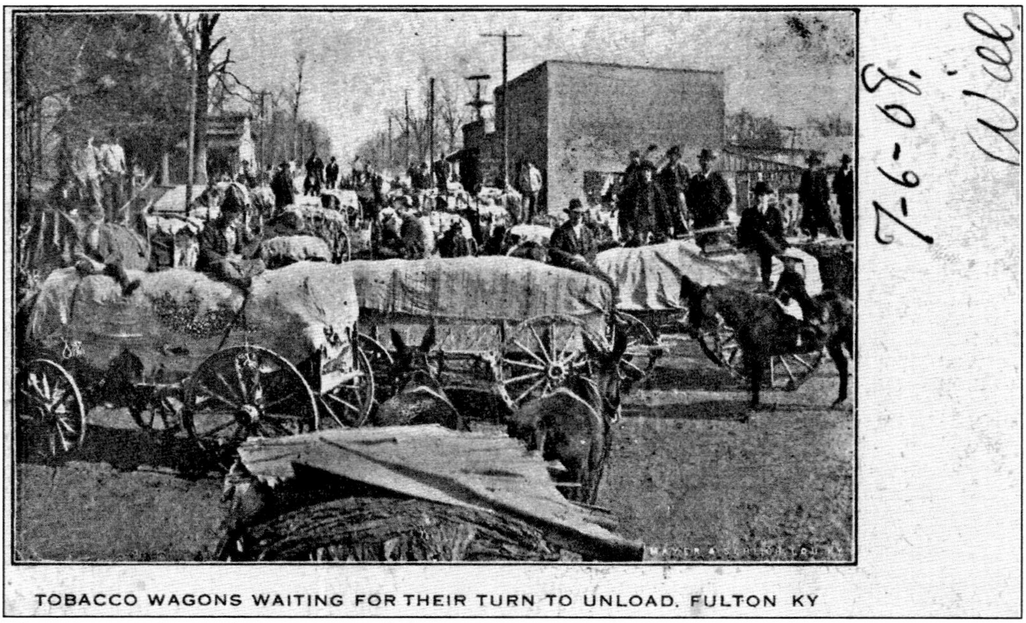

There were tobacco barns scattered throughout Fulton: the Fields-Hamlett barn stood where the present First Methodist Church now stands, and the Browder barn was at the corner of Carr and Valley Streets. It was not uncommon to see wagons lined from one end of the street to the other waiting their turn at the scales. The market was eventually lost because black patch tobacco, desired by the Italian government, could no longer be grown thanks to soil depletion.

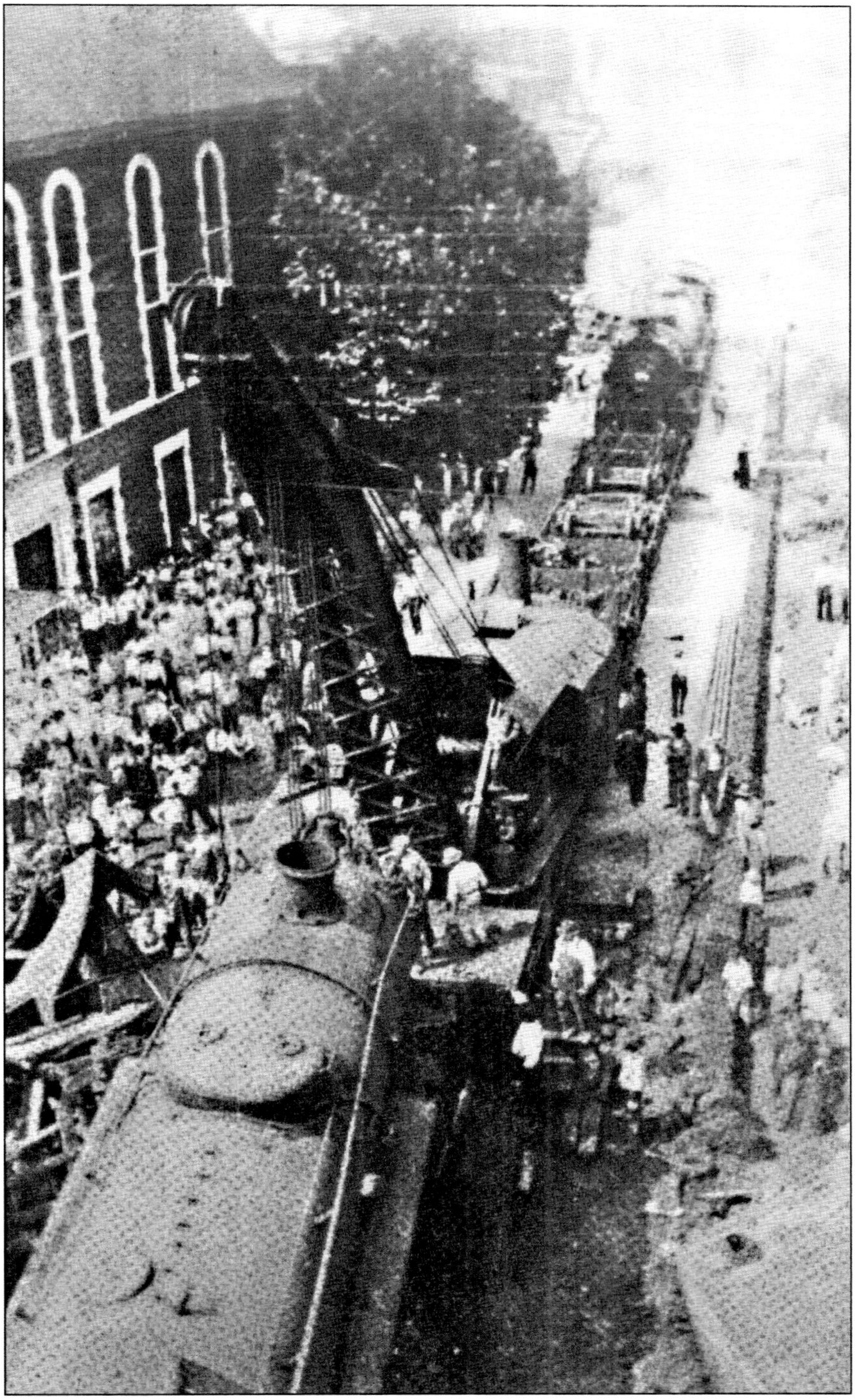

This image captured a train derailment in the early 1900s, with the USONA Hotel seen to the left. Derailments such as this were not uncommon, thanks to the heavy amount of traffic seen on the ICRR lines at the time.

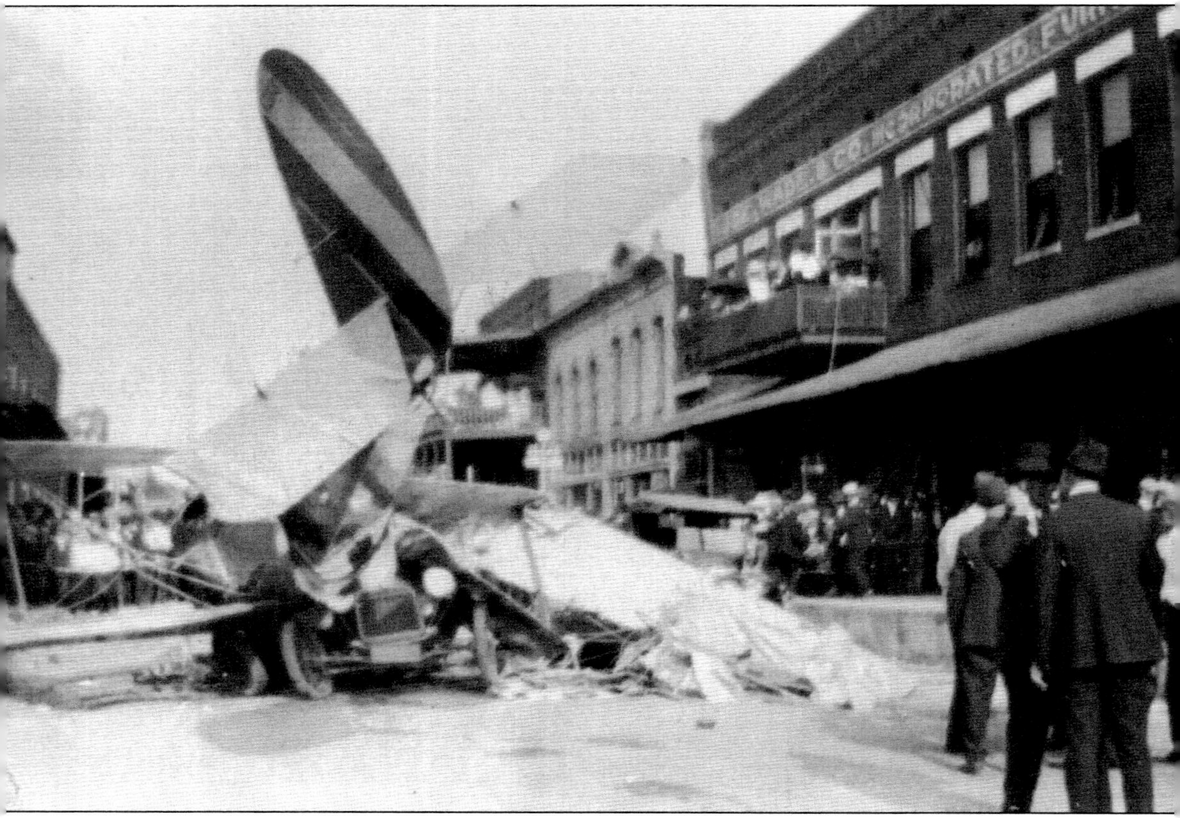

The airplane crash of 1919, at the intersection of Walnut and Mulberry (Nelson Tripp Place) Streets, caused a great deal of excitement within the community. The plane tore the roof from a building and killed a horse belonging to Walter Ridgeway. The incident gained national prominence when a picture of the crash was shown in many newspapers as a warning to avoid "Fulton, Kentucky Air Pockets." The myth of "air pockets" became so common that it was with a fair amount of nervous apprehension that pilots approached the "magnetism" that seemed to literally suck planes out of the sky in our vicinity. Around the time Fulton was attracting attention with its air pockets, Capt. Charles Lindbergh came to town. He and Lt. Charles E. Smith, the husband of a Fulton native, dreamed of a transatlantic flight together. Smith was killed in a plane crash in St. Louis, Missouri, on Easter Sunday, April 1926. In May, a 22-year-old Lindbergh came to town to pay his respects to the family and is said to have scattered flowers from his plane over the grave of Lieutenant Smith in Fairview Cemetery upon his departure.

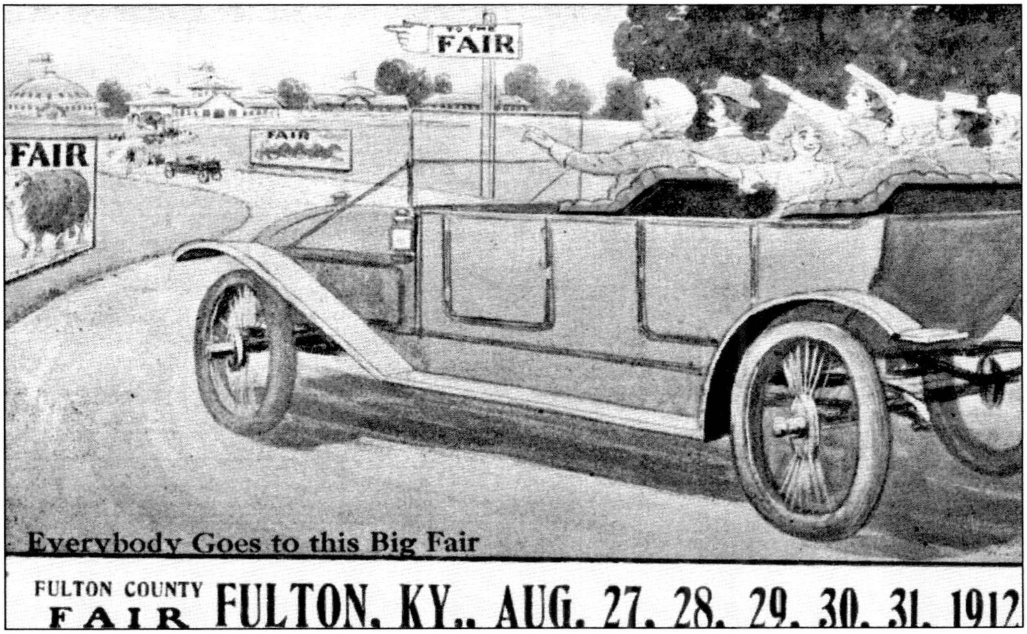

Over 10,000 people arrived in Fulton for the opening of the Fulton County Fair in 1911. They came to see horse racing, the carnivals, exhibits, balloons, automobiles, and airplanes. Once the fair opened, the people crowded the grandstand each day to watch the horse races. Perhaps the most popular attraction was the "balloon ascension." One man would ascend in a large, colorful, gas-filled balloon and descend in a parachute. The crowd would chase the balloon and retrieve it after all the gas had been expelled.

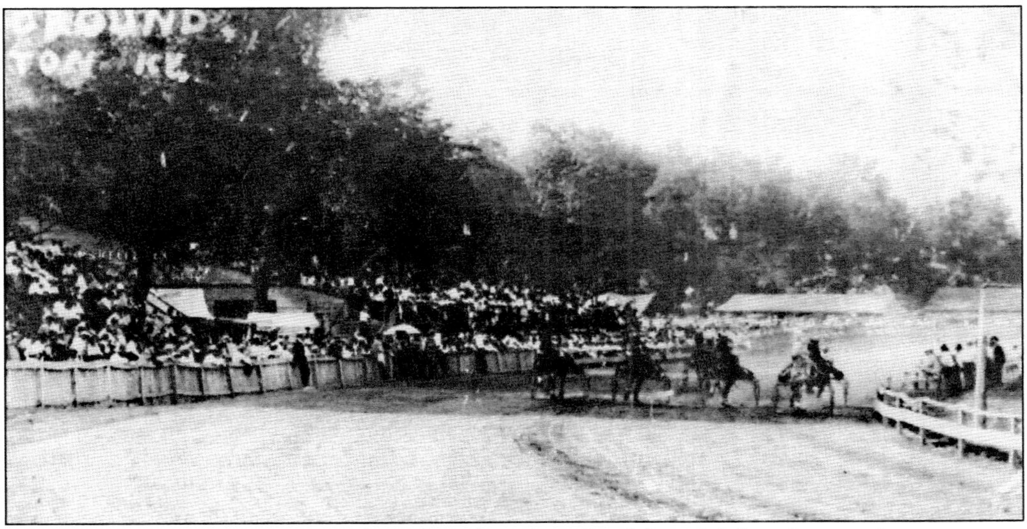

The fair's racetrack was half a mile in length and made of dirt. Adult tickets to the races were 50¢. The Fulton County Fair was among the first to draw horse owners who followed the fair circuit. There were three heats to each race, and horses raced two laps for each heat. The racetrack was never big enough for pari-mutuel, but betting pools were always available. Plug races were also held for the locals, with the best horses and mules competing against each other for excitement and prizes.

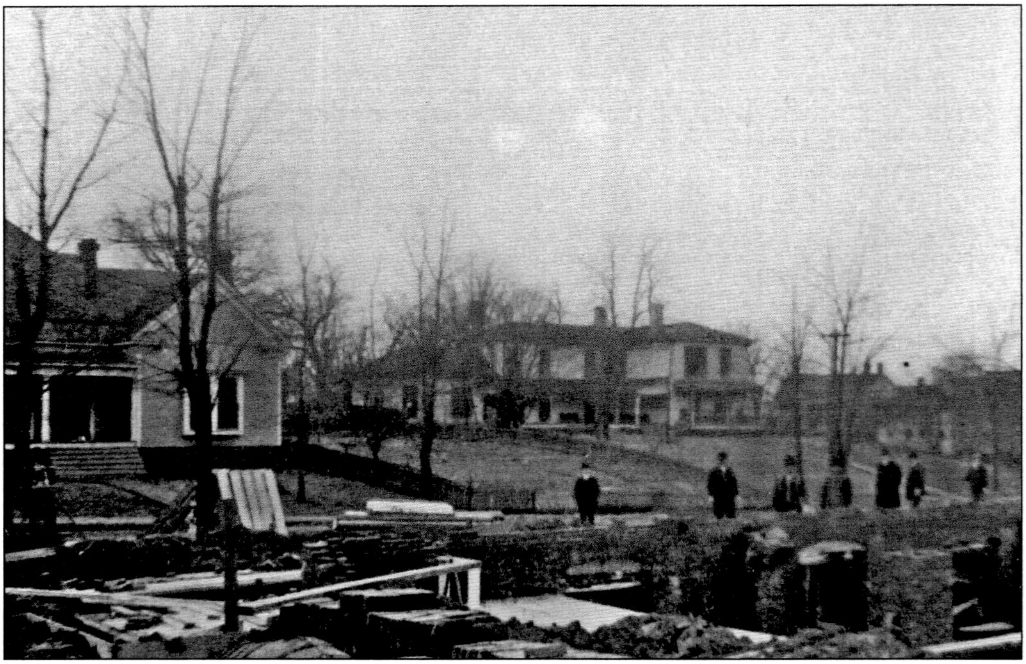

This image depicts the building of Dr. Gideon Paschall's home around 1858, a white, two-story frame structure at 311 Main Street. The land, on the Kentucky side of State Line Road, was known as Paschall Hill. Dr. N.J. Paschall built Forest Dale around 1928 on the Tennessee side. There was another white, two-story frame house lived in by nephew Jesse Rutledge Paschall on Central Avenue as well.

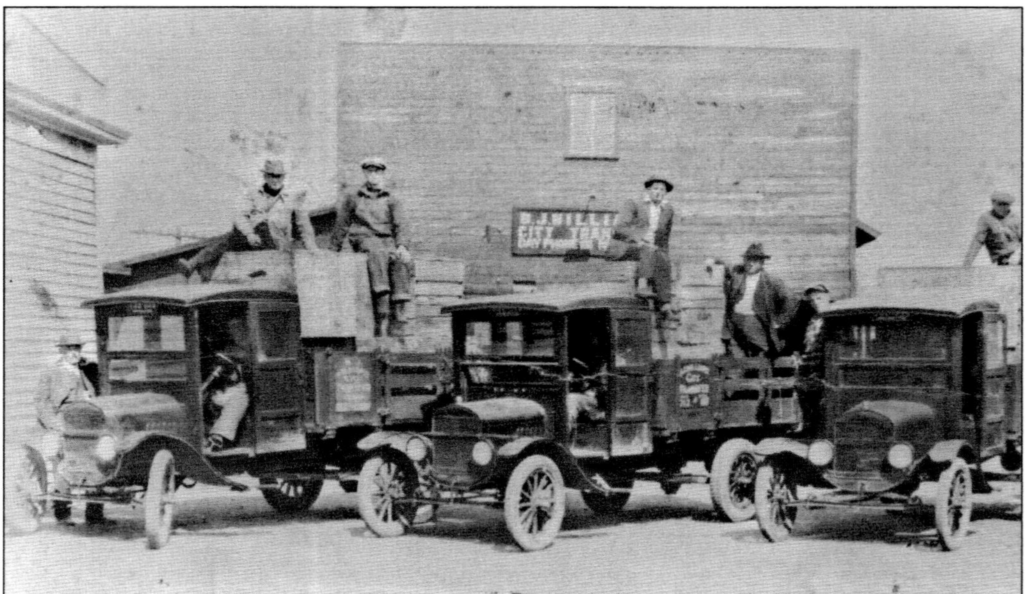

Williams City Transfer was perhaps the 1920s version to today's FedEx or UPS for the Twin Cities community. The pickup trucks would run from the home office to the trains and back again, making whatever deliveries or storage of shipped freight was required.

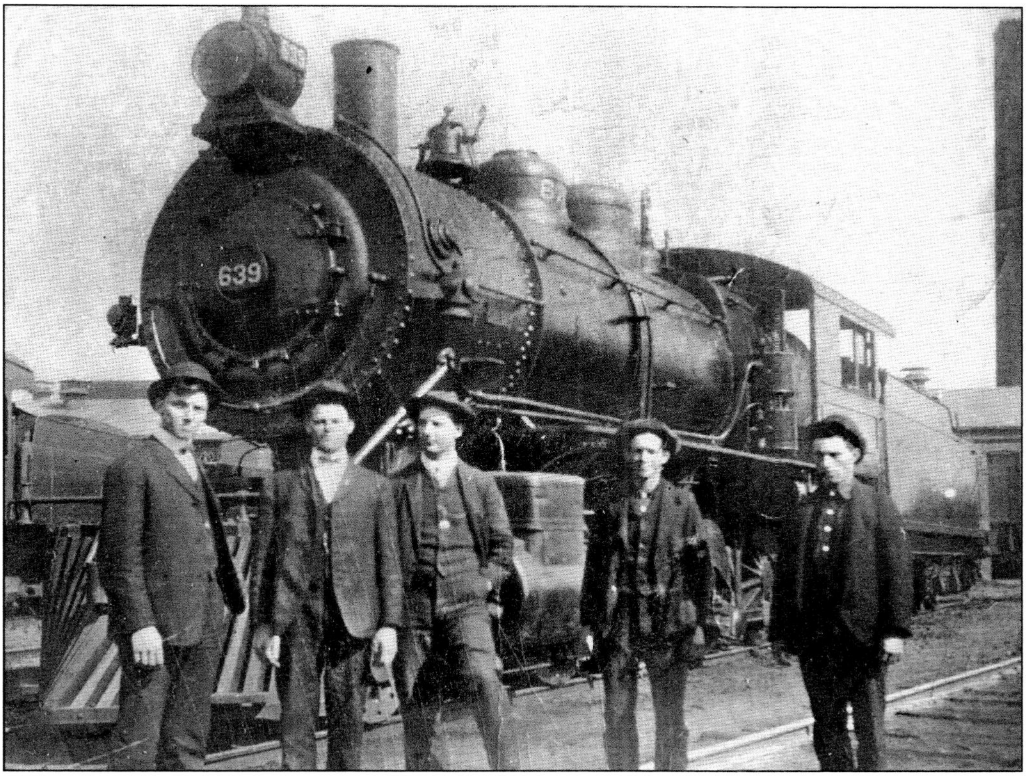

Steam powered the locomotives in the early years of the railroad. Seen here is a 1930 yard engine with tender and water tank attached. Coal chutes were located in the vicinity of today's Amtrak Station on U.S. Highway 51, and coal was supplied from western Kentucky coalmines. There were several water tanks scattered along the lines, one prominently located near the USONA and the division office.

TIPS...
ON SUMMER TRIPS

The following Round Trip rates will be in effect daily, with return limit October 31, 1915.

FROM

FULTON

TO

Chautauqua, N. Y.	$30.15
Chicago, Ill.	17.25
Battle Creek, Mich.	22.35
Denver, Colo.	32.00
Detroit, Mich.	24.55
French Lick, Ind.	11.55
Muskegon, Mich.	24.05
Niagara Falls, N. Y.	32.16
Norfolk, Va.	33.40
St. Paul, Minn.	30.10

PANAMA EXPOSITION RATES

TO

San Francisco, Los Angeles, San Diego and return $57.50

Tickets on sale daily, return limit three months.

These are only a few of our Summer Tourist Rates. We are prpared to quote rates to all points of interest, furnish information and arrange delightfal pleasure trips for you.

Let Us Plan Your Summer Trip.

Call on or Write Our Local Ticket Agent

ILLINOIS CENTRAL R. R.

G. H. BOWER, G. P. A., Memphis, Tenn.

A clipping from the news of the day announces rates for summer travel on the ICRR, c. 1915.

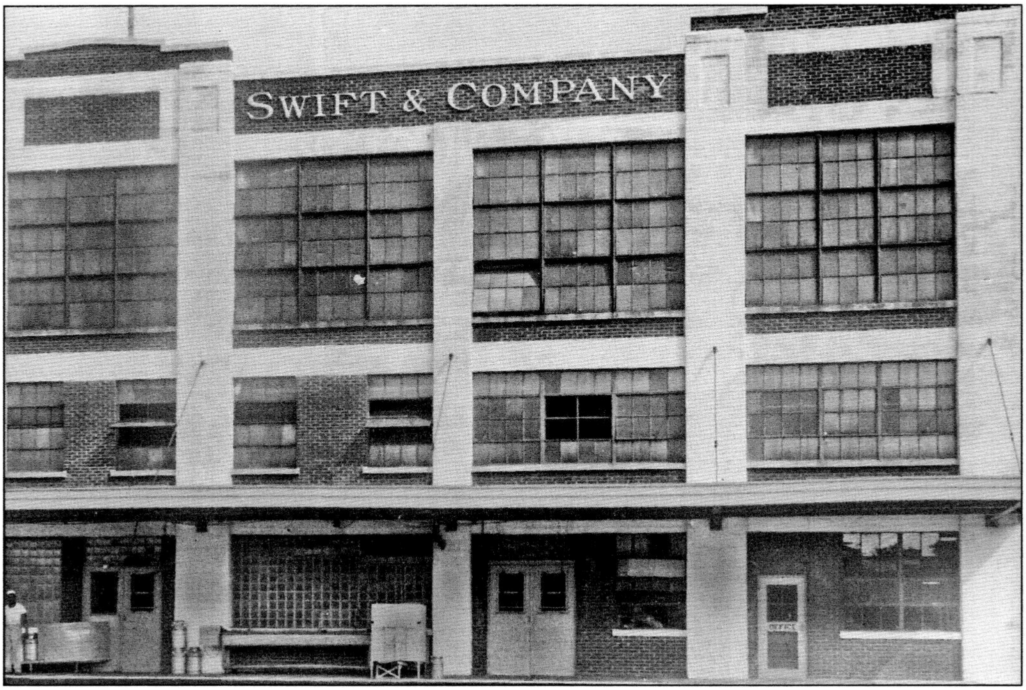

Swift and Company prospered after its opening in 1929. An ice cream plant was added in 1931, and ice cream operations serviced West Tennessee and Kentucky as well as Southwest Missouri and Evansville, Indiana. A new cheese-manufacturing factory was added in 1958. Milk for the factory was purchased from local farmers, providing a regular daily market for their dairy cattle.

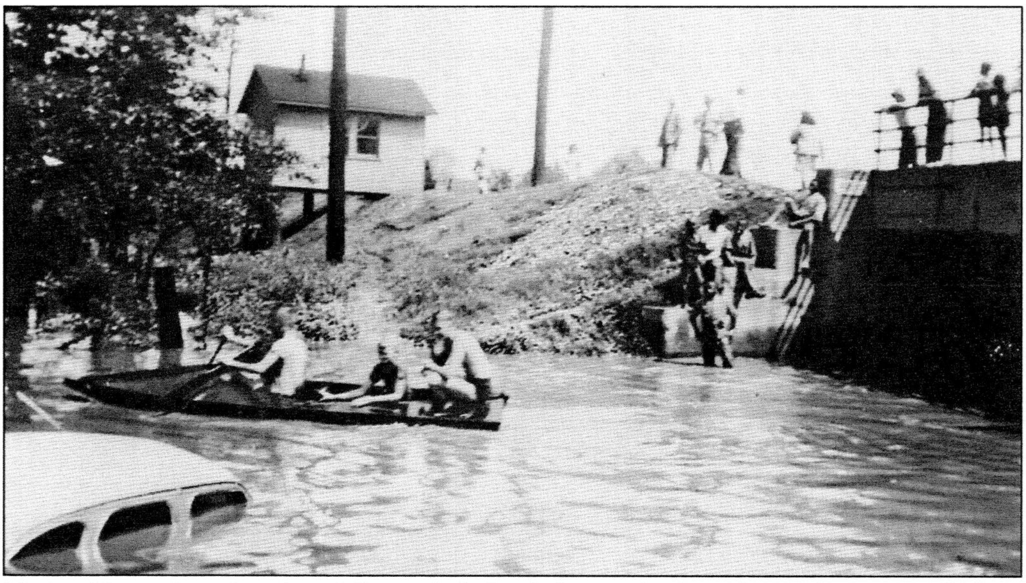

Mother Nature has often forced Harris Fork Creek from its banks and into the streets of Fulton through the years. Pictured here is the low area around the railroad overpass on Mears Street, with men in a rowboat surveying damage from floodwaters. Note the automobile almost completely submerged in the foreground.

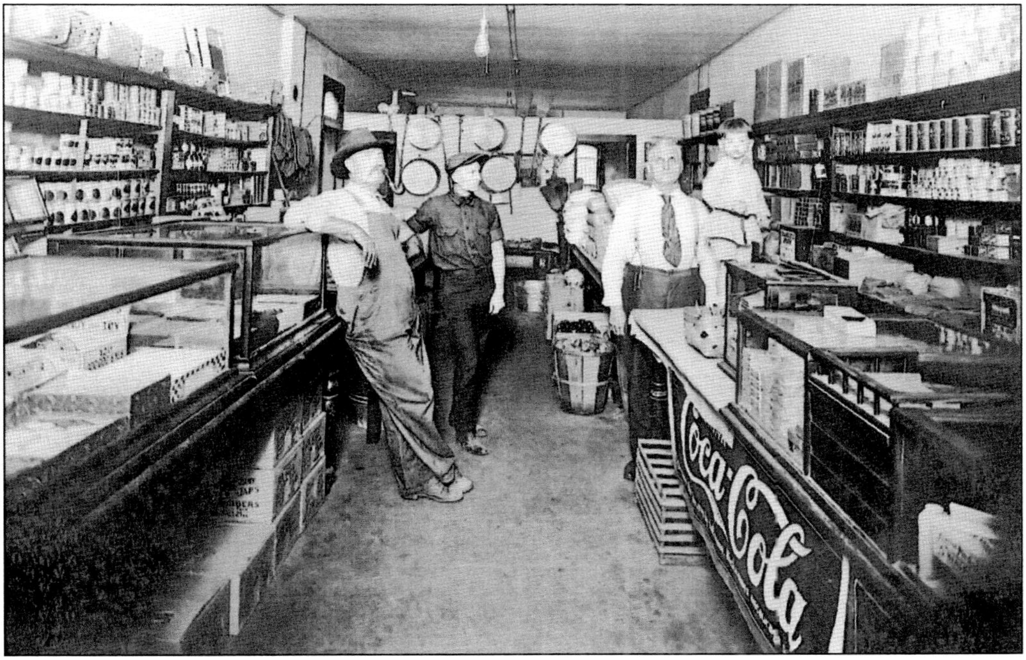

Scattered about the Twin Cities were many family or neighborhood grocery stores patronized by locals. The Rawles Grocery Store of South Fulton was one such establishment, pictured here sometime between 1920 and 1930.

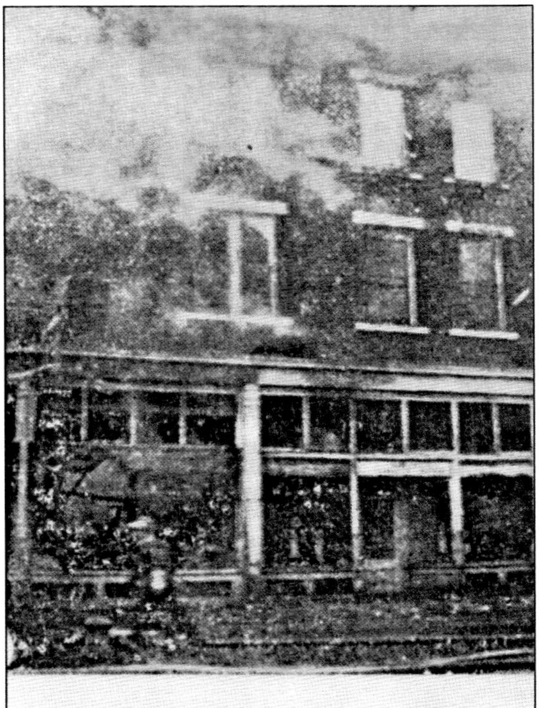

Meadows Hotel Fire—1933

The Meadows block was a staple of downtown commerce and travel, with its business establishments and 100-room hotel. The building faced three streets—Church, State, and Main—with its entrance in the middle of the block on Church Street. Plagued by a fire soon after opening in 1900, it was again consumed in flames in 1933 (pictured at right). People said to see it in flames the second time was to realize it would never be restored. A portion of the Meadows still remains and is used as an auto parts store.

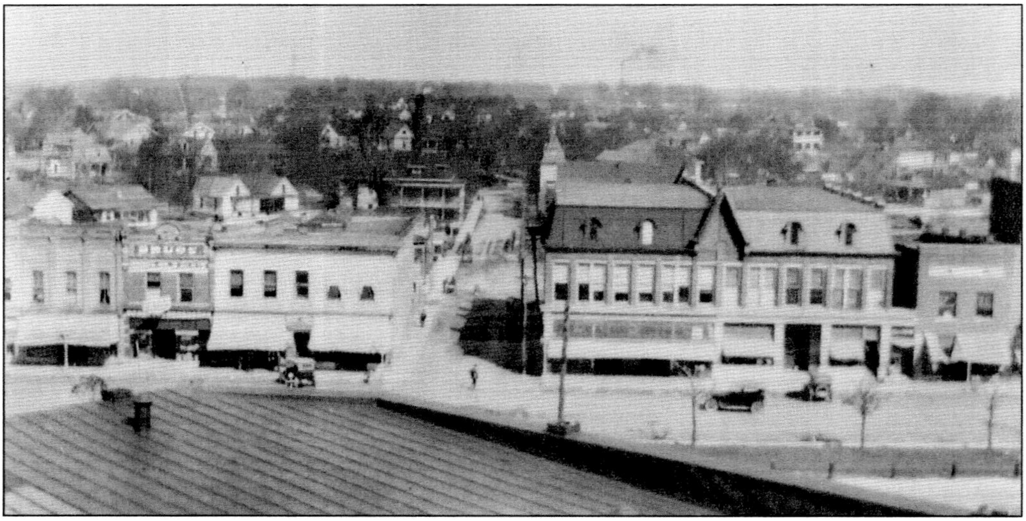

This excellent view of downtown Lake Street and West Fulton was taken atop the Vendome roof. Note Paschall Drug and the Carr Building on one side of Commercial Avenue and P.H. Weaks Dry Goods, Clothing, and Shoe Store opposite. Dr. R.T. Rudd's Sanitarium can also be seen in the background.

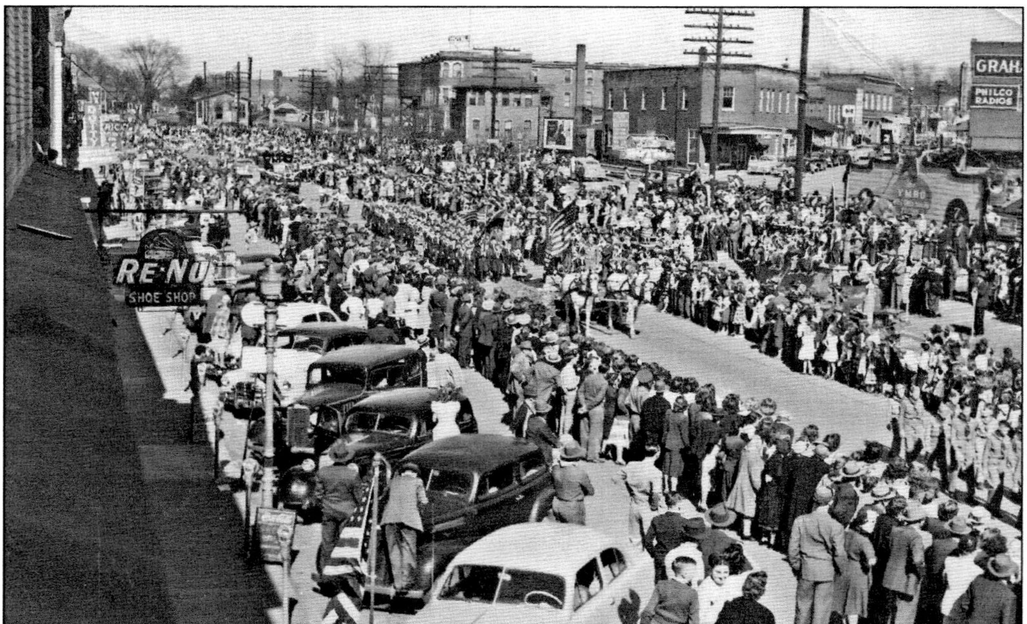

This fantastic view of Lake Street in the 1940s illustrates a variety of interesting landmarks. The old bandstand can be seen in the upper right-hand corner, as well as the Graham Furniture Store and other businesses located on Walnut Street. On the left side is the USONA Hotel. Longtime residents recall that the streets downtown were "packed with cars" on Saturday nights, and often the businesses were open until midnight to accommodate the crowds. Many would arrive in town early to find a good parking spot and spend the weekends people-watching from the windows of Smith's Café on Lake Street.

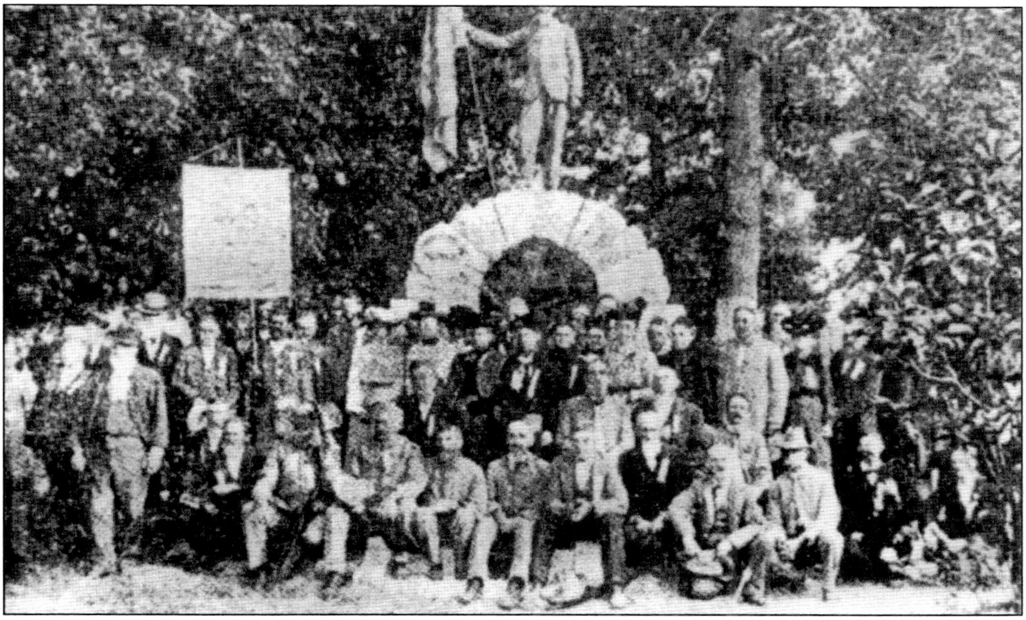

When the members of the United Confederate Veteran's Camp in Fulton gathered in 1902 to dedicate the monument, the arch and keystone were present, but the statue was missing. One of the veterans, J.T. Stubblefield, posed as the statue, holding a flag. One can see below that the real statue holds a rifle and not a flag. The memorial was given by the United Daughters of the Confederacy (UDC) 1902 Col. Ed Crossland Chapter No. 347, organized in Fulton in 1899.

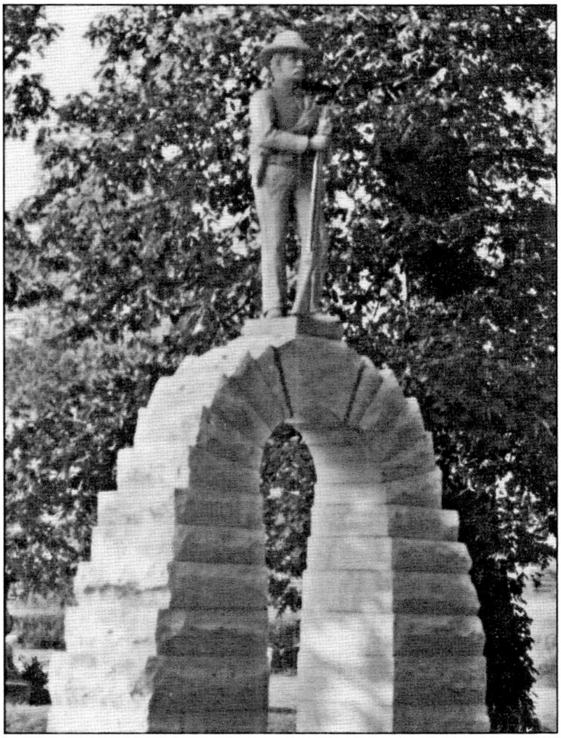

Confederate monuments were erected throughout the Deep South by the UDC to memorialize those brave soldiers who fought in the Civil War. The monument located at the entrance to Fairview Cemetery has an arched base constructed from rough-hewn limestone. The statue it supports is zinc and is typical of stock soldier figures. The keystone on the arch reads "Confederate Memorial 1861–1865" on the face and "erected by UDC 1902" on the arch interior.

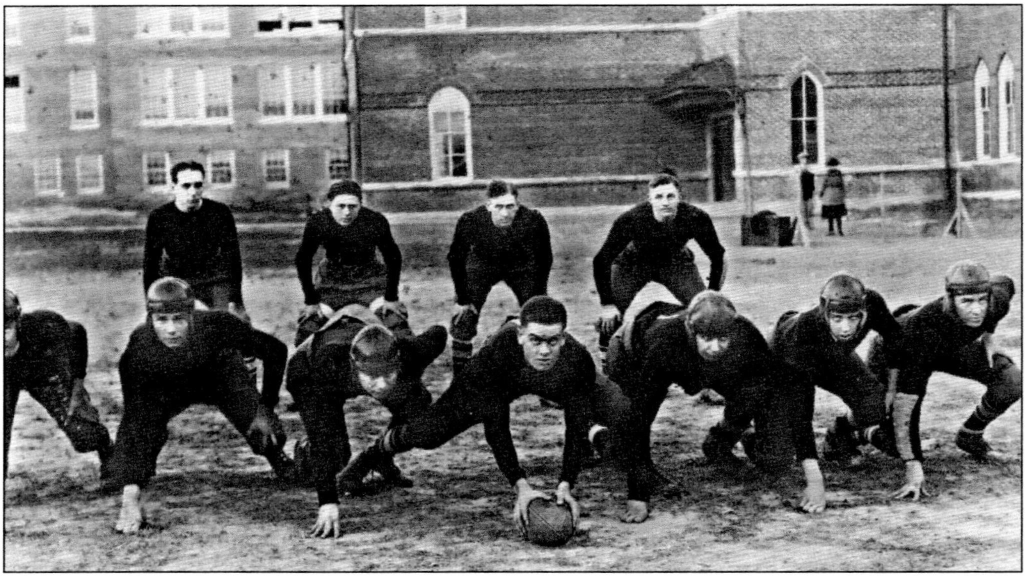

Fulton and South Fulton both have a rich history of competitive sports. Football, basketball, tennis, and golf were all popular in the early 1920s. The year 1922 not only marked the first organized football team of Carr Institute, but it also saw the first organized basketball teams for both girls and boys at the school.

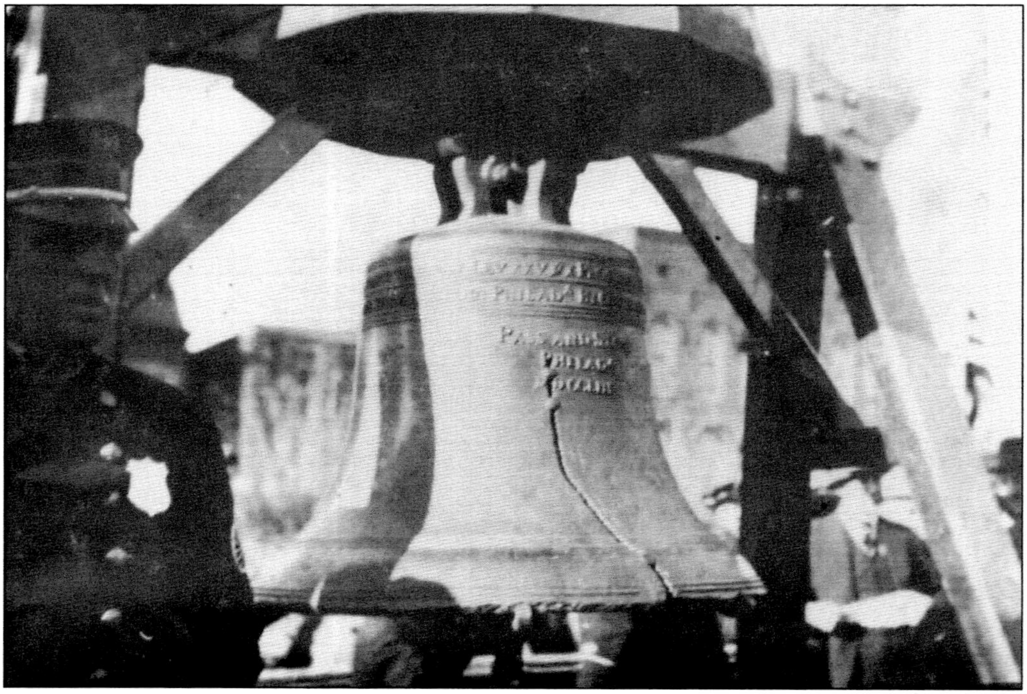

Brought to Fulton on a flatbed rail car in 1915, the Liberty Bell was displayed during a Fourth of July parade in the Twin Cities. It was not uncommon for items such as this to be brought into town by the railroad. A small fee would be charged for viewing, and then the article would head to the next stop. In this way, the citizens were provided a glimpse of the larger world.

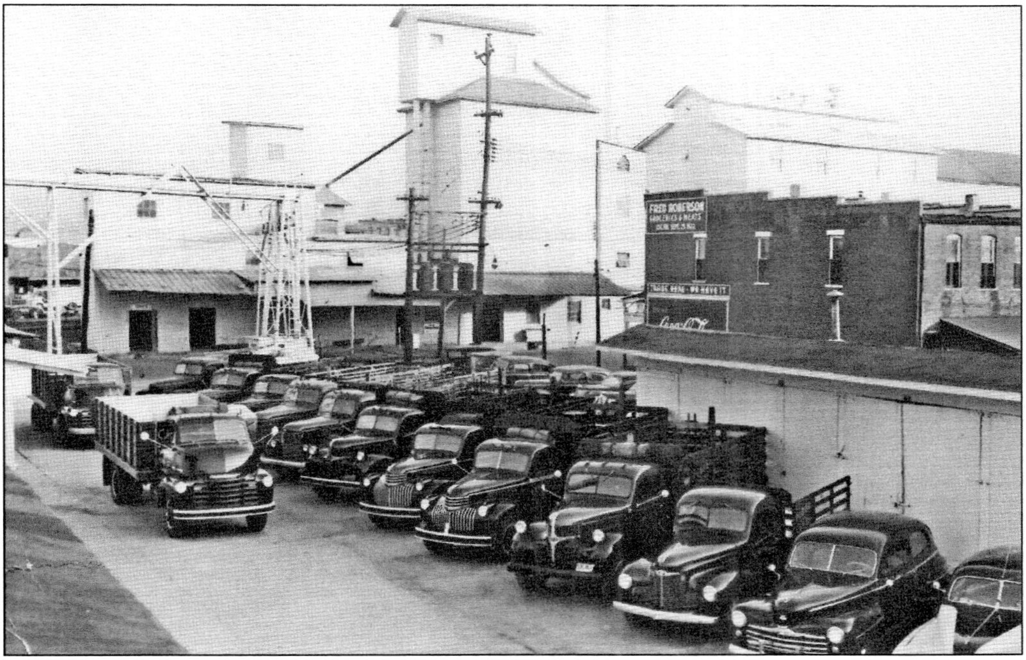

Charley and Commodore Brann established the State Line Mill near the site of the old water wheel for the community. The mill was sold to J.T. Burton in 1898. Burton, in turn, sold it to the Browder brothers, Joe and Enoch, in 1908. The Browder Mill quickly became one of the leading industries in Fulton, manufacturing flour, corn meal, and other foodstuffs. It was located at 112 East State Street. In 1946, the mill became owned entirely by the residents of Fulton.

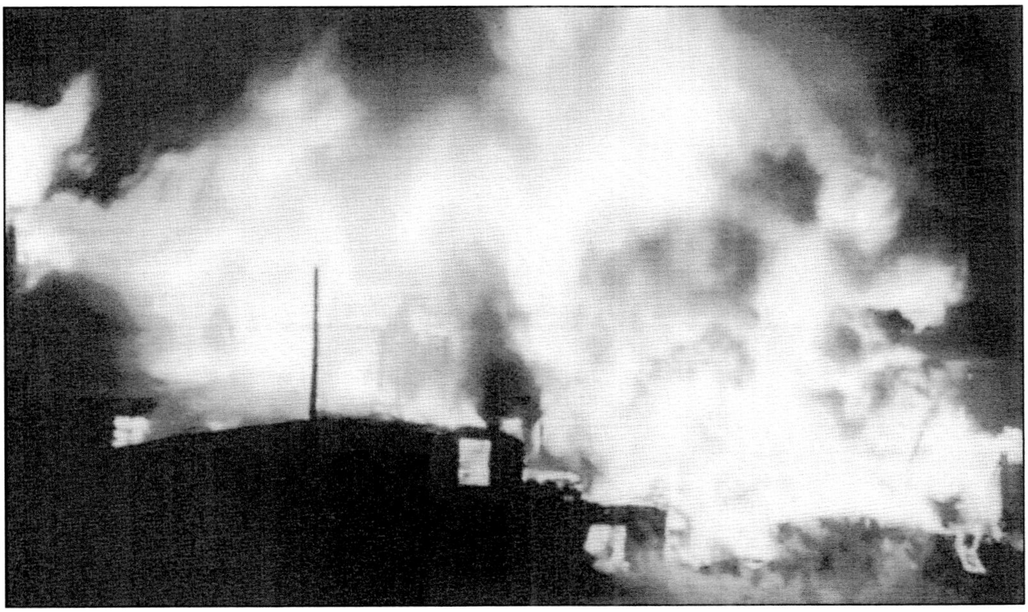

Tragically, the mill was destroyed by fire in December 1950, as depicted in the image above. The flames were said to threaten the entire business block and brought five fire departments to battle the blaze.

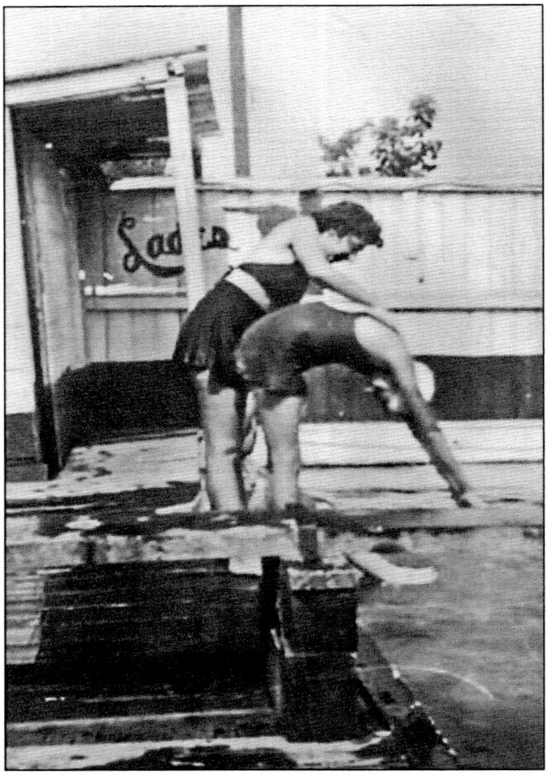

The Sunny Dip was a swimming pool of legendary coolness because of the fact it was filled by runoff from the R.H. Wade Ice Plant on Norman Street. The pool was located across the street from the plant. Here Barbara (Homra) Smith is learning how to dive from instructor and cousin Pam (Homra) Shdeed.

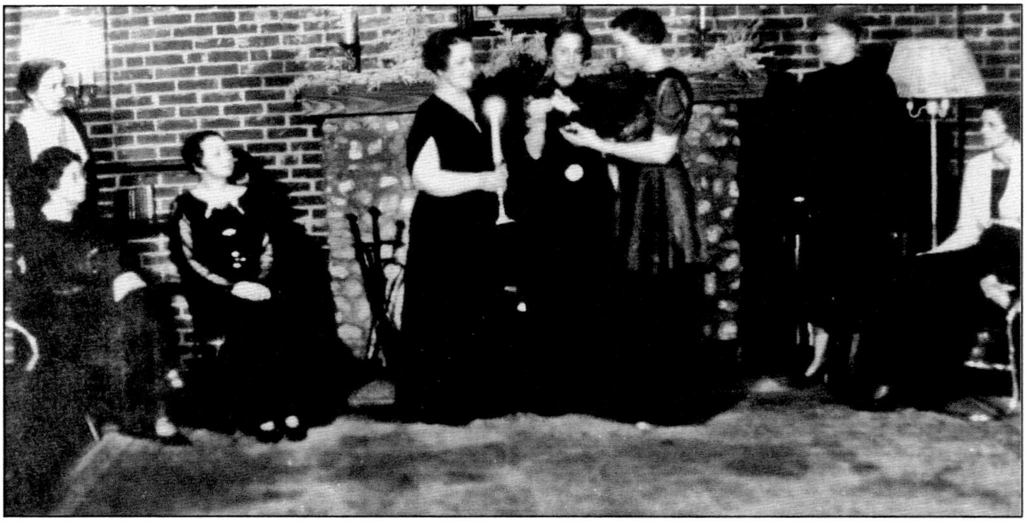

Nine small clubs—Sans Souci, Twentieth Century, Fortnightly, Shakespeare, Magazine, Philomathean, As You Like It, Thimble Club, and Art Club—combined their efforts and joined the State Federation of Women's Clubs in 1922. Meetings were held in the Commercial Club—a forerunner of the Chamber of Commerce—on Main Street. Years of hard work and good management led to construction of the Women's Club Building, which housed the Fulton Library. The clubhouse on Walnut was completely paid off in 1936, leaving it debt free to the community. The image above depicts a 1937 Women's Club dedication service.

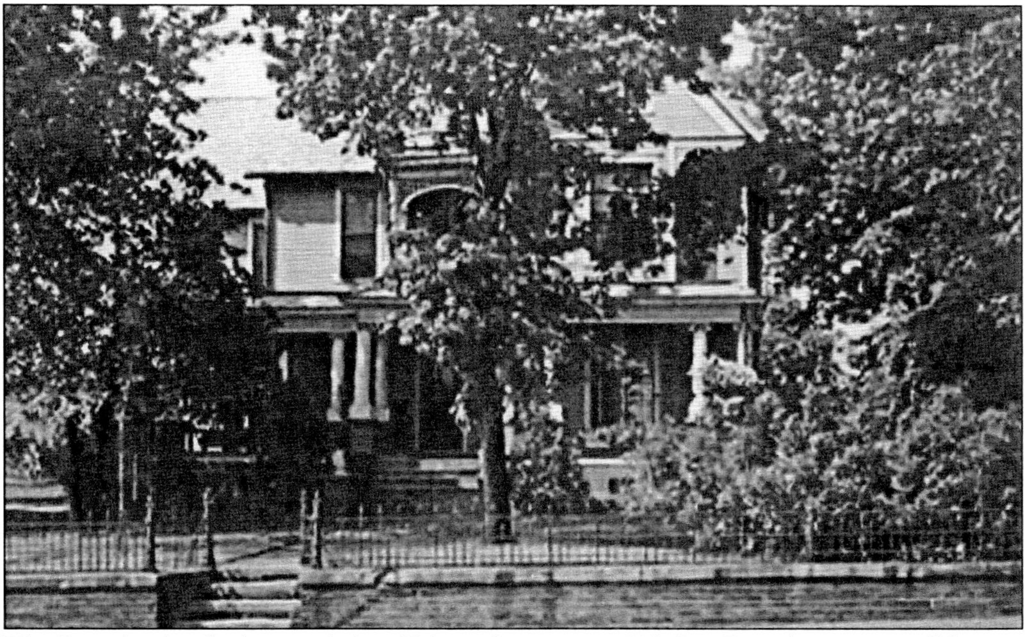

The Browder family first settled in Fulton County in 1825. Joe Browder was a well-known businessman in Fulton, and the frame house at 100 Reed Street, with its retaining wall and wrought-iron fence, paid homage to his success in commercial business ventures.

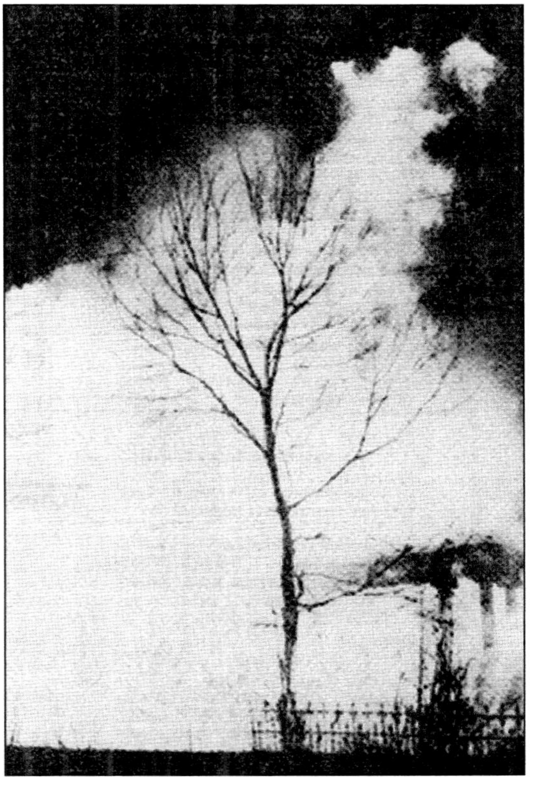

When the residence at 100 Reed Street burned, the Browder homestead was owned by Ben Triplett. High winds and floating sparks from the blaze contributed to the house fire and added additional combustion. The fire department was put on alert but to no avail. By the time the fire chief had walked to the back of the yard, the house, including the basement, was engulfed in flames. The home, one of the oldest in Fulton, succumbed to fire.

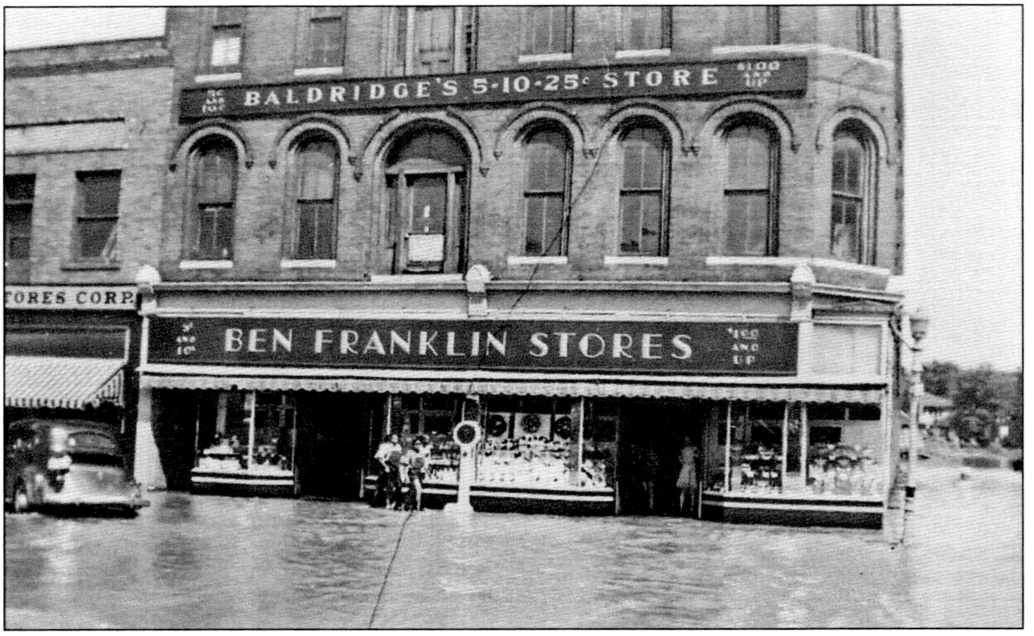

It was usually a given that Lake Street would be a victim of Harris Fork Creek when torrents of rain caused the creek to leave its banks. Seen here is the Ben Franklin Store under water. A channel was constructed to help prevent this leading business street from flooding, but sometimes the floodwaters would come regardless.

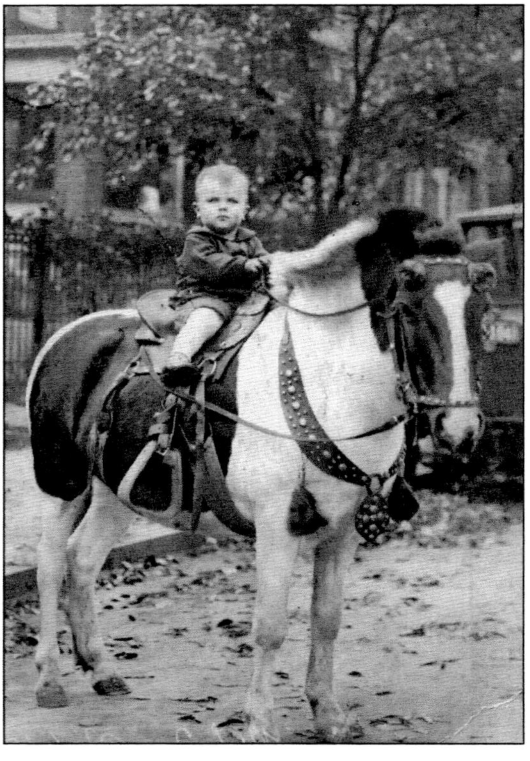

Joe Hall, father of Fulton resident Sally Hall Bondurant, poses on a drummer's (peddler's) pony in 1907.

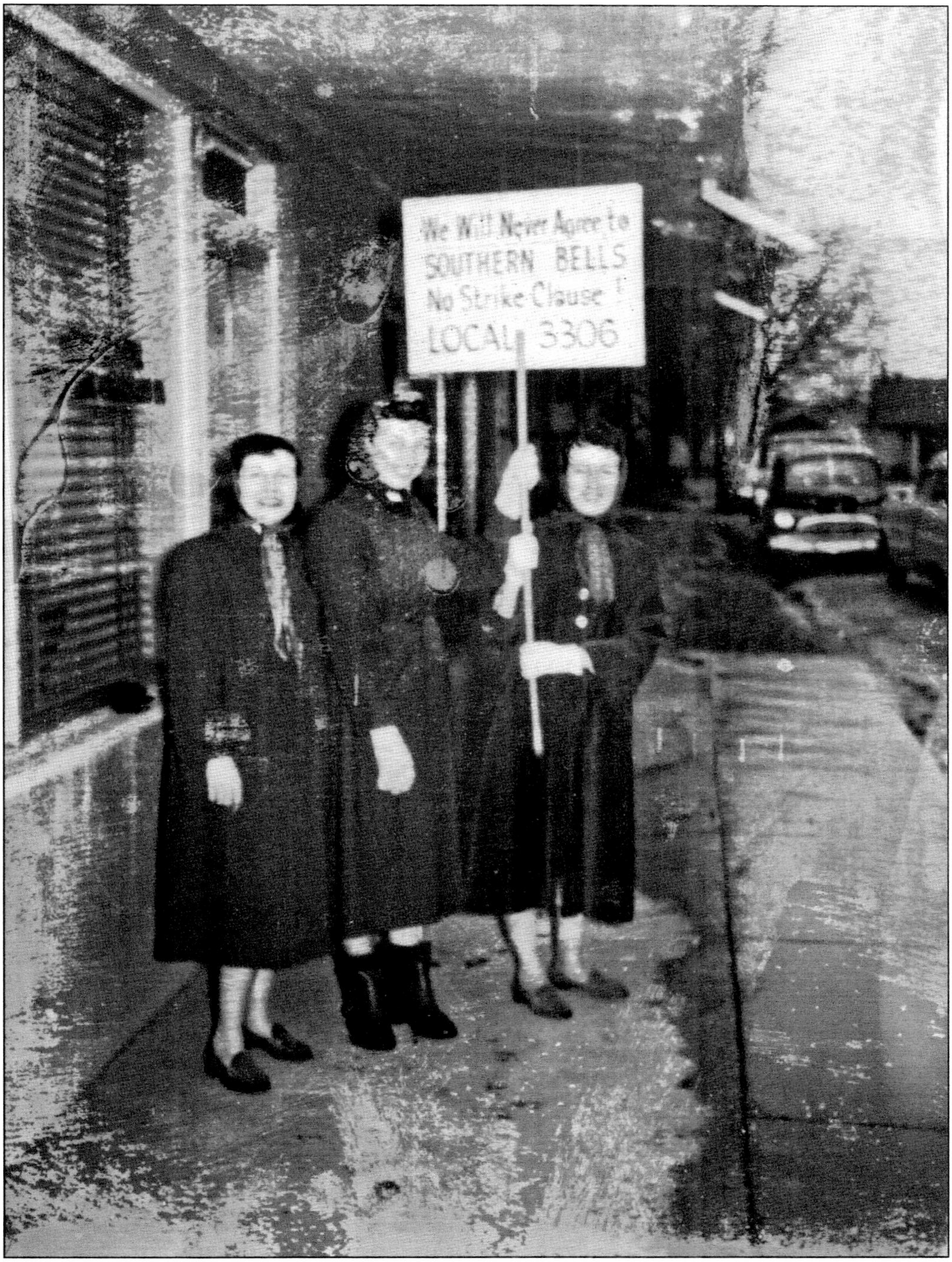

In 1955, a record-breaking strike throughout Kentucky and nine other Southern states lasted for over two months between operators and the telephone company Southern Bell. The jobs in general meant good pay and advancement opportunities for people in the community, but the hours were long and the shift work grueling.

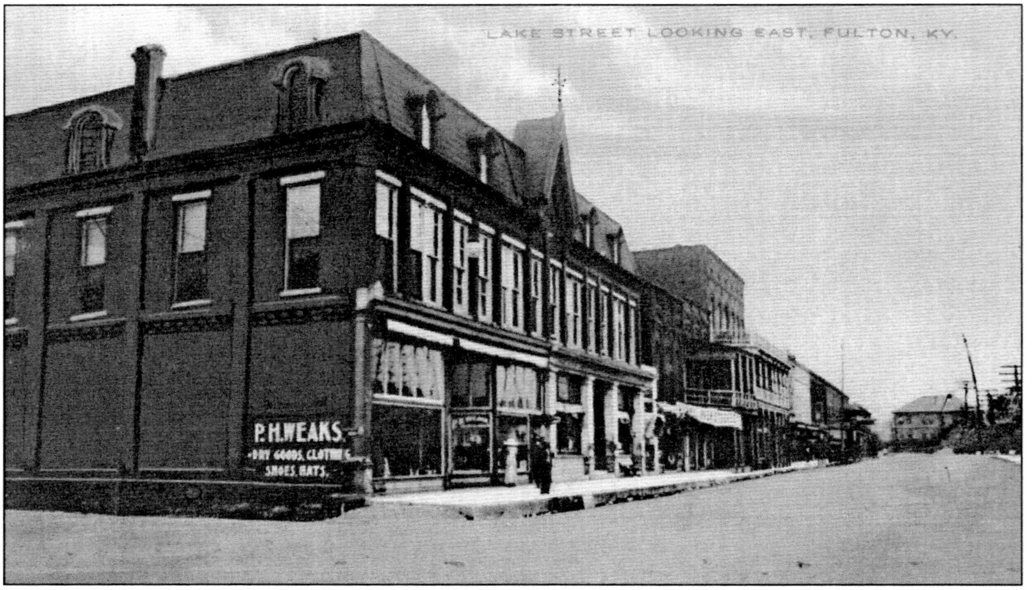

Established in 1863 and holding the western Kentucky record for oldest continuous business in operation by the same family, P.H. Weaks Dry Goods, Clothing, and Shoe Store was from the outset a "house of distinction." The 1863 store began in Feliciana, Kentucky, which used to serve as the trading center and post office for this section of West Kentucky. Porter Herchel Weaks, son of founder George Dodd Weaks, moved to Water Valley, eventually relocating the store to Fulton in 1894. The building pictured was originally French mansard in design, built by W.W. Meadows in 1880; P.H. Weaks purchased the building 14 years later.

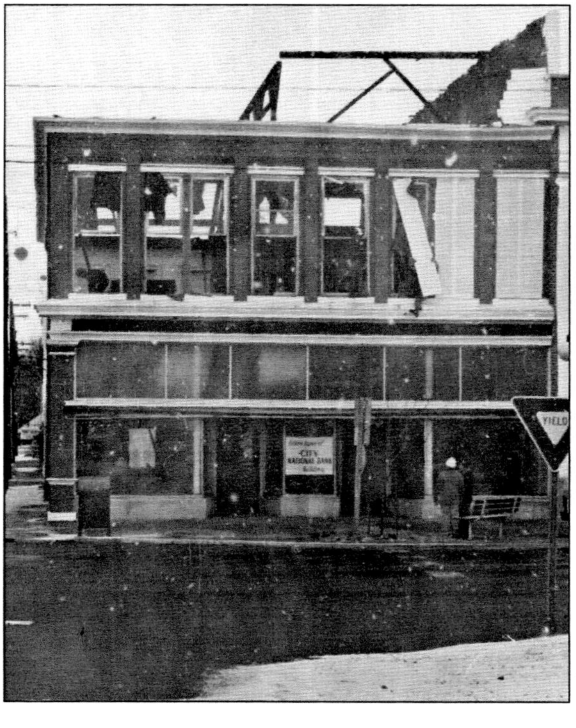

On January 11, 1977, City National Bank purchased the Weaks Department Store building for a planned expansion of the bank, which would double its size. When P.H. Weaks died in 1922, ownership of the business passed to his sons, Leslie and Louis Weaks, and then to his grandson, Lexie Parks Weaks. This image depicts the razing of this Fulton landmark.

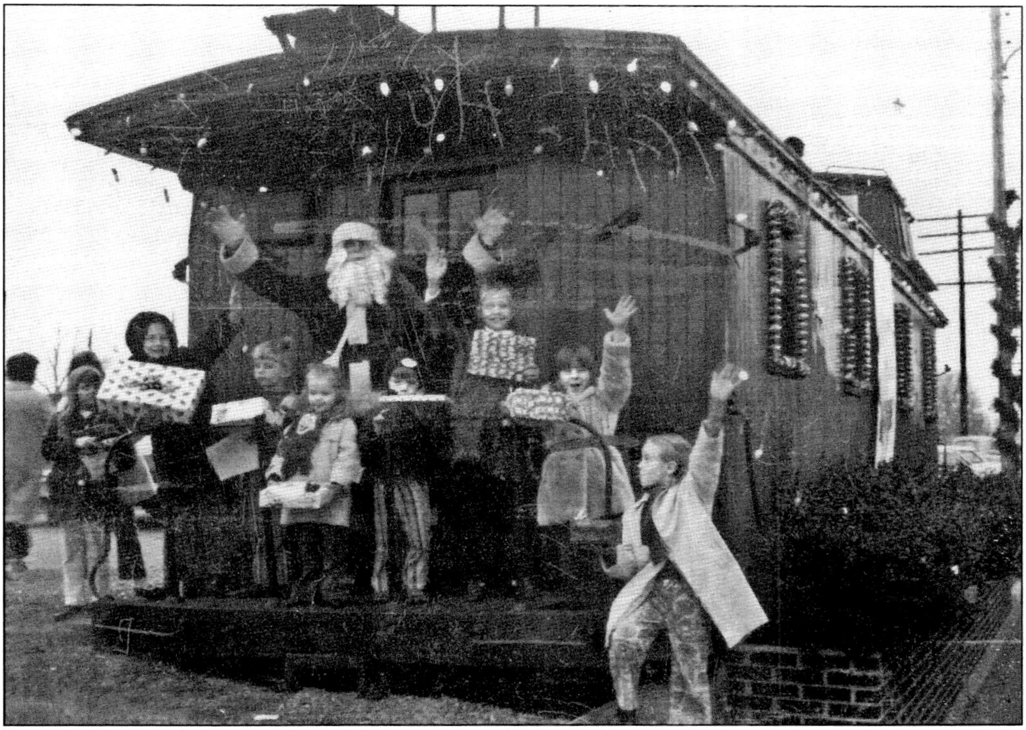

You never know where old St. Nick might turn up! For this Christmas parade, the children of Fulton found him giving out presents from the back of an old wooden caboose donated to the city by the ICRR.

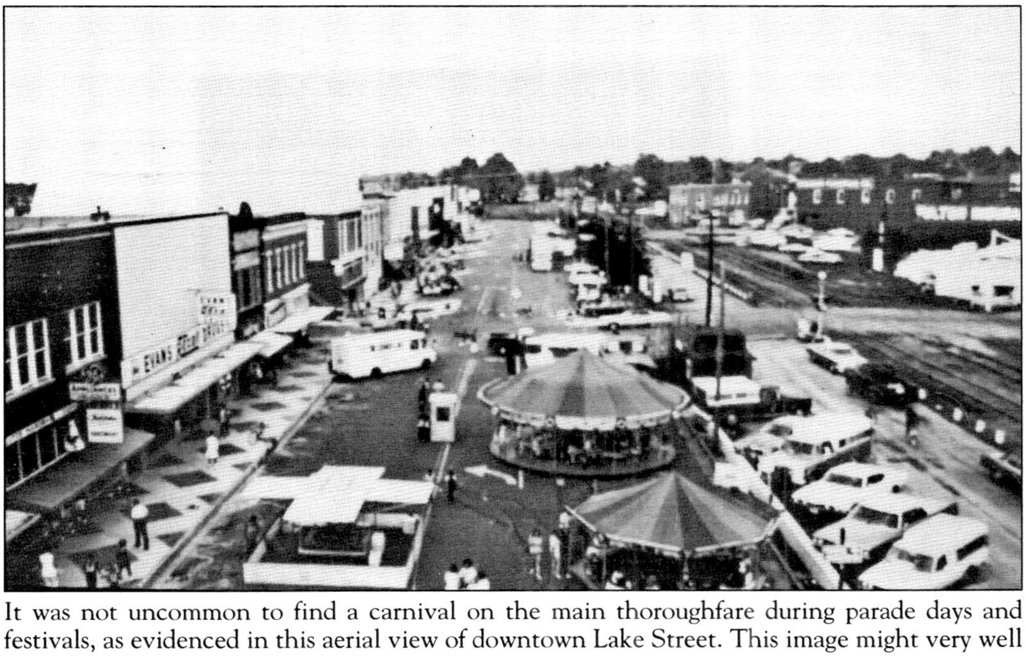

It was not uncommon to find a carnival on the main thoroughfare during parade days and festivals, as evidenced in this aerial view of downtown Lake Street. This image might very well show preparation for the first Banana Festival in 1963.

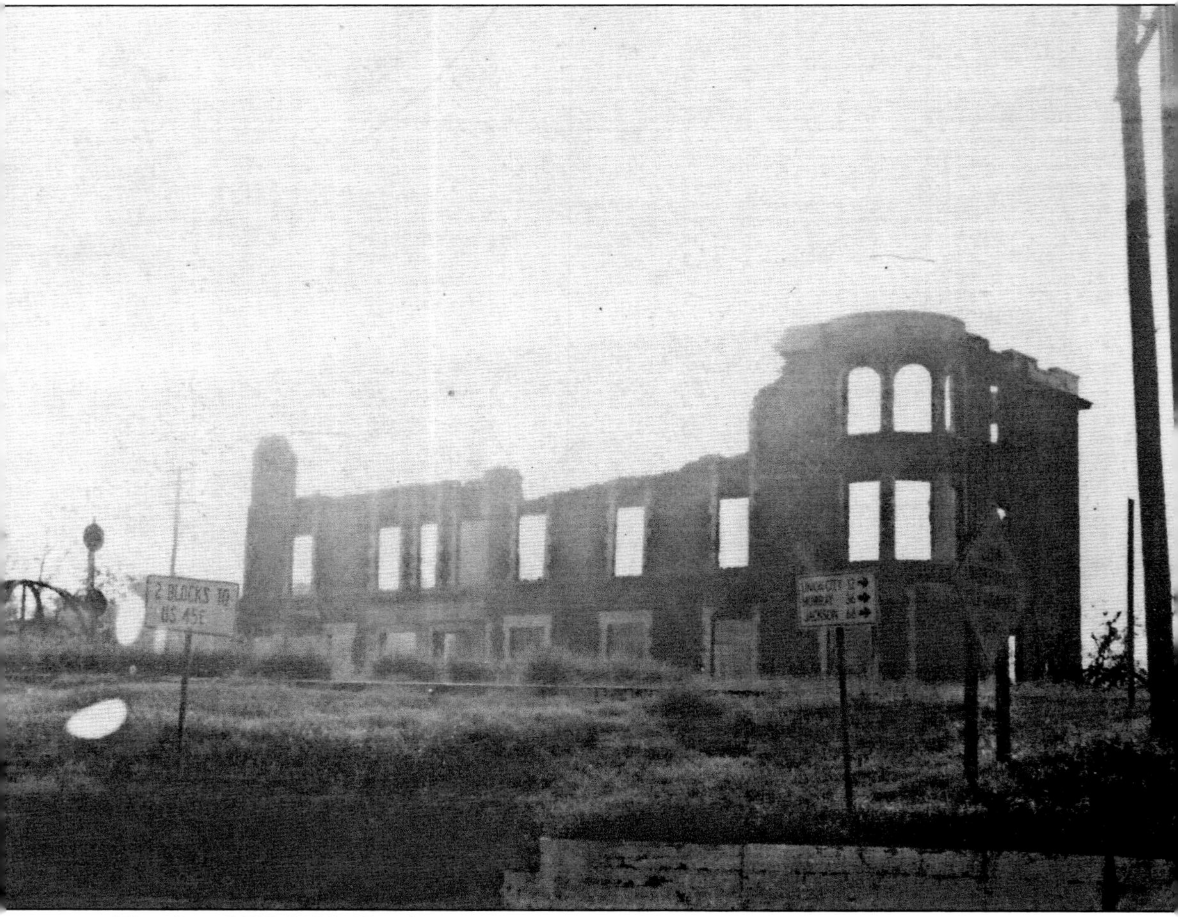

The famed USONA Hotel came to a very inconspicuous end. After the passenger rails left Fulton, the hotel's upkeep became cost-prohibitive, and it fell into a state of disrepair. Area residents were able to salvage some of the woodwork and other mementos from the lobby before demolition crews finished their job. The building was used as a training exercise for the local fire department and then razed. The new post office on Walnut Street occupies some of the ground on which the USONA stood. There remains no trace of the beautiful green space created by the groundskeepers of the ICRR for the pleasure of the viewing public.

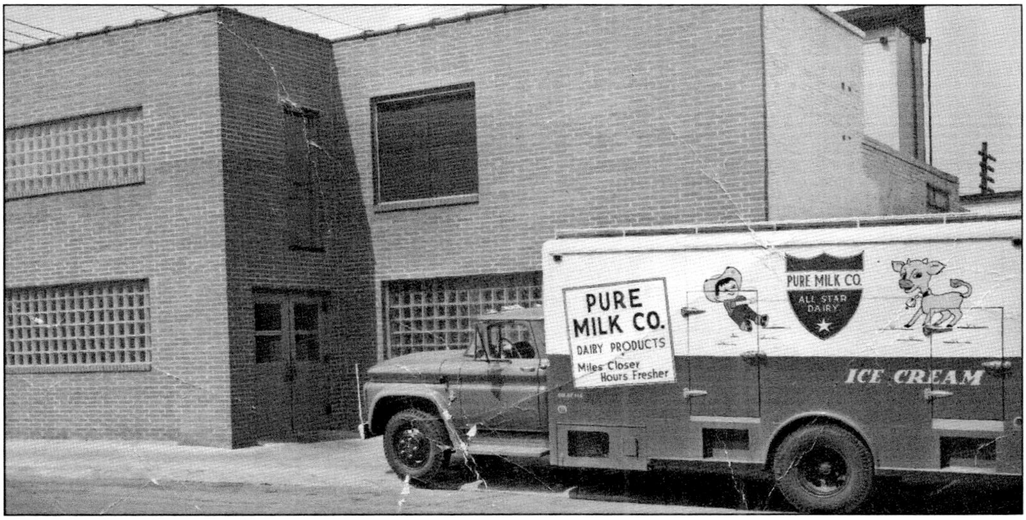

Pure Milk Company came to Fulton in 1939 and was the cornerstone for the International Banana Festival's preparation of the One Ton Banana Pudding. The company was also a corporate sponsor of floats and dairy princess crowns for the Twin Cities, helping to make the festivities a huge success. Located on the same block of Fourth Street, it is now Turner Dairies, with a reputation equally as dedicated to the present community as Pure Milk had in the past.

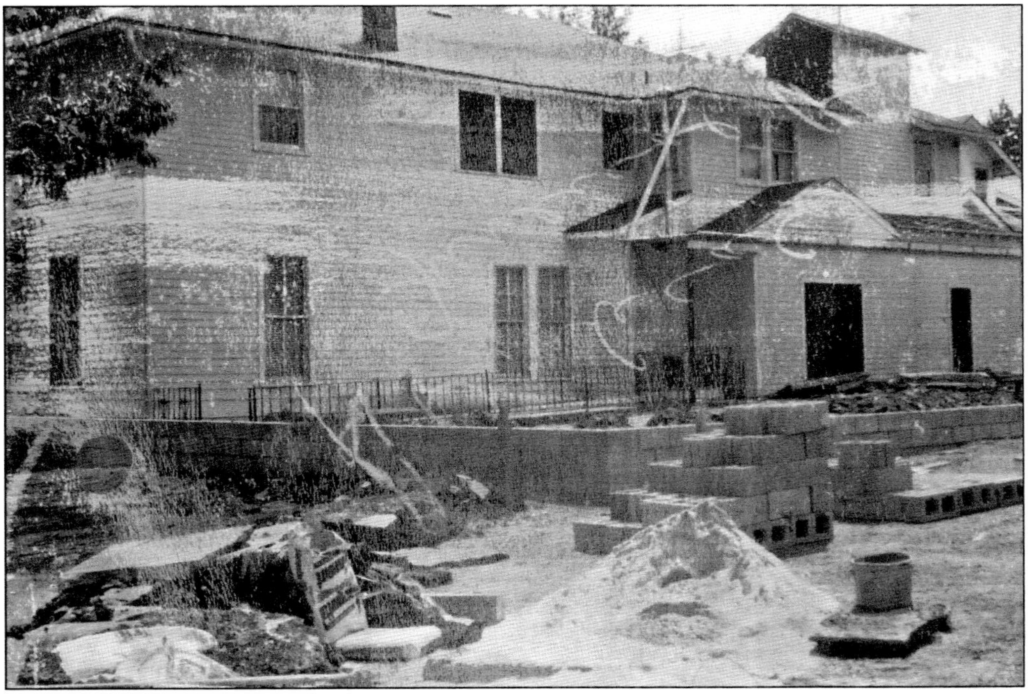

Paul Hornbeak, founder and director of Hornbeak Funeral Home in Fulton, dabbled with his brother in both the baking and undertaking businesses after serving on active duty in both world wars. In 1931, Paul opened a funeral parlor on Carr Street in the Gid Willingham home, moving it to its present location at 302 Carr Street in 1934. The image above shows the renovation of the current site, which is still in use today.

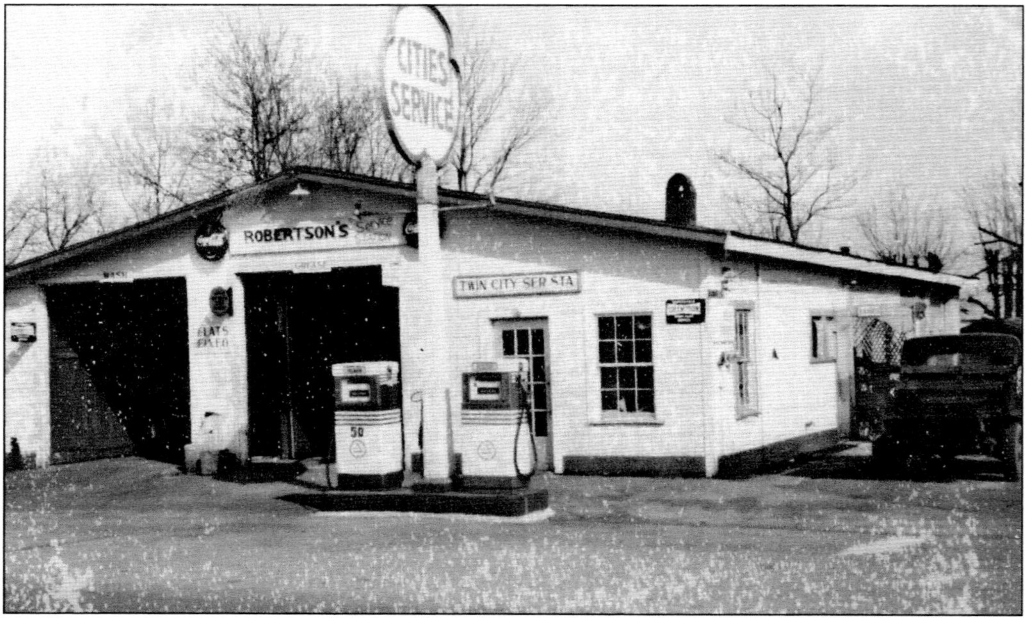

Twin Cities Service Station was a well-known establishment on the Fourth Street extension that provided fuel for many vehicles in the good old days.

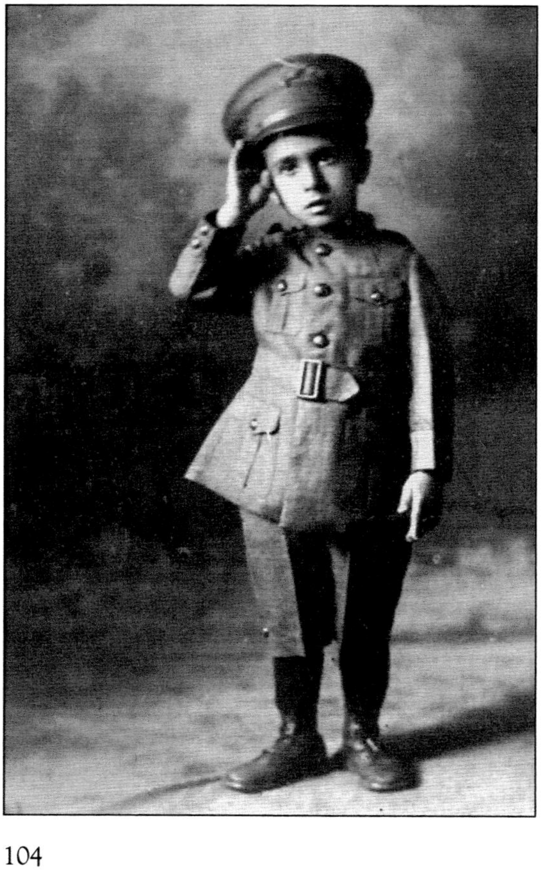

Saluting crisply and in dress typical of the turn of the century in this c. 1917 photo is five-year-old Ernest Khourie, son of Fulton business merchant Alexander Michael Khourie and Rumsey Haddad Khourie.

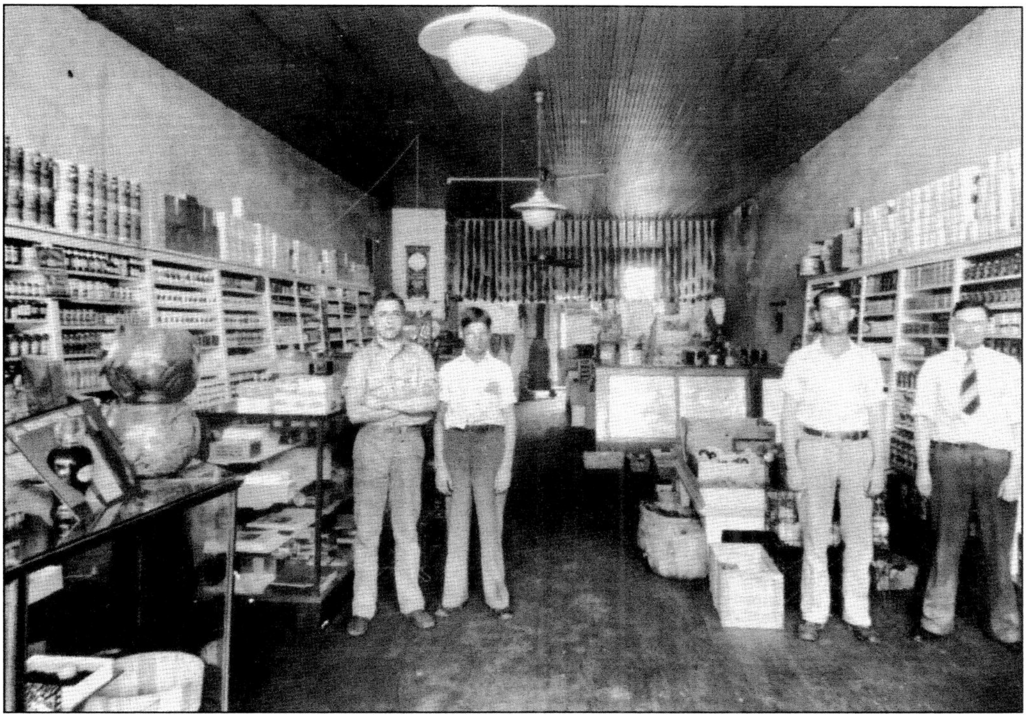

Buggs Grocery was a family-owed and -operated business on Walnut Street during the late 1940s. It had many loyal neighborhood patrons, as did most of the "mom and pop" grocery establishments located in chiefly residential areas of the Twin Cities during this time.

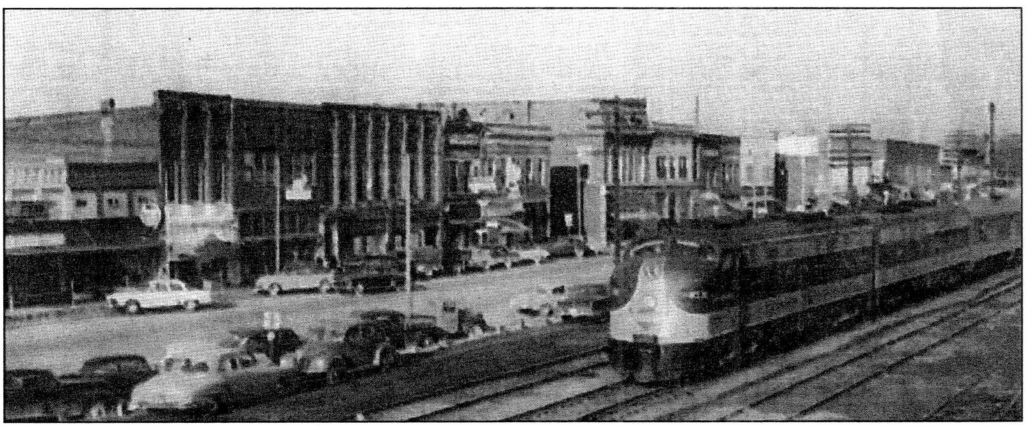

Seen on January 10, 1954, downtown Fulton was the picture of a prosperous center of commerce. Many passenger and freight trains crossed through the town daily, and the railroad was a prime source of employment.

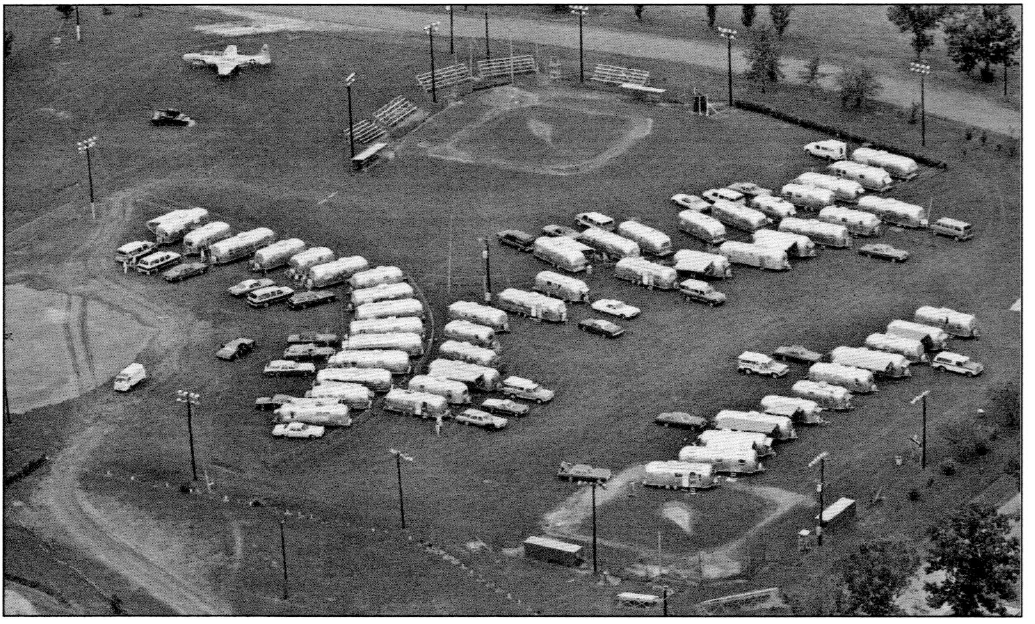

Fulton City Park is seen here in an aerial view from 1975. The land passed from the Fulton County Fair Association to the Fulton Board of Education and, in June 1946, on to the City of Fulton for a purchase price of $7,000. In 1959, the old fairgrounds were bisected with a bypass connecting U.S. Highways 45 and 51. At that time, the land was converted to a city park.

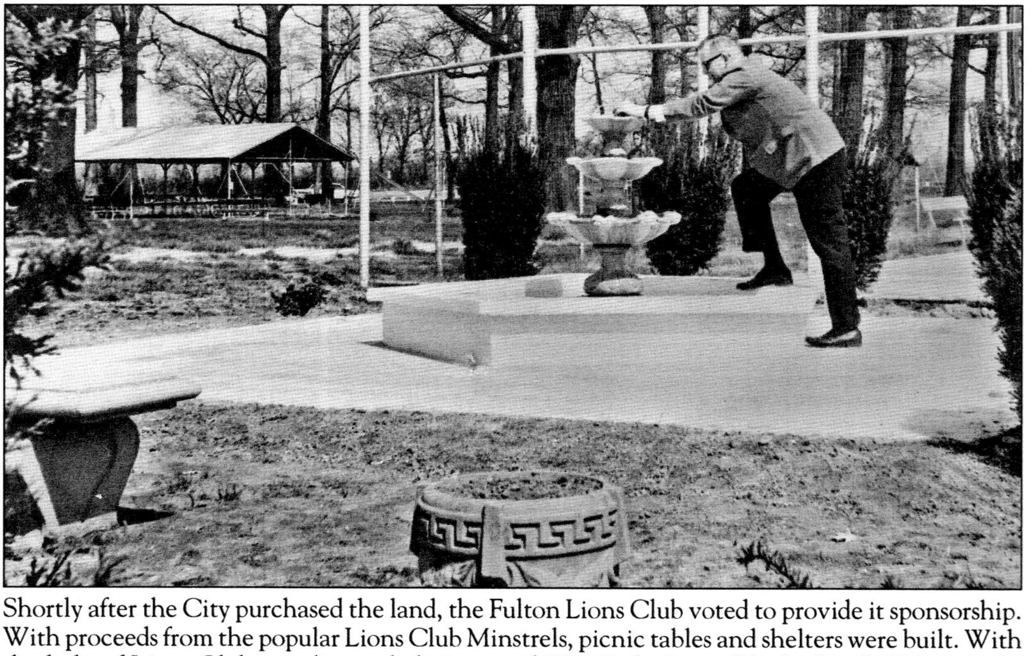

Shortly after the City purchased the land, the Fulton Lions Club voted to provide it sponsorship. With proceeds from the popular Lions Club Minstrels, picnic tables and shelters were built. With the help of Lions Club member and chairman of City Parks Louis Weaks, baseball diamonds, tennis courts, and playground equipment were added. A memorial to Mr. Weaks was dedicated April 6, 1980. The fountain pictured above is no longer in existence, but the platform and a wrought-iron arch are still on display.

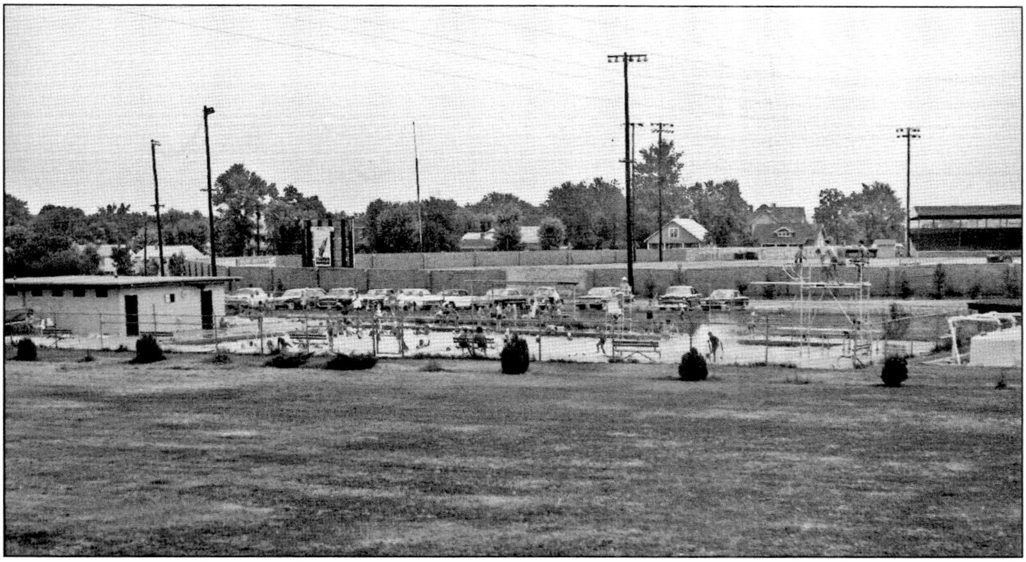

Willow Plunge, a community swimming pool built for $20,000 under the direction of the Willow Plunge Corporation, held its grand opening July 4, 1959, and enjoyed great popularity among youth and adults alike until its closing in the 1990s. In the background is the Kitty League Fairfield Stadium and the fence encircling the park, which contained area advertisements. The fence was taken down around the time the new police and fire department was built on Browder Avenue in 1975.

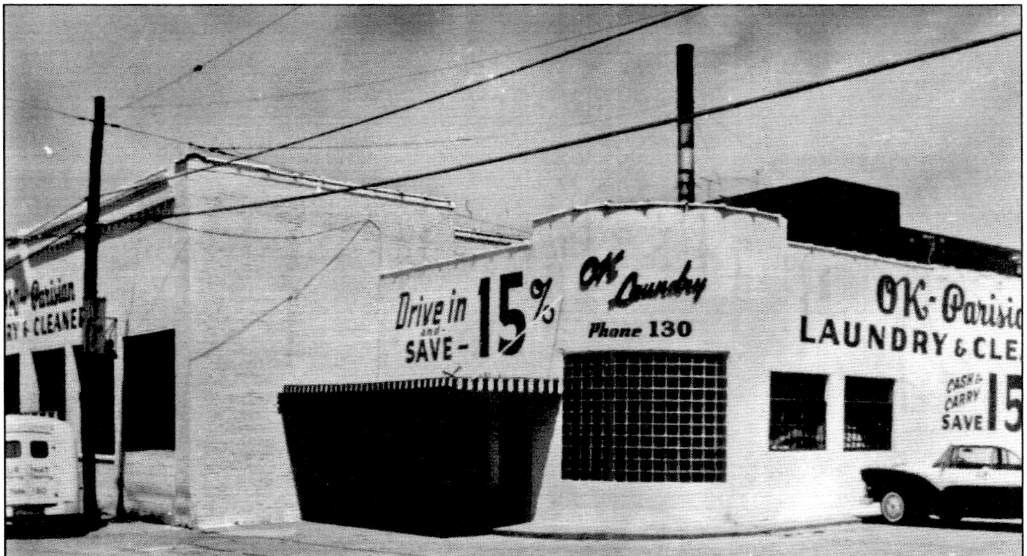

The O.K. Steam Laundry at 208 East State Street was founded in 1898. Proprietor J.J. Owen, of Paducah, and his three sons, Vernon, Harold, and Johnnie, were in business together. Featuring French dry-cleaning and sanitary steam pressing, the service became very popular among men who "did not care to wear wrinkled and uncreased trousers." The plant itself was a large brick structure, which housed the latest machinery and cold storage vaults for furs and winter wearables.

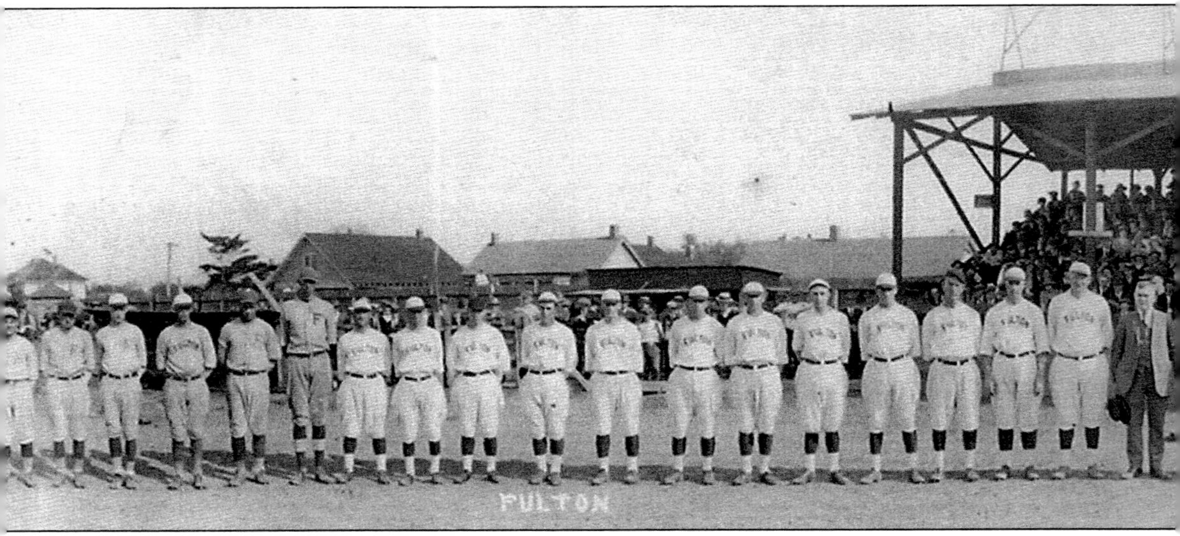

The opening day of Kitty League baseball season always created a stir in the Twin Cities. Even though the Fulton team disbanded and reorganized several times between 1911 and 1935, rooters were always in the grandstand cheering the men on. Eventually this grandstand was torn down and replaced with an improved structure. Featured here are the Fulton and Dyersburg

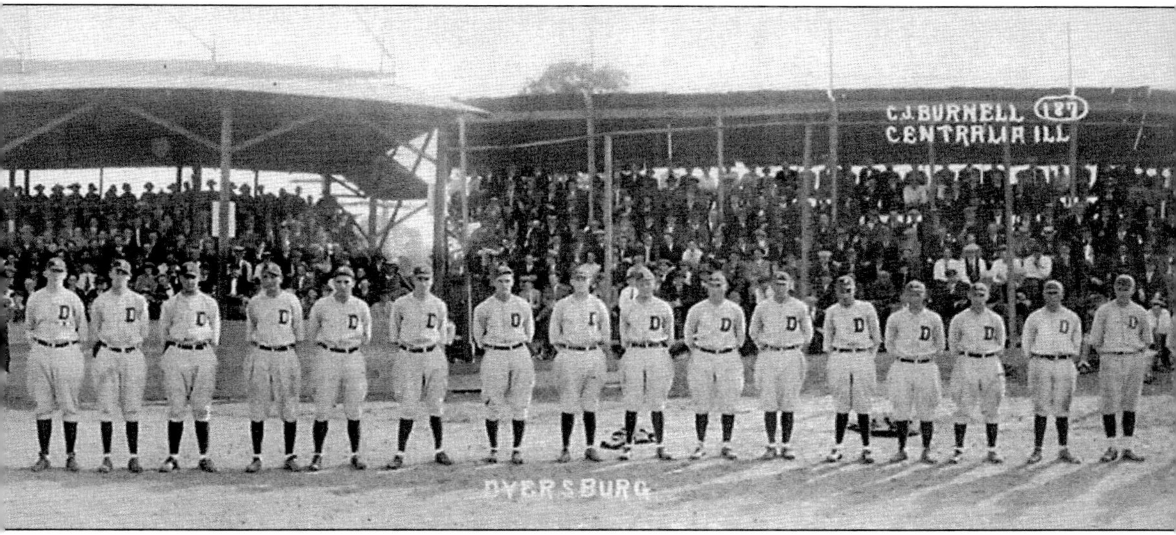

teams on May 18, 1923, at Fairfield Park. The Kitty League drew many young men interested in a professional baseball career to the area. These men often ended up marrying local girls and calling Fulton their home when their baseball careers ended.

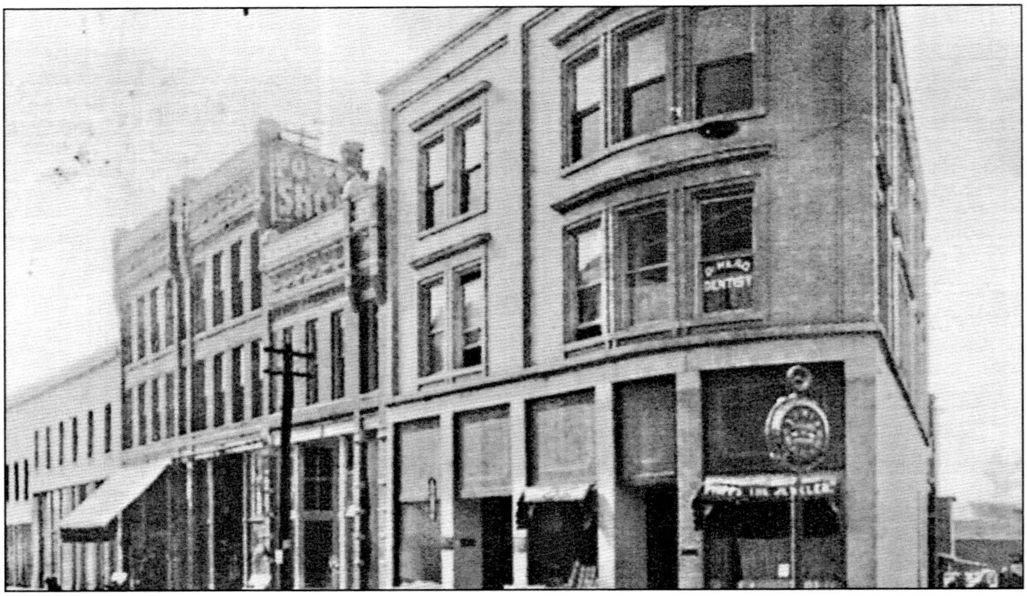

The R.N. Phipps Jewelry Store at 226 Church Street was in the Flat Iron Building. This Fulton business house enjoyed as much popularity locally as New York's famed Flat Iron Building. The three-story building was erected by Mr. Phipps, who occupied the first floor. Phipps Jewelry was the site of Jimmie Roper's accidental shooting death in 1902. Mr. Phipps was the official watch inspector for the Illinois Central Railroad. The store also had a special optometry department where "scientific fitting of eye glasses" was conducted.

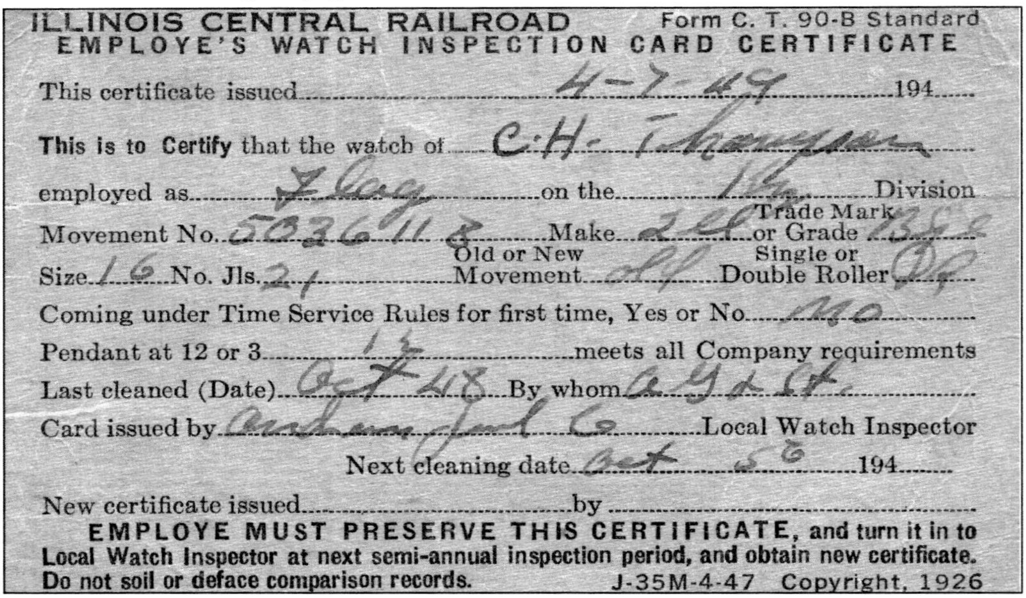

ILLINOIS CENTRAL RAILROAD Form C. T. 90-B Standard
EMPLOYE'S WATCH INSPECTION CARD CERTIFICATE

This certificate issued 4-7-49 194

This is to Certify that the watch of C.H. Thompson

employed as Flag on the [illegible] Division

Movement No. 5036118 Make Ill Trade Mark or Grade Bunn

Size 16 No. Jls. 21 Old or New Movement old Single or Double Roller DR

Coming under Time Service Rules for first time, Yes or No no

Pendant at 12 or 3 12 meets all Company requirements

Last cleaned (Date) Oct 48 By whom [illegible]

Card issued by Andrews Jewel Co. Local Watch Inspector

Next cleaning date Oct 50 194

New certificate issued by

EMPLOYE MUST PRESERVE THIS CERTIFICATE, and turn it in to Local Watch Inspector at next semi-annual inspection period, and obtain new certificate. Do not soil or deface comparison records. J-35M-4-47 Copyright, 1926

Each employee with the ICRR whose watch was subject to inspection was required to obtain a semi-annual inspection card certificate, an example of which is pictured above, to present to the local watch inspector. The record was sent to the division superintendent for permanent recordkeeping. R.N. Phipps, and later Andrews Jewelry in the same location, provided this service for the railroad employees.

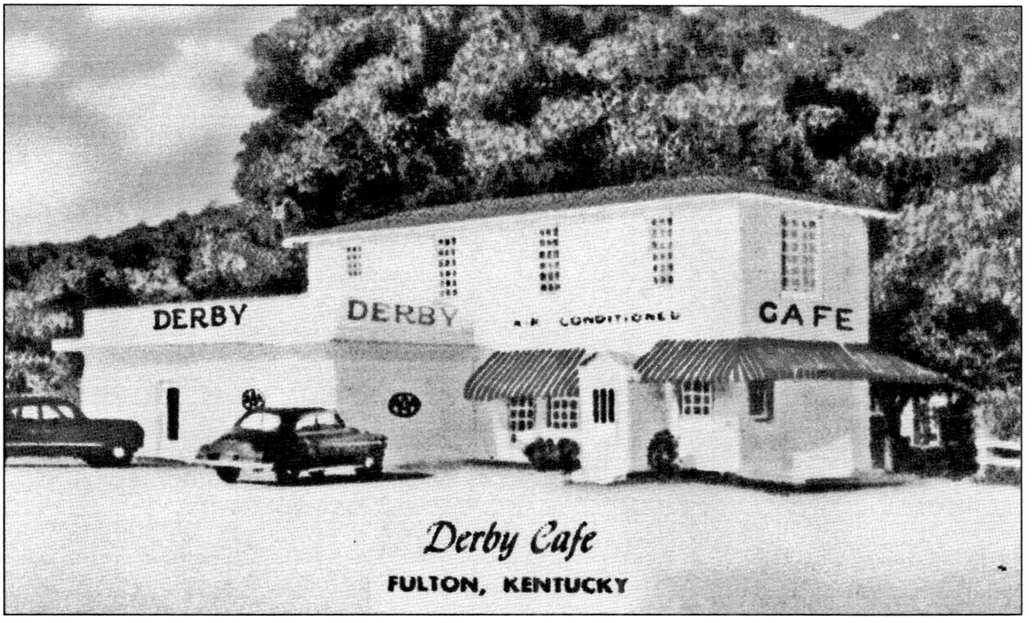

The Brown Derby, located on Highway 51, was originally a two-story, concrete-block drive-in with curb service. It was built by Tucker Brown and had limited booths and counter space for indoor dining. Tucker Brown went on to build a "modern" tourist court on the Union City highway in 1950, which still stands today.

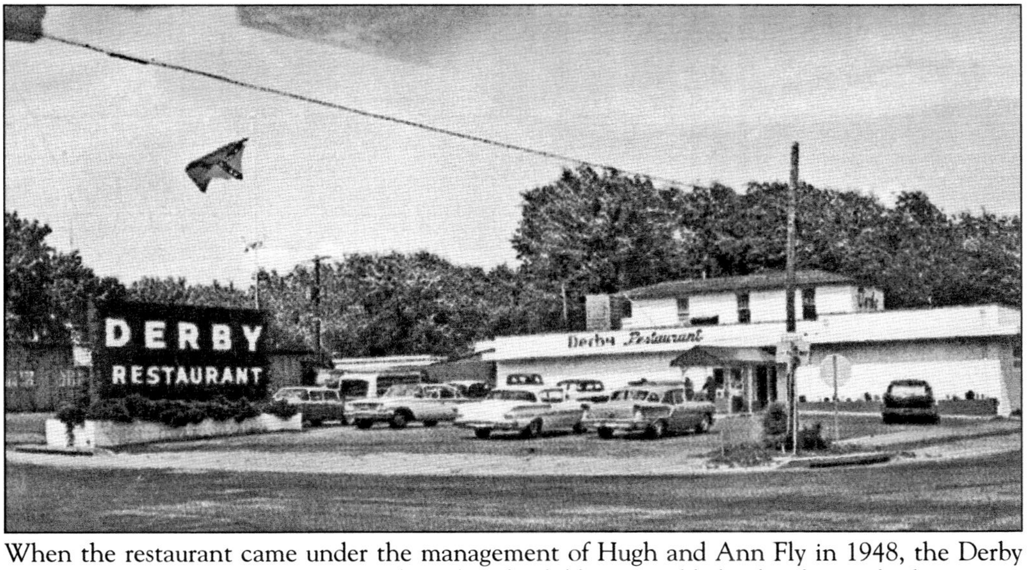

When the restaurant came under the management of Hugh and Ann Fly in 1948, the Derby was renovated. The kitchen was enlarged and a lobby was added. The dining facilities were expanded to "The Pit," "The Rebel Room," the "Kentucky Room," a coffee shop, and the Rebel gift shop. The Derby could seat 300 and offered live music and a dance floor. Delicacies like fresh seafood and Chinese dishes were made possible by Fulton's rail connections. For authentic cuisine, Mr. Fly brought in a Chinese cook from Chicago, who lived in the small apartment above the restaurant. During the Banana Festival, the Derby hosted a Governor's Breakfast to honor festival dignitaries that was always well attended.

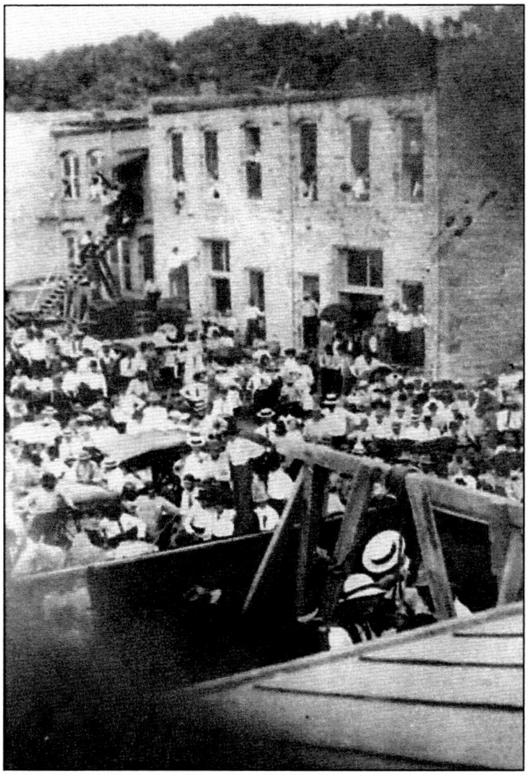

In the early 1890s, those opposed to liquor united in a prohibition effort that will go down in the annals of Fulton history. It was told that two of Fulton's most popular men—Mott Ayers, editor of the newspaper, and professor J.C. Cheek, superintendent of Fulton City Schools—were engaged in a heated conversation over the alcohol issue in the middle of the street. At the end of the day, prohibition won with a mere 20 votes. Seen here is the public hanging of John Barleycorn in celebration of the vote.

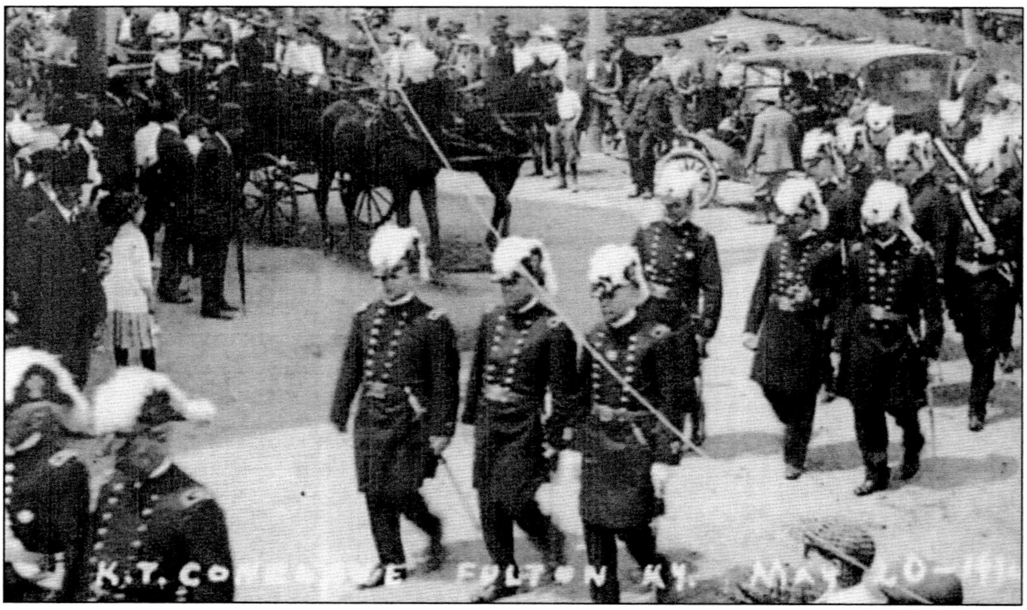

The Grand Commandery of Kentucky chartered Fulton Commandery No. 34 Knights Templar with 36 members on May 20, 1909. The Knights were prominent citizens of the community and willing participants in many of Fulton's parades, proudly displaying full dress regalia. In this image, the group is gathered to celebrate their charter on May 20, 1914.

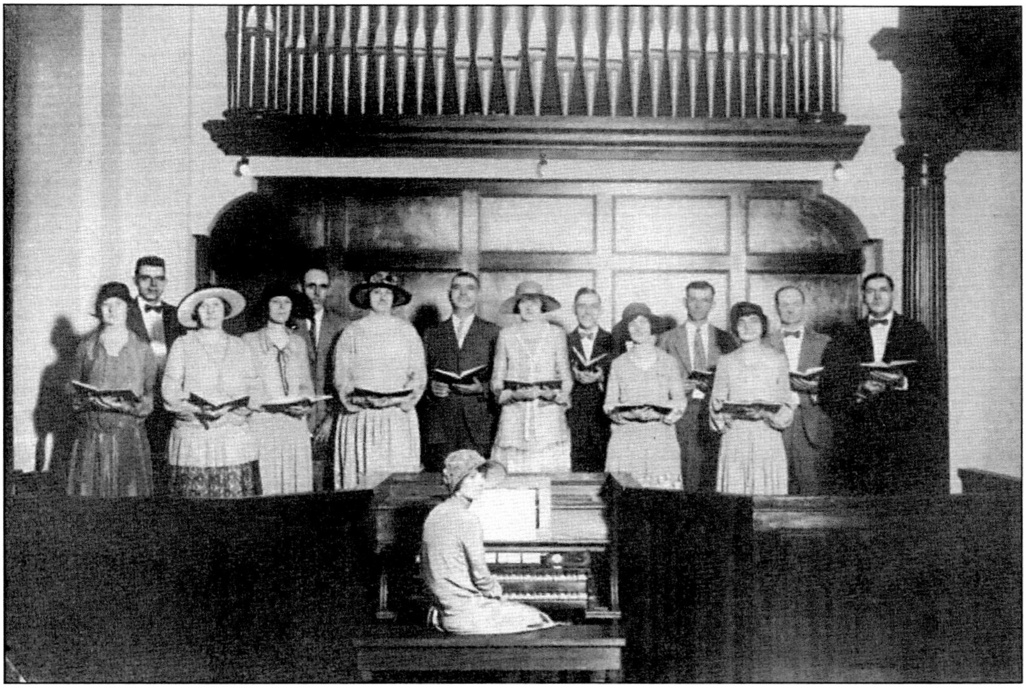

The sanctuary shown here is the Baptist Church chancel, on the corner of Second and Eddings Streets, completed in 1925. This was the second sanctuary constructed, the first having been built in 1901.

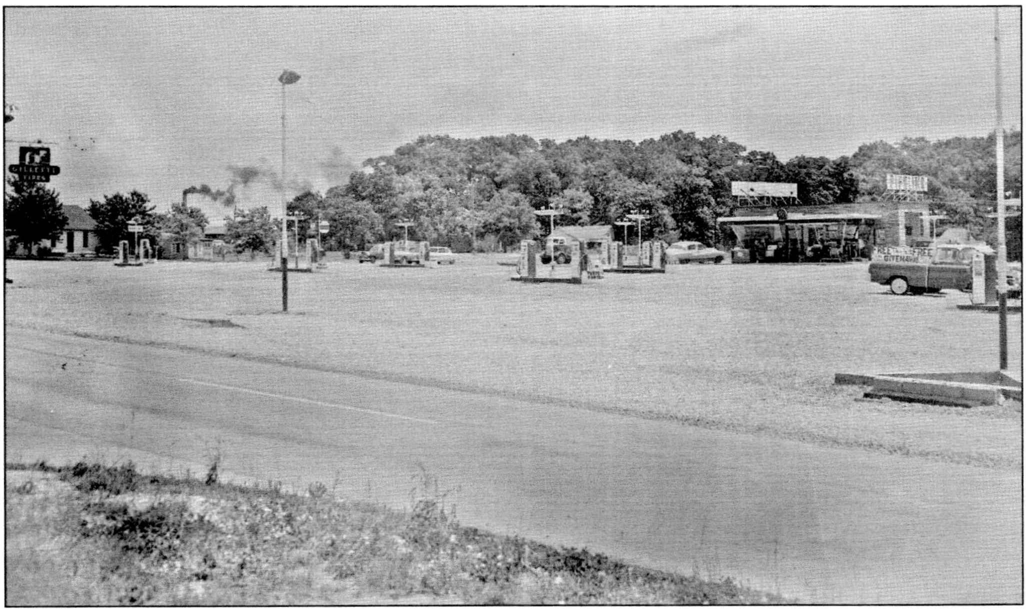

Pipeline Gas and Oil Company was located on the north bypass through Highlands joining Highways 45 and 51 in the lot across from where the Whistlin' Pig Restaurant stands today. Traffic was heavy, and the well-known Pipeline Café was a popular draw for truckers and travelers alike.

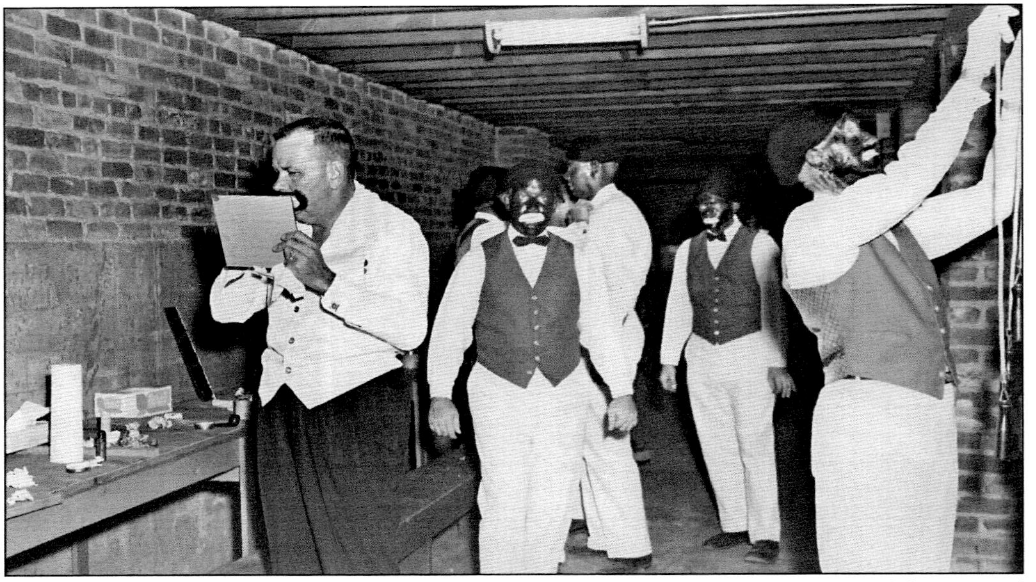

Enlivening the Twin Cities in the 1940s and 1950s were the annual Lions Club Minstrel productions. Carr Elementary gymnasium hosted two consecutive nights of these popular shows. The entertainment was modeled after the early traveling minstrels and had a vaudeville feel. Great pains were taken to appear authentic in every aspect. Seen here are members of the Lions Club putting finishing touches on makeup in the basement of the school before arriving on stage to perform.

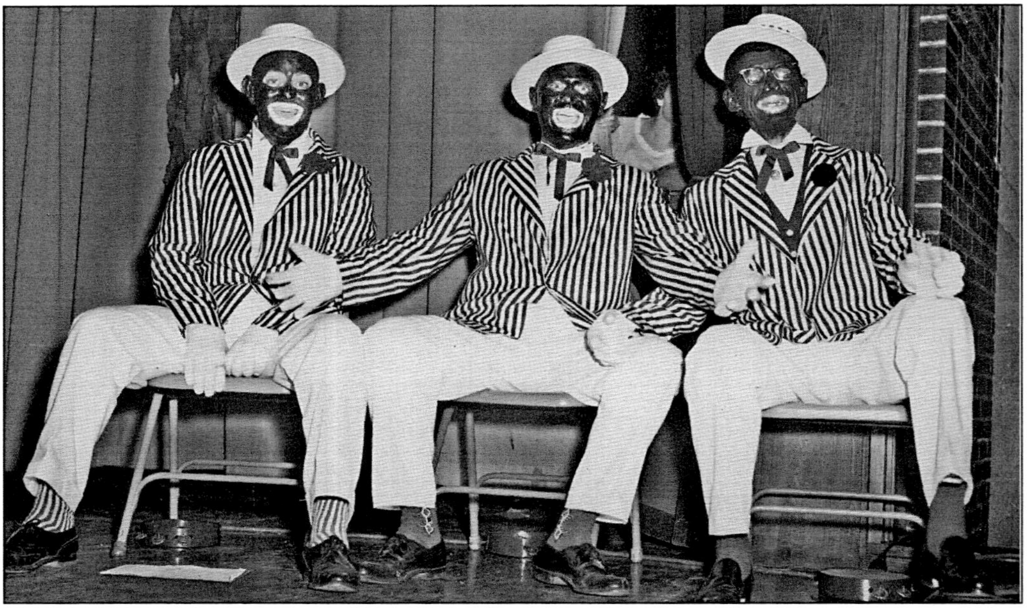

The Lions Club Minstrel Show began in 1938, was discontinued during World War II, and was brought back around 1948, to the pleasure of the citizens of the Twin Cities. Through the years many talented community members helped to make the production a huge success. Area talent was showcased in chorus, quartet, comedy, monologues, and dance numbers. Seen in this image are minstrel performers in black face having a good time on the Carr Elementary stage.

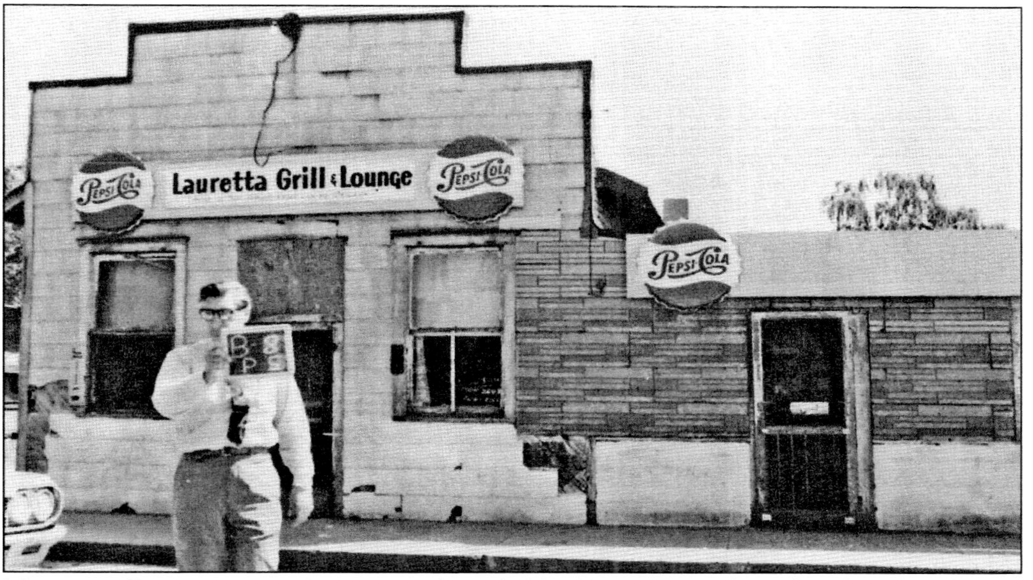

Missionary Bottom was a 43-acre tract bounded by Vine Street, the railroad tracks adjacent to Carr Street, and North Highland Drive. Missionary Bottom was known as the African-American section of town. A separate community developed, complete with grocery stores, nightclubs, and schools. An urban renewal grant placed families in more modern sanitary living conditions and razed all existing structures. Seen here is the Lauretta Grill and Lounge being slated for destruction.

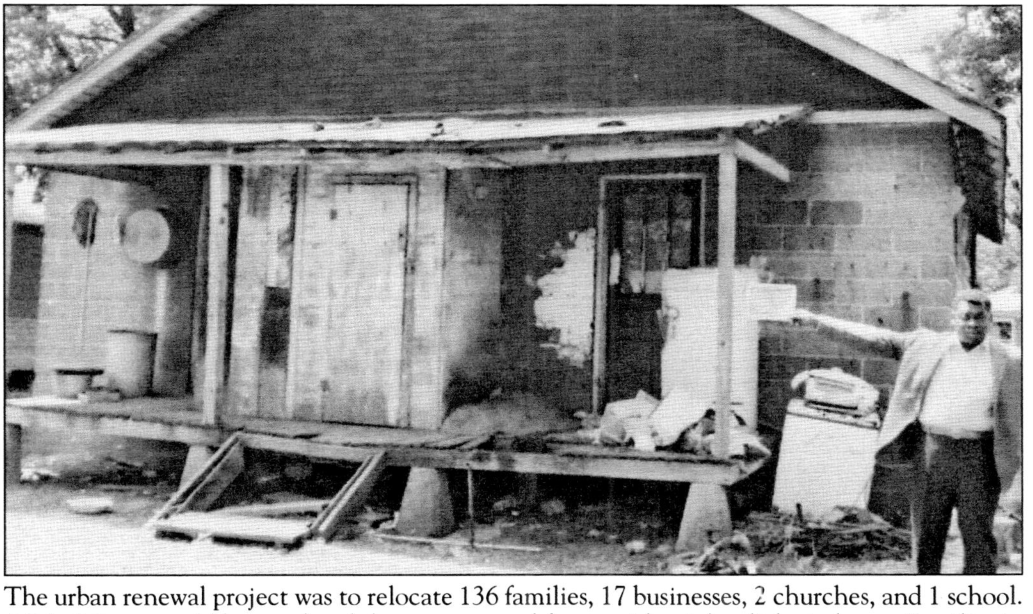

The urban renewal project was to relocate 136 families, 17 businesses, 2 churches, and 1 school. All buildings would be razed and the area rezoned from residential to light industry. Families in groups of houses that shared one outside water faucet and one outdoor toilet (that discharged into Harris Fork Creek) now had better living environments. Water Street, Burton Row, and Burns Avenue no longer existed, and Norman Street was significantly straightened (Martin Luther King Drive), transforming the landscape to its appearance today.

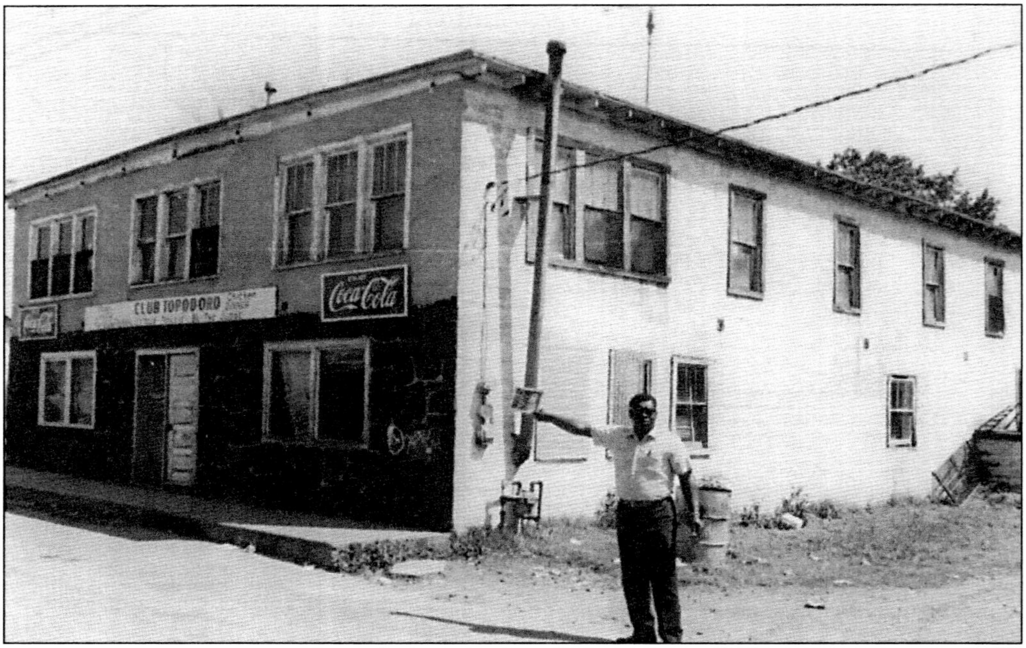

Also with the urban renewal project, gone were the various night spots that attracted large crowds, particularly groups from surrounding "dry" counties looking for entertainment. The Club Topodoro was a particular favorite on Burns Avenue in Missionary Bottom. Reportedly "all the action" was on Burns Avenue, which ran adjacent to the railroad tracks parallel to Fourth Street on the northeast side of the Mears Street Viaduct. Remnants of the street can be viewed in this area today.

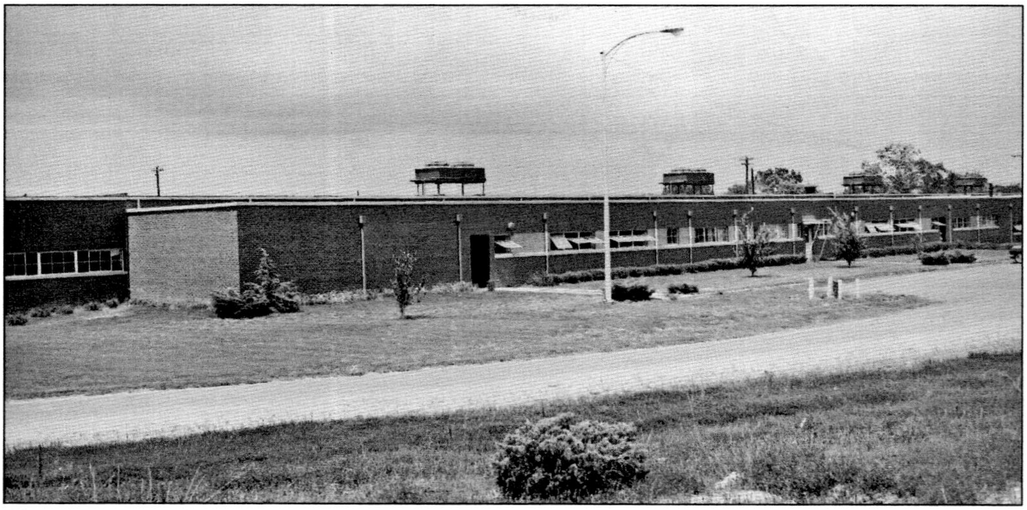

The American Cigar Factory on Fourth Street became the Henry I. Siegel garment factory in 1937. A new plant would cross the State Line into Tennessee. For a period of time, the Siegel Company operated two factories in the Twin Cities. The Fourth Street building was refurbished, and CHIC jeans were produced from the South Fulton plant. Now the Fulton building stands decaying, but the South Fulton plant has found new life as the South Fulton Municipal Building, dedicated in 2004.

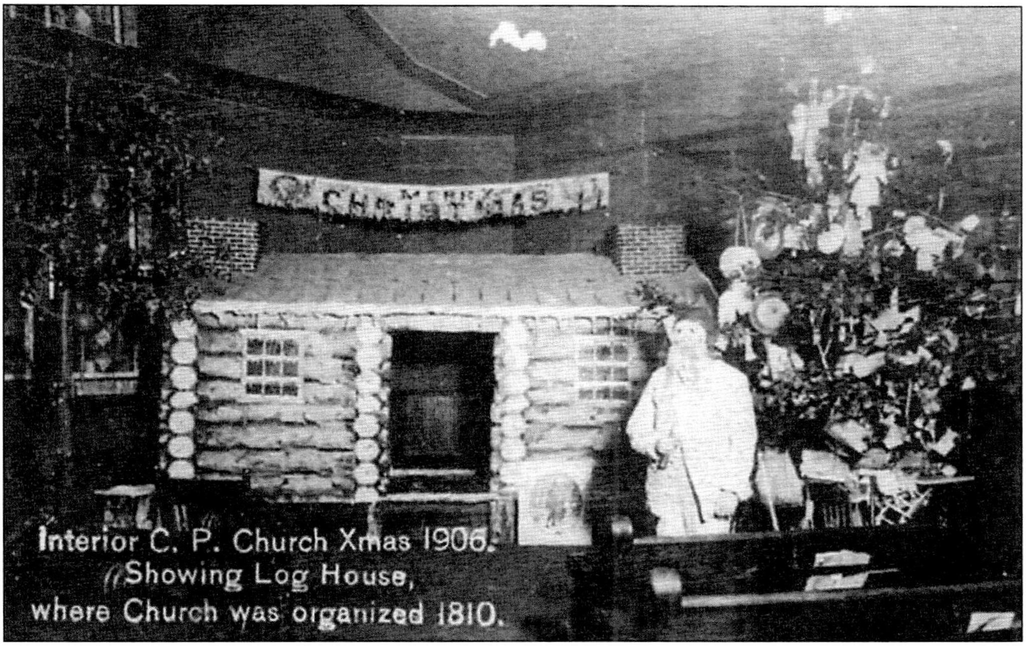

On Highway 1125 is the site of what may be the oldest church in Fulton County. Union Cumberland Presbyterian Church was originally built of logs around 1840 and stood in the corner of Old Union Cemetery across the road from the present church. The oldest stone is for Henry Ashburn, born 1765 and died 1846. The Union Cumberland Presbyterian Church was formally organized in 1842 with 32 members; the two-story frame building housed Masons and Good Templars on the second floor. It is felt the featured image depicts the original log cabin.

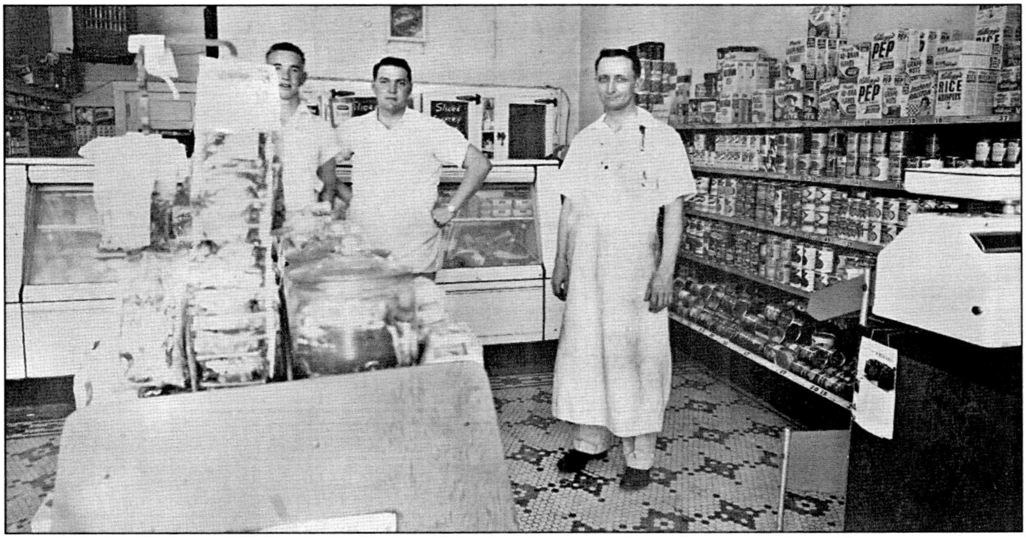

De Meyer's Grocery was located around the corner from Smith's Café, facing what is now Mears Street looking towards the parking lot of The Keg. Many groceries have gone into business in this area over the years. In the late 1940s and 1950s, the grocery would rent frozen food lockers in which one could store meats and other perishable. From left to right in the photograph are unidentified, Jimmy Lawson, and Gilbert De Meyer.

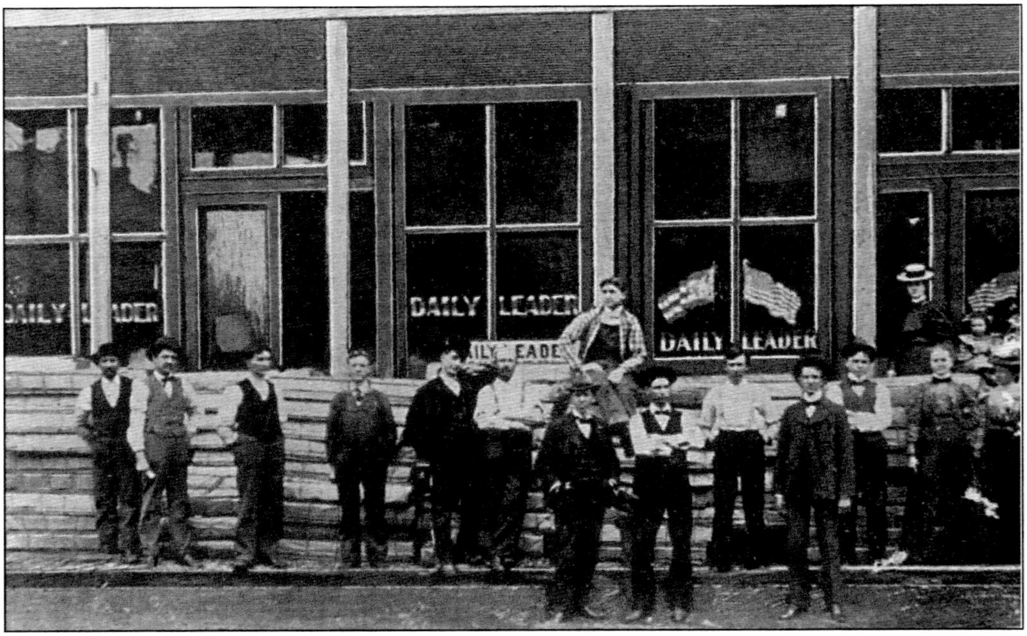

Established by Mott Ayers on June 25, 1898, the *Fulton Daily Leader* occupied a two-story brick building on Walnut Street. In 1919, the paper was purchased by Rev. T.F. Moore and his two sons for $5,000. The *Fulton Daily Leader* was the smallest daily newspaper in Tennessee or Kentucky. In 1989, the Fulton Publishing Company switched to printing the paper once a week, but many in the community are just now learning to drop the "Daily" from its name.

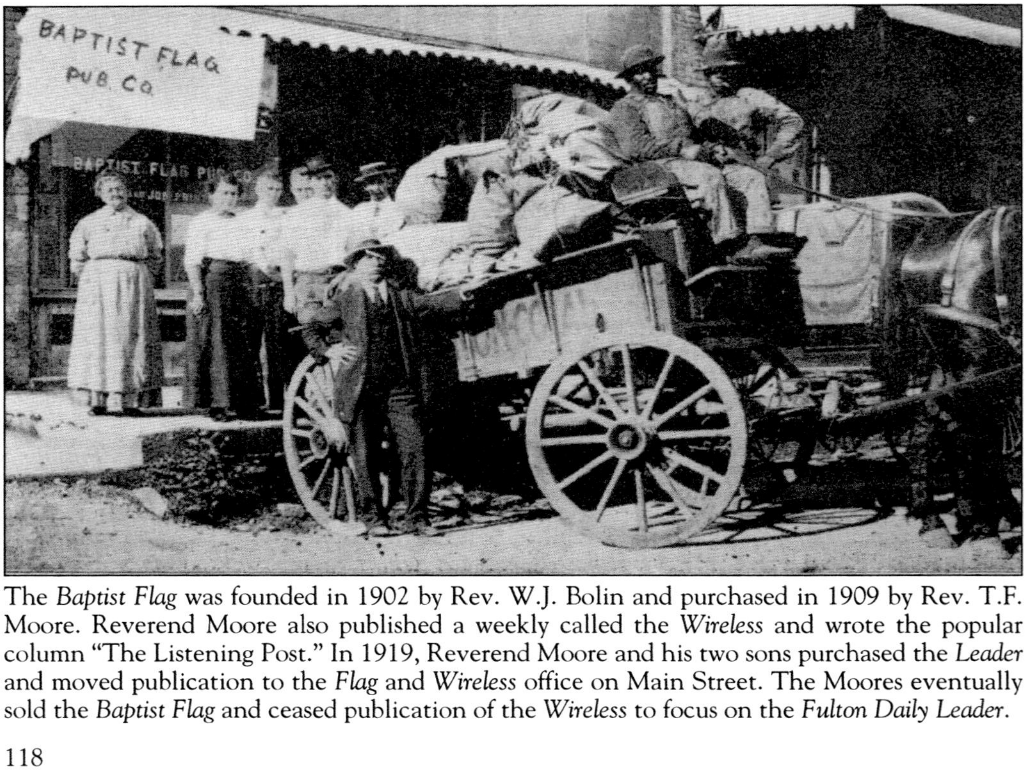

The *Baptist Flag* was founded in 1902 by Rev. W.J. Bolin and purchased in 1909 by Rev. T.F. Moore. Reverend Moore also published a weekly called the *Wireless* and wrote the popular column "The Listening Post." In 1919, Reverend Moore and his two sons purchased the *Leader* and moved publication to the *Flag* and *Wireless* office on Main Street. The Moores eventually sold the *Baptist Flag* and ceased publication of the *Wireless* to focus on the *Fulton Daily Leader*.

Even today, one can find vestiges of the Banana Festival in its heyday. Still around are live banana trees growing in the community of the Twin Cities. Citizen volunteers of all ages planted banana trees throughout town during the early years of the festivities in an attempt to create scenery for the visitors who poured into Fulton for the annual event.

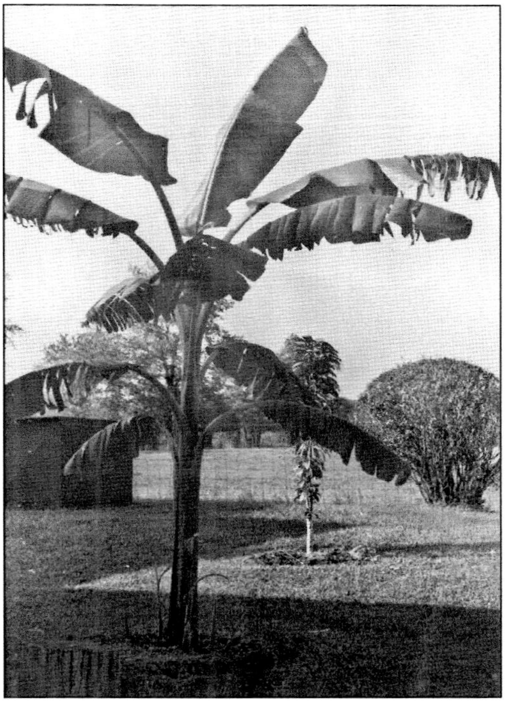

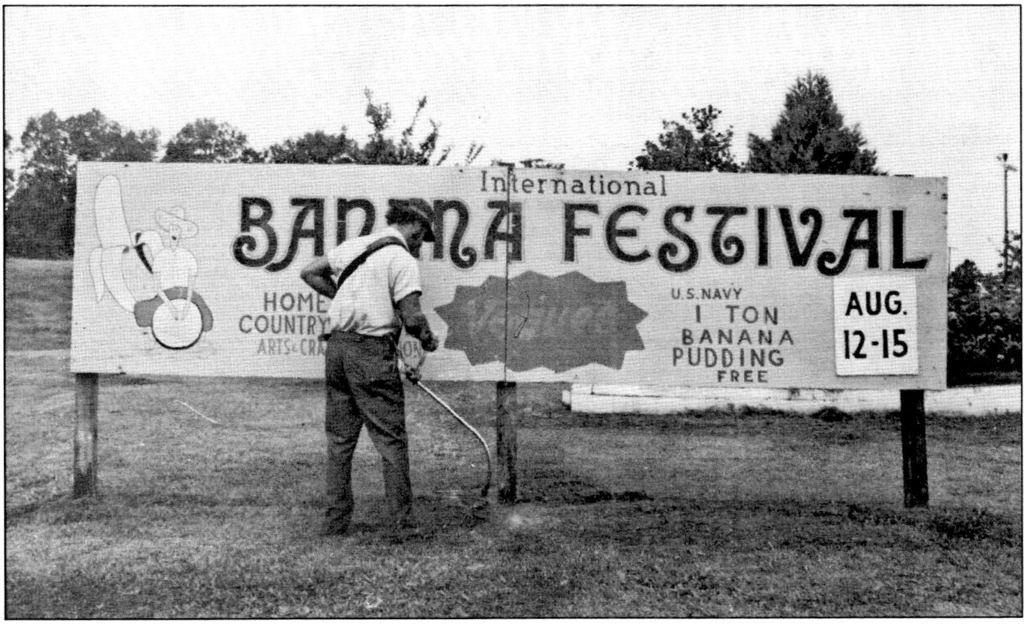

Billed in the 1964 Paducah *Sun* as "a worthwhile civic project with imagination, depth and potential for endurance," the International Banana Festival of the Twin Cities enjoyed success from the outset. Upwards of 40,000 visitors celebrated the importance of the import-export trade and reminded all of just how many jobs depended on this healthy exchange of goods across borders in foreign trade economy. Signs such as the one above were posted throughout Fulton and South Fulton to remind people of the festival dates.

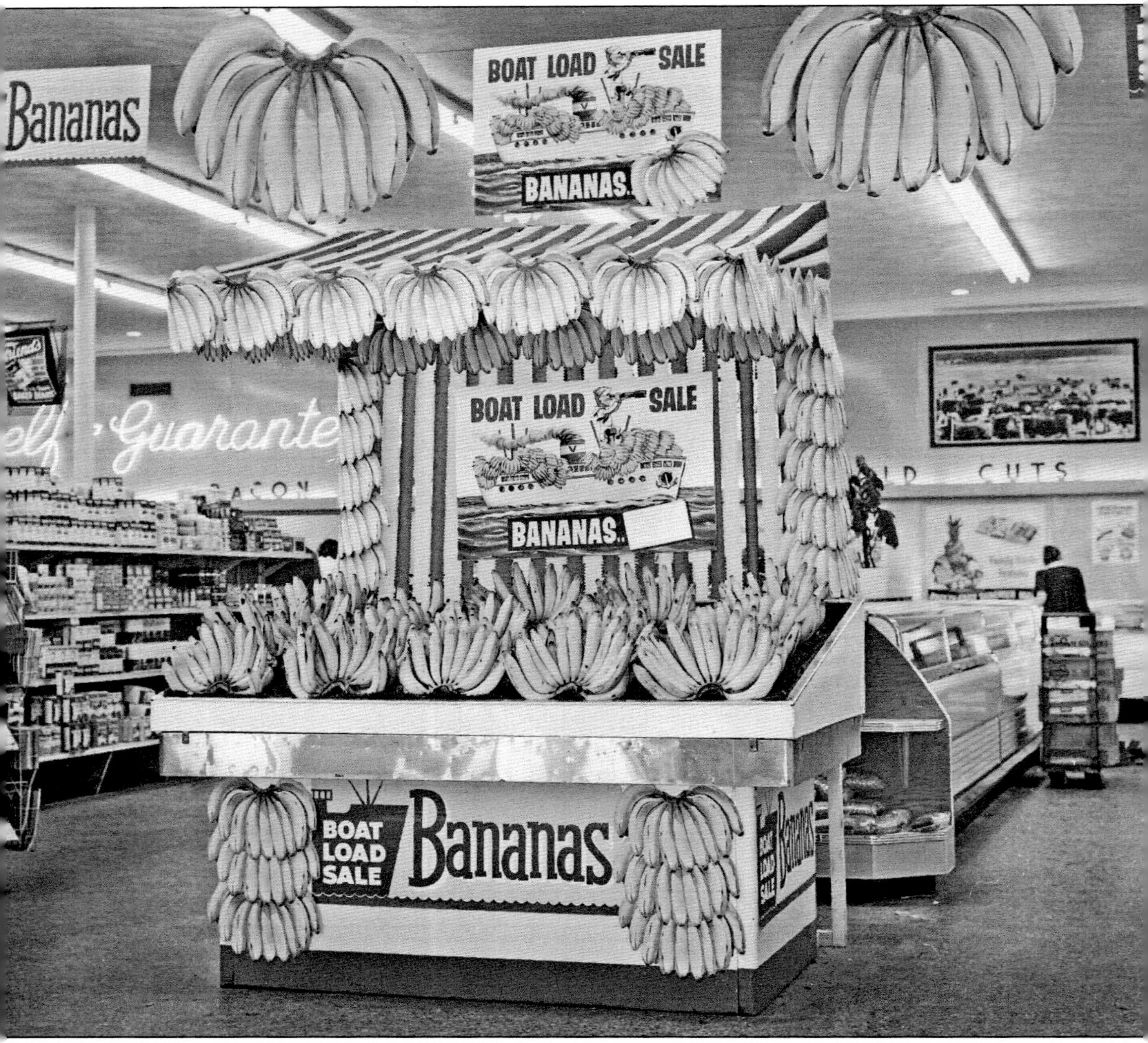

With financial backing from the National Banana Association, there was a veritable "banana bonanza" in the Twin Cities during festival time. Seen here is a display typical of a 1964 grocery produce department, in which banana sales reached record levels to supply the varied schedule of events. Numerous charts, posters, pamphlets, and bulletins on all aspects of the banana were available at point-of-sale displays to any interested store customer. Even the Fulton Ice Plant on Fourth Street, a successor to the R.H. Wade Ice Plant on Norman Street in the earlier years, advertised for the public to "come see the banana icing process on the rail cars" as a festival activity.

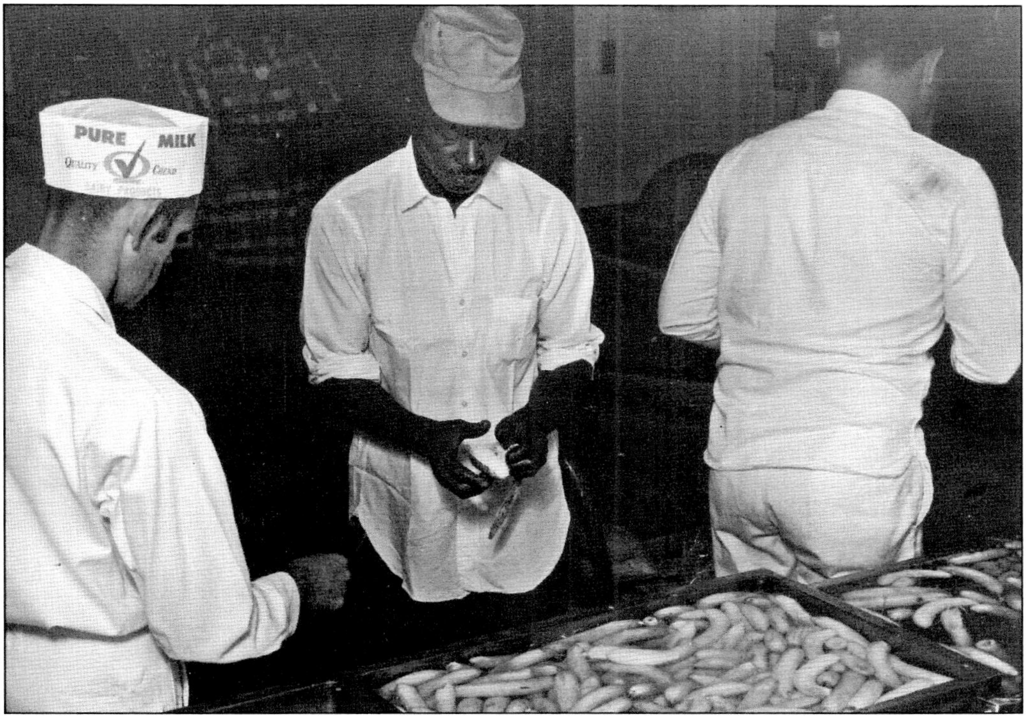

Drafted under the direction of "Chef" Dub Burnette, the crew of workers at Pure Milk Company was hard at work several days in advance of the festival date. Seen here, about 3,000 ripe bananas were peeled by hand and put in a solution to keep from browning.

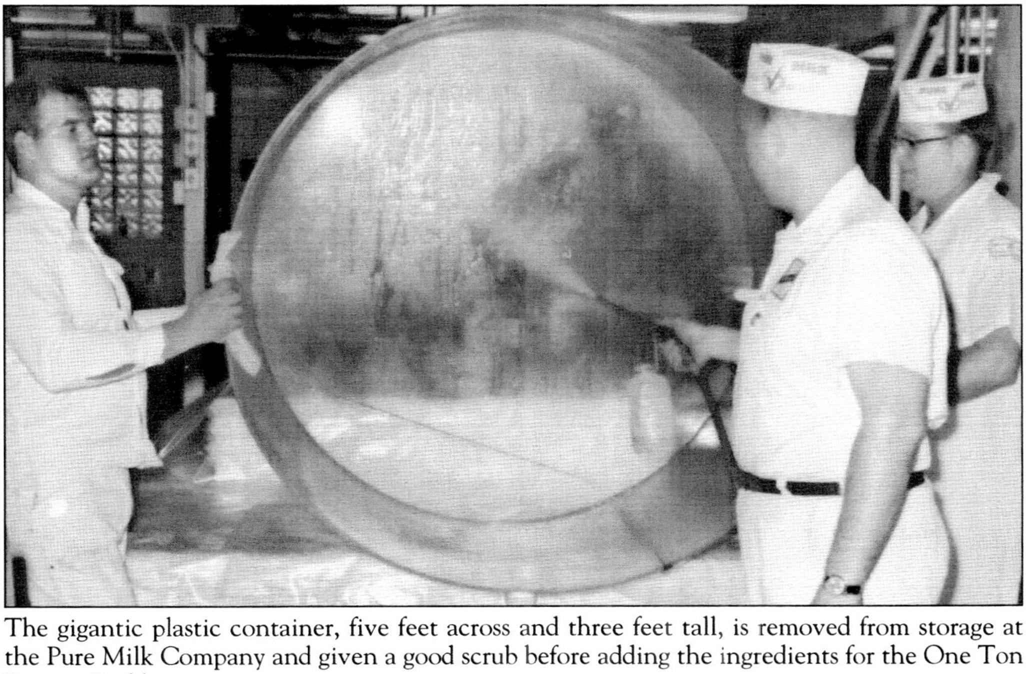

The gigantic plastic container, five feet across and three feet tall, is removed from storage at the Pure Milk Company and given a good scrub before adding the ingredients for the One Ton Banana Pudding.

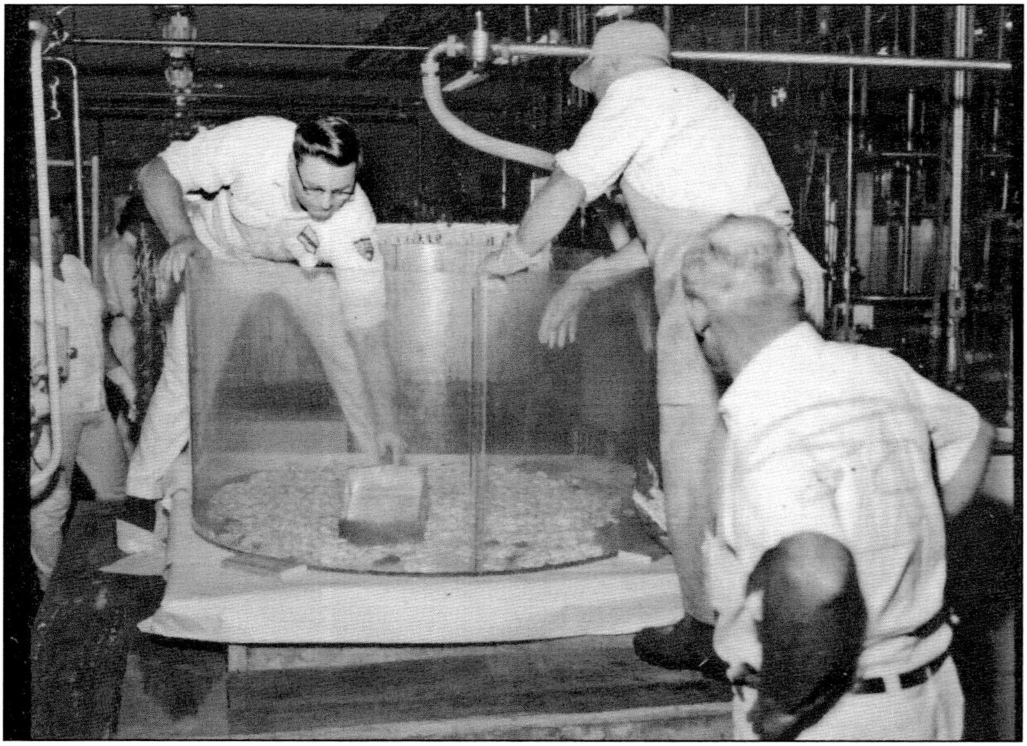

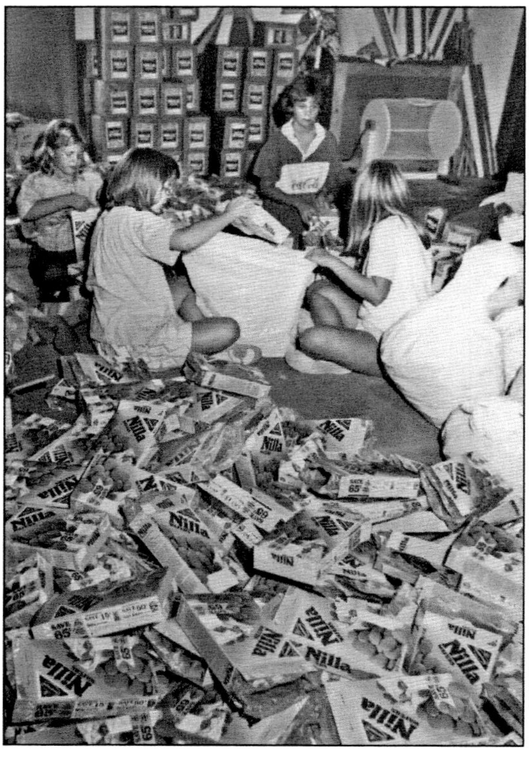

In the container, about 250 pounds of vanilla wafers—about 29,000 cookies—are spread in alternating layers over 850 pounds of boiled custard and 3,000 hand-peeled, sliced bananas. For many years, the Nabisco Company donated much of the wafers needed to prepare the dessert.

This photo shows the involvement of local children enlisted to help empty vanilla wafer boxes in preparation for the One Ton Banana Pudding. It was a sought-after job among the younger crowd of the Twin Cities, helping make the festival a community-wide event.

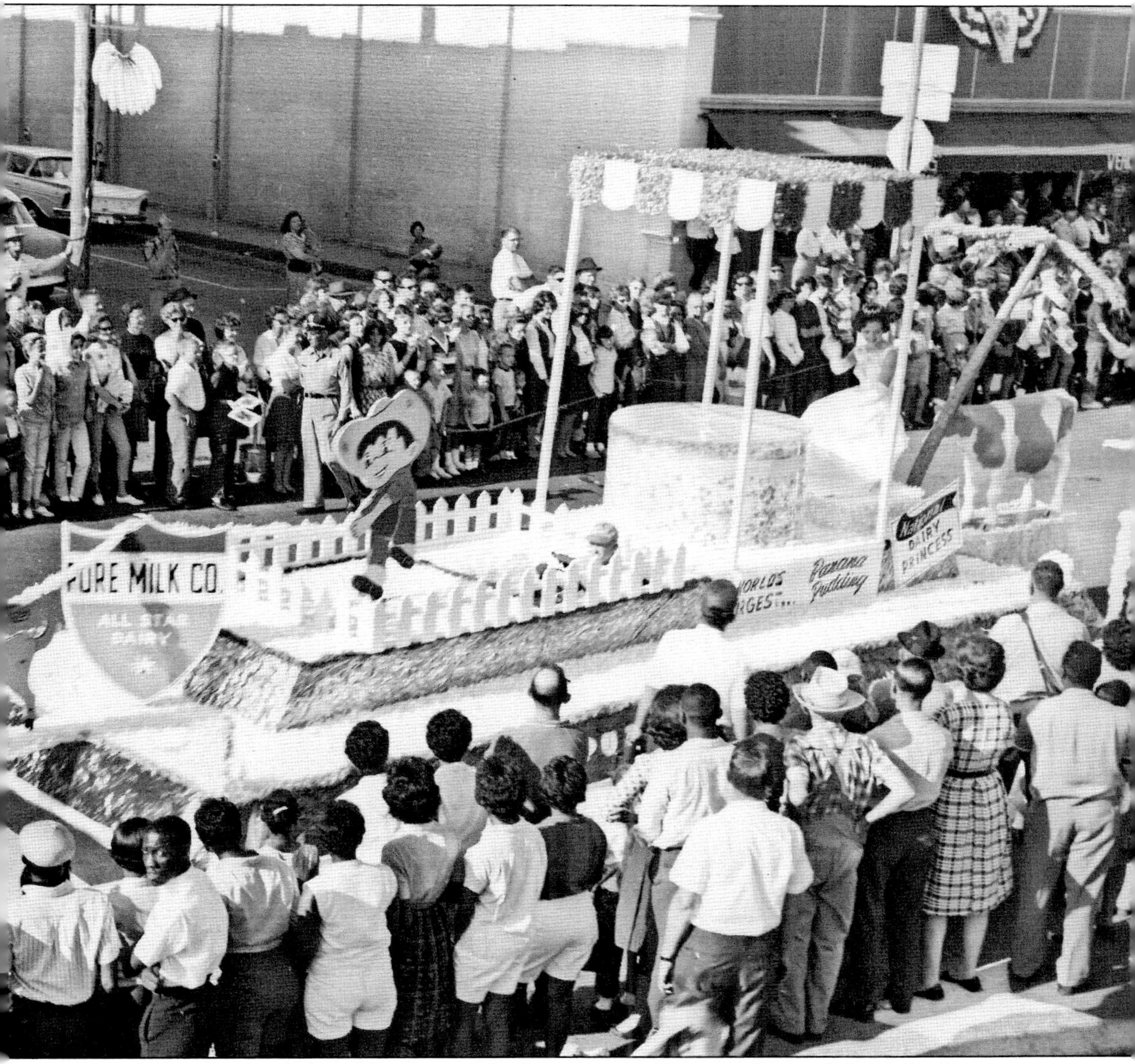

One of the most talked-about features of the International Banana Festival through the years has been the One Ton Banana Pudding. Introduced as a surprise at the very first festival in 1963, the pudding came to be an icon of the celebration, and if you did not have a taste of this delicious specialty, served up by a bevy of local, national, and international beauties on the bandstand at the end of the Grand Parade, then somehow, your festival experience was lacking. The recipe was a well-kept secret and stored in a safe at the Pure Milk Company until time to begin the pudding preparations. The One Ton Banana Pudding of the International Banana Festival has made its place in the *Guinness Book of World Records* as the world's largest banana pudding, an enduring marker of a festival that has long since fallen by the wayside.

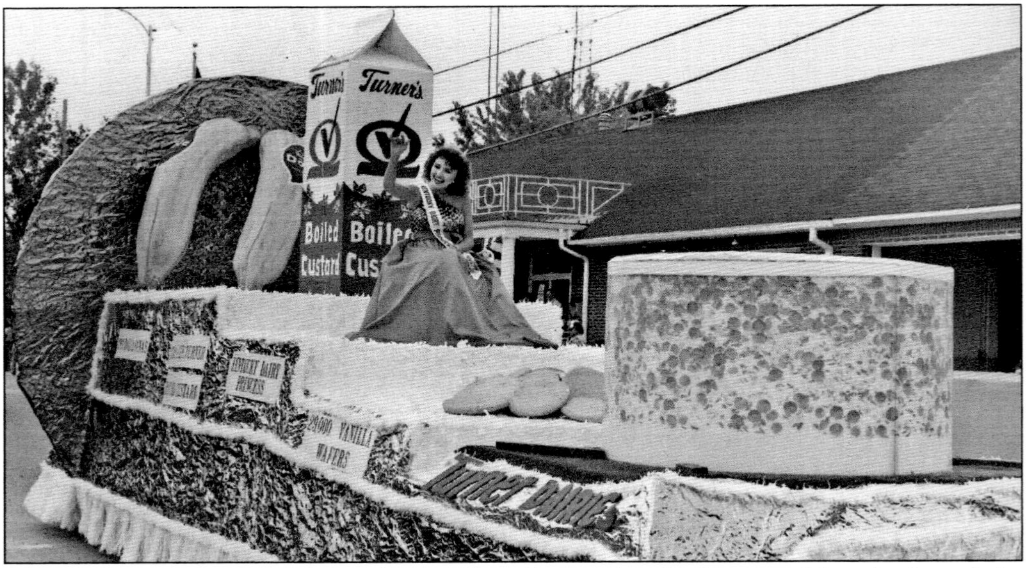

The International Banana Festival typically culminated with the Grand Parade down Lake Street on Saturday morning and the finals of the Princess Pageant in the Fulton City School Auditorium that evening. It was customary for the American Dairy Princess to ride on the float with the pudding during the Grand Parade. In this image Pure Milk Company has become Turner Dairy, but the tradition of an American Dairy Princess and a float for the pudding does not miss a beat.

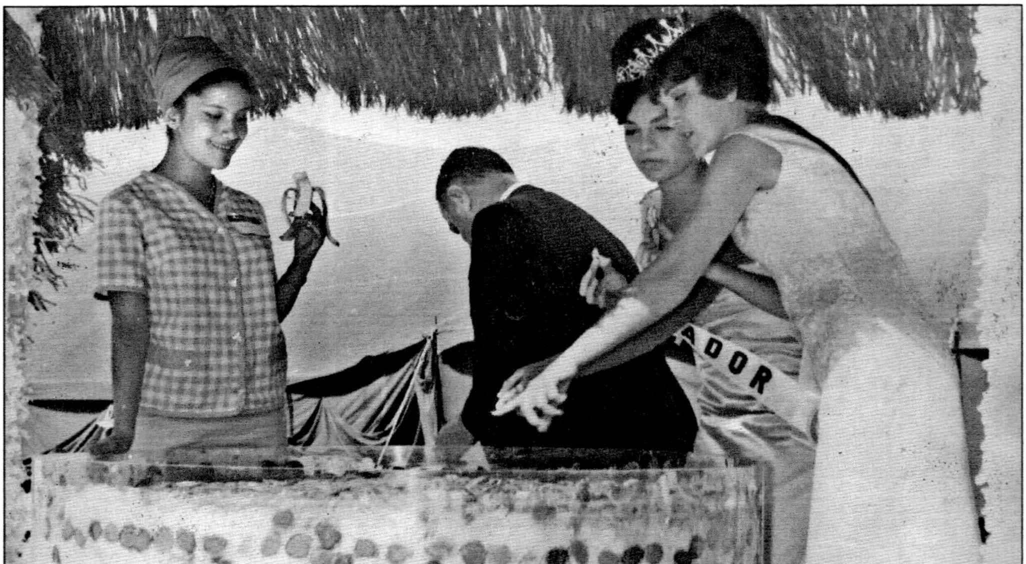

The Fulton Rotary Club conducted a yearly Princess Pageant. The lavish event attracted entrants from Kentucky and Tennessee and from as far away as Florida, Texas, Michigan, South Carolina, Mississippi, Illinois, and Nicaragua. Vonda Kay van Dyke, Miss America 1965, was a special guest of honor at the Banana Princess Pageant of the Second Annual Banana Festival. Perhaps the princess's most well-known responsibility was dishing the first servings of the One Ton Banana Pudding, as pictured above, to an eagerly waiting crowd.

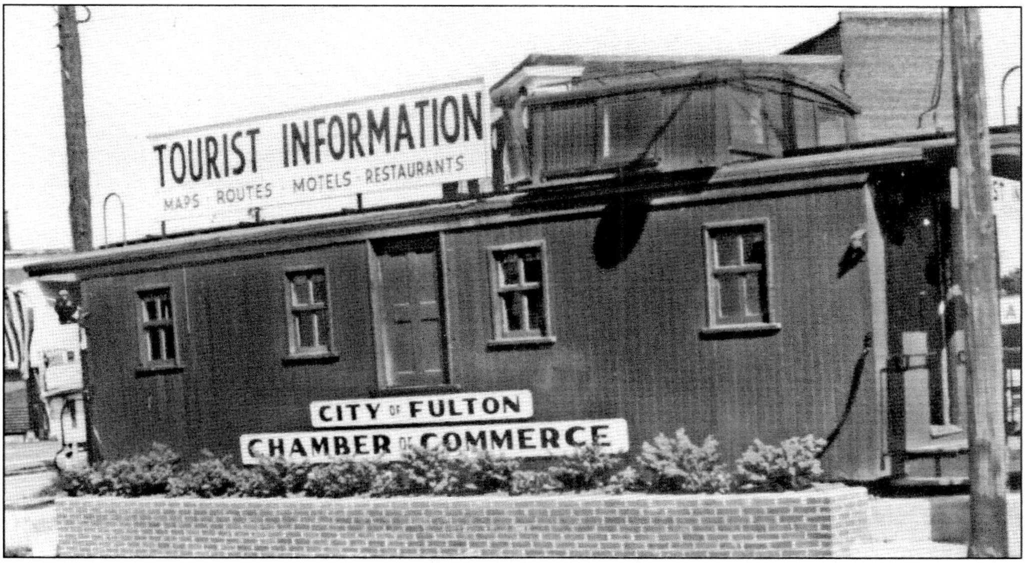

The Illinois Central Railroad donated the caboose seen above to the city of Fulton, bringing it to rest on Lake Street from the lines that crisscrossed downtown. It was used as the first office of the chamber of commerce in the 1950s. The office deteriorated in the weather, and for a time a second caboose was donated by the Norfolk Southern Railway. The Chamber of Commerce is now located in the South Fulton Municipal Complex.

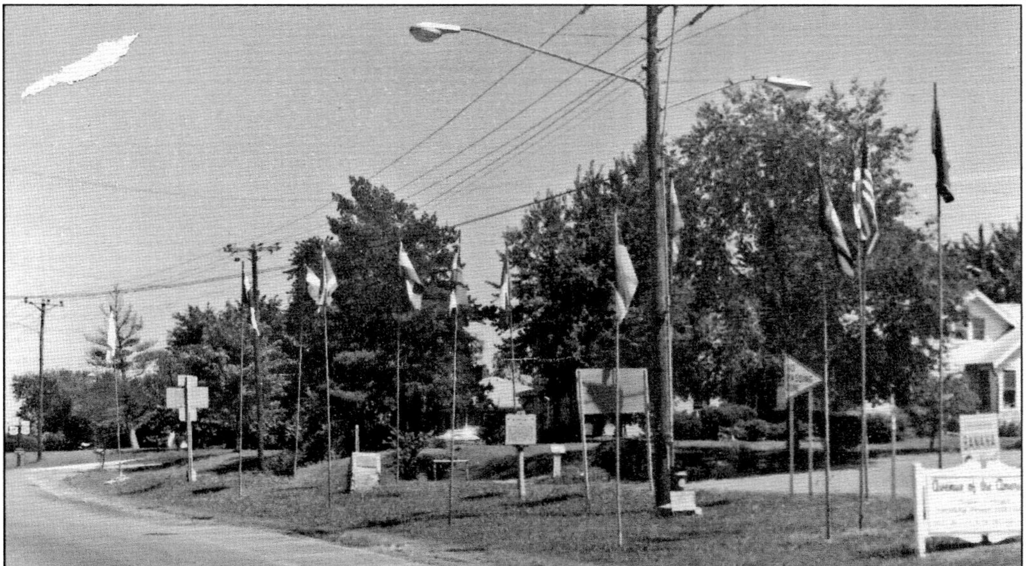

The Avenue of the Americas served as a daily reminder of Latin-American friendships. The flags of nine banana-producing countries, along with the flags of Kentucky, Tennessee, and the Banana Festival, flew on West State Line Road. W.D. Powers built the avenue, and Mrs. E.E. Williamson designed the festival flag. It was green with a yellow border, featuring bunches of bananas encircling North and South America with "International Banana Festival" written around the outside edge. A banner underneath read, "Project Unite Us Fulton, Kentucky–South Fulton, Tennessee."

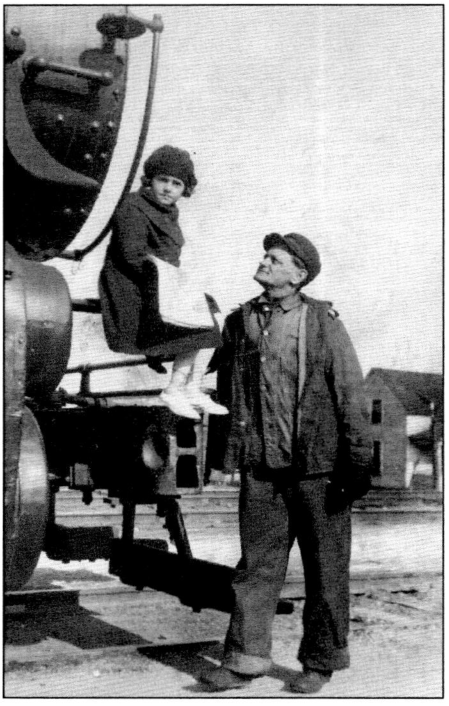

The Illinois Central Railroad made scheduled stops in Pearl's Village on Burton Row, where many of the train engineers lived with their families. This image is dated 1918 and features a young Margaret Shuck Hall and her father, Arch Shuck, an engineer for the railroad.

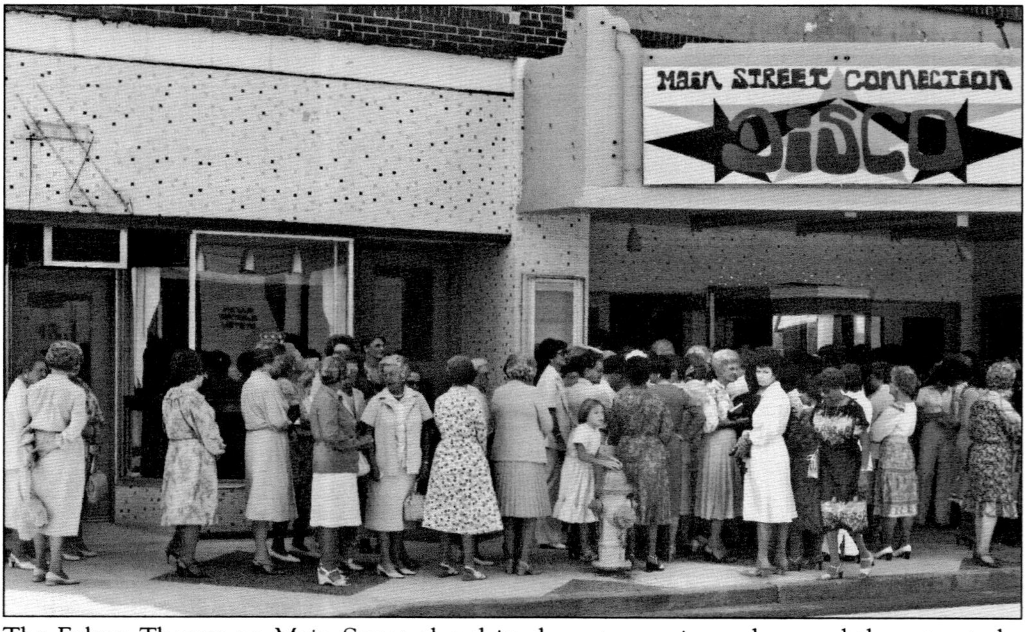

The Fulton Theater on Main Street closed its doors to movies and opened them to strobe lights and disco music in the 1970s. Gone are many of the pioneering families who settled this community. Gone are many of the magnificent buildings that filled the early landscape. And sadly gone is much of the interest in preserving the history of Fulton, Kentucky, and South Fulton, Tennessee. As we head into the new millennium, let us have renewed focus, energy, and the necessary courage to perpetuate what remains of our shared past in the Twin Cities.

INDEX